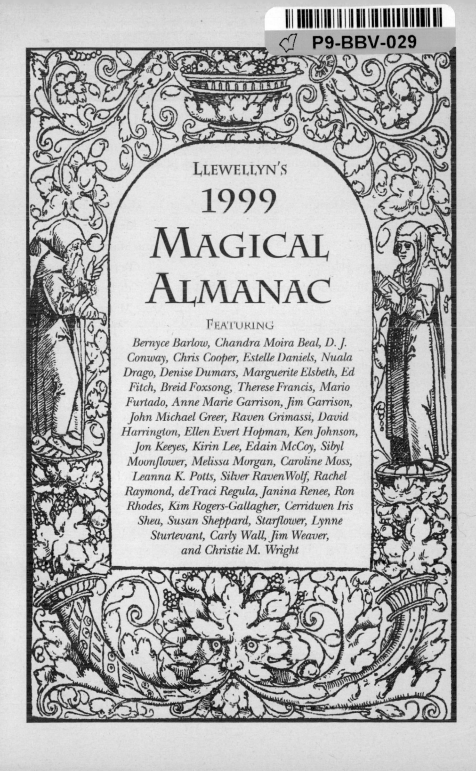

Llewellyn's
1999
Magical
Almanac

Featuring

Bernyce Barlow, Chandra Moira Beal, D. J. Conway, Chris Cooper, Estelle Daniels, Nuala Drago, Denise Dumars, Marguerite Elsbeth, Ed Fitch, Breid Foxsong, Therese Francis, Mario Furtado, Anne Marie Garrison, Jim Garrison, John Michael Greer, Raven Grimassi, David Harrington, Ellen Evert Hopman, Ken Johnson, Jon Keeyes, Kirin Lee, Edain McCoy, Sibyl Moonflower, Melissa Morgan, Caroline Moss, Leanna K. Potts, Silver RavenWolf, Rachel Raymond, deTraci Regula, Janina Renee, Ron Rhodes, Kim Rogers-Gallagher, Cerridwen Iris Shea, Susan Sheppard, Starflower, Lynne Sturtevant, Carly Wall, Jim Weaver, and Christie M. Wright

LLEWELLN'S 1999 MAGICAL ALMANAC

ISBN 1-56718-940-7. Copyright © 1998 by Llewellyn Worldwide. All rights reserved. Printed in the United States of America.

Editor/Designer:	Cynthia Ahlquist
Calendar Pages Design:	Corrine Kenner
Cover Illustration:	Merle S. Insinga
Cover Design:	Anne Marie Garrison
Photos, pages 241–3:	Bernyce Barlow
Photos and illustrations, pages 78–81; 274–6:	deTraci Regula
Illustrations, pages 304–5:	Anne Marie Garrison
Illustrations, pages 324–7:	Jim Garrison
Illustrations, pages 1–3; 6–8; 31–4; 46; 50–3; 54–6; 62–3; 75–7; 84–6; 98–9; 104–5 106–7; 187–91; 201; 202–3; 236; 254–6; 262; 264–8; 269; 272–3; 286–8; 292–3; 294; 295–7; 301; 302–3; 306–7; 308–9; 310–13; 314–17; 320–2; 323; 328–31; 332–3; 344:	Carrie Westfall
Clip Art Illustrations:	Dover Publications

Special thanks to Amber Wolfe for the use of daily color and incense correspondences. For more detailed information, please see *Personal Alchemy* by Amber Wolfe.

Moon sign and phase data computed by Matrix Software.

Llewellyn Publications
Dept. 940-7
P.O. Box 64383
St. Paul, MN 55164-0838

Welcome to the *1999 Magical Almanac*. It is a little known fact that although the *Magical Almanac* hits the store shelves in August or September, it is compiled and designed in the spring. While many people are thinking of rabbits, eggs, and the IRS, the thoughts of those of us who work on this publication run more toward, "How can I fit the entire Qabala into four pages?" and "Why are there no pictures of Pagan altars or disembodied glowing astral beings in the readily available clip art collections?" This is why the Spring Equinox at Llewellyn is really more like Thanksgiving—we're feeling pretty darned thankful toward the people who make this book possible. I extend heartfelt appreciation to the authors for their expertise and inspiration, which make these pages diverse, informative, and fun. Thank you also to our artists, in particular Merle Insinga for her delightful cover art and interior illustration artist Carrie Westfall, who is a wiz at drawing disembodied glowing things and whose art adds both depth and wonder to the pages it graces. Finally, thank you to the readers, whose interest and feedback keep this book vibrant and evolving. Now, meet the authors!

BERNYCE BARLOW is the author of *Sacred Sites of the West,* from Llewellyn. She researches and leads seminars on sacred sites of the ten western states. Bernyce is currently working on a CD of music for the sacred sites. She is also involved in in-depth research on the use of the mallet and anvil as mystical symbols of spontaneous enlightenment.

CHANDRA MOIRA BEAL is a freelance writer. She has also been published in the magazine *Texas Beat.* The name Chandra means Moon.

D. J. CONWAY is the author of the Llewellyn books *Celtic Magick; Norse Magick; Maiden, Mother, Crone; Dancing with Dragons; Animal Magick; Moon Magick; Flying Without a Broom; By Falcon Feather and Valkyrie Sword; By Oak, Ash, and Thorn; Lord of Light and Shadow; Magick of the Gods and Goddesses; Magickal, Mythical, Mystical Beasts; The Mysterious, Magickal Cat; Perfect Love; Dream Warrior; Soothslayer;* and *Warrior of Shadows.* She is also co-author of *Shapeshifter Tarot.*

CHRIS COOPER is a writer of the comic books *Darkhold: Pages from the Book of Sins,* and *Star Trek: Starfleet Academy.* He is an unaffiliated Pagan who would be Wiccan if only he could get his Talking Self to shut up.

He is currently tweaking a myth cycle involving goddesses and gods of his own invention, since none of the others would have him.

ESTELLE DANIELS is a professional, part-time astrologer and author of *Astrologickal Magick,* from Weiser Publications. Estelle has a small select private astrological practice and travels to festivals and conferences in the U.S. She is available for lectures and book signings with advance planning. She has been practicing astrology professionally since 1972, and also teaches the Craft with her High Priest.

NUALA DRAGO is a self-initiate and has been a practitioner of her own form of Witta for more than thirty years. Majoring in anthropology as a college student led to her love of folklore, particularly Celtic. She is passionate about animal rights, the study of herbal medicine, Druids, and ancient cultures.

DENISE DUMARS is a widely published poet, critic, and author of science fiction, fantasy, and horror stories. Her articles on strange phenomena have appeared in *The Gate,* and she is the author of the section on Santeria in Merrimack Books' writer's guide to religions, titled *A New Age.* She teaches college English and intends to write a lot more about magic, women's spirituality, and occult phenomena.

MARGUERITE ELSBETH (Raven Hawk) is a professional diviner and a student of Native American and European folk healing. She is co-author of the Llewellyn books *The Grail Castle: Male Myths and Mysteries in the Celtic Tradition* and *The Silver Wheel: Women's Myths and Mysteries in the Celtic Tradition* with Kenneth Johnson, and author of *Crystal Medicine: Working with Crystals, Gems and Minerals.* Marguerite is a hereditary Sicilian strega, and is proud of her Delaware Indian ancestry.

ED FITCH is one of the major figures in modern Wicca and neo-Paganism. He is the author of the Llewellyn books *Magical Rites from the Crystal Well; Rites of Odin;* and *A Grimoire of Shadows.* He has been an Air Force officer, an aerospace engineer, and a private investigator.

BREID FOXSONG is a British Traditional Wiccan who has been practicing for more than twenty years. She is the former editor of *Sacred Hart Magazine* and has had articles published in other magazines, ranging from *Green Egg* to *Craft/Crafts.* She is also active in her community, hosting open circles and introductory classes in Wicca.

THERESE FRANCIS is a third degree Wiccan (Turquoise Path), astrologer, teacher, shaman, and author. She is the designer of the *Age of Aquarius Astrology Game* and author of numerous books, including *Bless This House and All, Twenty Herbs to Take Outdoors: An Herbal First Aid Primer,* and *101 Things to Do During a Retrograde Mercury.*

MARIO FURTADO is a practitioner of solitary eclectic Wicca, as well as an herbalist, writer, devotee of the goddess Isis, and new dad. His work has been published in *Circle Network News* and *The Silver Chalice.*

ANNE MARIE GARRISON is Senior Creative Designer for Llewellyn Publications. Recently, Anne Marie has illustrated *Llewellyn's 1997 Astrological Calendar* and written *Gods and Goddesses of the Zodiac: A Coloring Book,* published by CrossQuarter Breeze, Santa Fe, NM. She is currently designing and co-publishing Pagan cross-stitch and needlepoint patterns.

JIM GARRISON is a professional consulting occultist and is in the middle of writing a science fiction novel and a book about prayer. He is a member of the American Tarot Association, the International Tarot Society, and ERAL. Jim welcomes letters from his readers and can be reached at Llewellyn, where he has his day job working on *New Worlds.*

JOHN MICHAEL GREER has been actively involved in the Western esoteric tradition since 1975. He teaches Cabalistic magic in the Golden Dawn tradition and is involved in the modern revial of magical lodge work.

RAVEN GRIMASSI is a hereditary Italian Witch practicing a family tradition of Stregheria. He is also an Initiate of Pictish-Gaelic Wicca, Gardnerian Wicca, and Brittic Witchcraft. Raven is the author of *Ways of the Strega; The Wiccan Mysteries;* and *Wiccan Magick.* He is the former editor of *Raven's Call Magazine.*

DAVID HARRINGTON has been a chronicler of the magical arts for the past fifteen years. He is the co-author, with Scott Cunningham, of the Llewellyn books *The Magical Household* and *Spellcrafts.* He is also the co-author of *Whispers of the Moon* and the forthcoming *Body Magic: The Art and Craft of Adornment and Transformation* with deTraci Regula.

ELLEN EVERT HOPMAN is a master herbalist and lay homeopath who holds an M.Ed. in mental health counseling. She is the author of *Tree*

Medicine, Tree Magic from Phoenix publishers in Custer, WA; *A Druid's Herbal for the Sacred Earth Year* from Inner Traditions/Destiny Books in Rochester, VT; *People of the Earth—The New Pagans Speak Out,* also from Inner Traditions/Destiny Books; and the videos *Gifts From the Healing Earth Volume I* and *Pagans,* both from EFP Services in Amherst, MA.

KEN JOHNSON holds a degree in comparative religions with an emphasis in the study of mythology. He is co-author of the Llewellyn books *The Grail Castle: Male Myths and Mysteries in the Celtic Tradition,* and *The Silver Wheel: Women's Myths and Mysteries in the Celtic Tradition* with Marguerite Elsbeth; and co-author of *Mythic Astrology* with Ariel Guttman. He is also the author of *Slavic Sorcery* and *Jaguar Wisdom.*

JON KEEYES lives in Texas and is the owner of Bell, Book, and Candle, an occult store. Practicing Wicca since the age of thirteen, Jon has spent the last three years involved in Celtic reconstructionalism. He is a member of the Clann Na Fhaoil Choin, IMBAS, and has written articles on the topic of Celtic Paganism.

KIRIN LEE writes and does graphic design for a science fiction magazine and is the managing editor for a rock n' roll magazine. When she is not writing articles she is writing science fiction, and she is currently working on a *Star Trek* novel and a Pagan parents' handbook.

EDAIN MCCOY has been a Witch since 1981, and today is a part of the Wittan Irish Pagan Tradition and is a Priestess of Brighid and elder within that tradition. Edain is the author of *Witta: An Irish Pagan Tradition; A Witch's Guide to Faery Folk; The Sabbats; How to Do Automatic Writing; Celtic Myth and Magic; Mountain Magic; Lady of the Night; Entering the Summerland; Inside A Witches' Coven; Making Magic; Celtic Women's Spirituality;* and the forthcoming *Astral Projection for Beginners.*

SIBYL MOONFLOWER is a poet and artist who gives poetry readings and has had poems published in the *Tyler Literary Review* and *Transcendent Vision.* She grows moonflowers and loves to read. Her house is full of books on topics ranging from Celtic magic to Tibetan Buddhism.

MELISSA MORGAN is an internationally acclaimed harpist and composer. Morgan has produced several recordings, including *Erin's Harp, happenstance dance, Gateways,* and the New Age classic *Invocation to Isis.* Morgan has created new frontiers with the harp collaborating

with other artists, including choreographer Julie Morgan, and experimental underwater composer Michael Redolfi.

CAROLINE MOSS runs workshops and gives talks on herb growing, cookery, crafts, history, and folklore. She lives in England and designs herb gardens to commission. She also teaches law.

LEANNA K. POTTS is a freelance writer who writes about Native American culture and herbs. She enjoys reading, powwows, hiking in the Rockies, gardening, cooking, writing, and lecturing about herbs.

SILVER RAVENWOLF is the Director of the International Wiccan/Pagan Press Alliance and the editor of the organization's mouthpiece, *The MidNight Drive*. She is also the National Director of WADL, the Witches Anti-Discrimination League. She is the author of the Llewellyn books *To Ride a Silver Broomstick; American Magick; Beneath a Mountain Moon; To Stir a Magick Cauldron; Angels;* and the forthcoming *Teen Witch: Wicca For a New Generation;* and *To Light a Sacred Flame.*

RACHEL RAYMOND is a writer, astrologer, herbalist, artist, bookkeeper, Pagan priestess, wife, and mommy. She lives in Northern California with her husband and two children.

DETRACI REGULA is the author of *The Mysteries of Isis* and co-author with David Harrington of *Whispers of the Moon,* a biography of Scott Cunningham, and the forthcoming *Body Magic: The Art and Craft of Adornment and Transformation.*

JANINA RENEE is the author of *Tarot Spells* and *Playful Magick.* She lives out in farm country, where daily life is full of opportunities to make a community with the animal, vegetable, and mineral worlds. One of Janina's main occupations is creating simple ritual practices that cultivate magical habits of mind.

RON RHODES is an eclectic practitioner blending shamanism, Wicca, angel and dragon magic in his spiritual belief system. His hobbies include jewelry making, herbal wildcrafting, and gardening. He can see and feel auras and uses this gift to enhance his healing work.

KIM ROGERS-GALLAGHER is the author of *Astrology for the Light Side of the Brain* from ACS Publications. She edits the astrology magazine

KOSMOS and contributes frequently to several other astrology magazines, including *Aspects* and *Dell Horoscope*.

CERRIDWEN IRIS SHEA writes in several genres under several different names. Her play *Roadkill* had successful runs in London, Edinburgh, and Australia. *Scrying* received four-star reviews in Edinburgh. *Plateau* is being adapted for the screen. She is currently working on a play based on the Iphigenia myth, and a feminist comedy for several of her priestesses in Circle of Muses called *Rock Chicks Rule*.

SUSAN SHEPPARD is the author of the *Phoenix Cards,* published in 1990 from Destiny Books. She writes articles for *Dell Horoscope* and *American Astrology* magazines. She has also written a novel called *The Gallows Tree,* published by Caramoor.

STARFLOWER is an initiated solitary, and has been interested in spirituality and Wicca since she was a small child. She loves to sing and write songs and she is working on a novel and a book for solitaries.

LYNNE STURTEVANT is a solitary Pagan practitioner. She has a B.A. in philosophy and has had a life-long fascination with ancient cultures, mystery cults, myths, fairy tales, and folk traditions. She is an accomplished craftswoman and an avid collector of folk art.

CARLY WALL is the author of *Naturally Healing Herbs* and *Setting the Mood with Aromatherapy,* both from Sterling Publishing. She leads aromatherapy workshops and has a large herb garden.

JIM WEAVER enjoys celebrating the past by adding to his collection of American folk art. Working in his herb and flower gardens helps him stay close to nature while marking the changing seasons.

Christie Wright sent in this bio: My name is **CHRISTIE M. WRIGHT** and this is my second major publication. I am seventeen years old, and at the time of publication will be a high school senior. I am an eccentric solitary following the Celtic Tradition. I would like to thank Silver RavenWolf for her encouragement. Mom, no one could have filled the job as well as you. Love ya.

I hope you enjoy this edition of the *Magical Almanac*. May the year bring you peace, joy, and enlightenment.

—Cynthia Ahlquist, Editor

TABLE OF CONTENTS

A Wiccan Creation Story

By Silver RavenWolf

Long, long ago, the world slept in the arms of the dark void. From this place of nothingness, Spirit drew together and created Our Lady of Infinite Love. The Lady danced among the heavens, Her feet beating out the rhythm of all creation. Sparks of light catapulted from Her hair, giving birth to the stars and planets. As She twirled, these heavenly bodies began to move with Her in the divine symphony of the universe. When Her dancing quickened She formed the seas and the mountains of Earth. She chanted words of love and joy, and as these sounds fell to the Earth, the trees and flowers were born. From the pure, white light of Her breath came the colors of the universe, turning all things to vibrant beauty. From the bubbling laughter in Her throat sprang the sounds of the pristine running water of the streams, the gentle lapping vibrations of the lake, and the roaring screams of the oceans. Her tears of joy became the rains of our survival.

When Her dancing slowed and She sought a companion to share the wonders of the world, Spirit created The Lord as Her lifemate and companion. Because She so loved the Earth, Spirit made Her companion half spirit, half animal, so that together the Lord and Lady

1

could populate our planet. The Lord's power moves through Her and She showers the Earth and all upon it with Her blessings. Together, the Lord and Lady gave birth to the birds, animals, fishes, and people of our world. To protect and guide the humans, the Lord and Lady created the angels and power spirits. These energies walk with us always, though we often cannot see them. Their speech creates a tapestry of positive energy, from which we draw strength. To each bird the Lady gave a magic song, and to each animal the Lord bestowed the instinct to survive. The Lord is the master of the animal and vegetable kingdoms, and therefore wears the antlers of a stag crowning His great head. This aspect of half man, half animal shows His joy in both the human and animal creations of the Spirit.

As the humans began to grow and prosper, the Lord and Lady saw the need for healers among them. And so they drew forth energy from the realm of the angels, the realm of the power animals, and the realm of the humans to create the Witches. The Witches brought with them the wisdom of the Lord and Lady, the ability to heal, and the art of magic. The Lady taught the Witches how to cast a magic circle and talk to Spirit, and the Lord taught the Witches how to communicate with the energies of air, fire, earth, and water, and commune with the animal and plant kingdoms.

At first, the humans accepted the Witches and treated them fairly; but because the Witches were different, humans began to fear the Wise Ones of the Lord and Lady, thus the Witches became the Hidden Children, conducting their rites of positive energy in secret lest they risk capture and death at the hands of uneducated humans.

As the world grew darker with ignorance and hate of human creation, The Lady took the body of the Moon to represent the gentle light of her perfect peace, and the Lord took the vibrant rays of the Sun as his symbol of strength in perfect love. And once a month, when the Moon is full, The Witches celebrate and remember the blessings our Mother has bestowed upon us. We call forth Her energy to help us take care of ourselves, our families, our planet, and our friends. Four times a year the Witches celebrate the festivals of fire and honor the Lord and His love for us—these are called the cross-quarters. At the four quarters of the seasons, the Witches honor the cycle of life and the gifts of the Earth with festivals to

both the Lord and Lady—signi-
fying the balance they have
brought us—the Equinox-
es and the Solstices.

The Lady has many
names—Isis, Astarte,
Bride, Diana, Aradia,
Hecate—and the
Lady walks within and
beside each woman of
every race. The Lord
has many faces, from
the strong Cernunnos
to the delightful Pan.
He guards and guides
us and resides in each
man of every race. When
thunder roars in the
heavens, and lightning
cracks from the
ground, the Lord and
Lady dance the divine myth of creation so that we may remember
them and know that we are never alone. When the Sun rises each
morning, we bask in the joy of His love for us, and when the Moon
moves through Her phases, we understand the cycle of birth,
growth, death, and rebirth

When it is our time, the Witches enter the Summerland. From
the Spirit that moves and flows through the Lord and Lady we continue to learn the mysticism of the Universe so that we may return,
life after life, to serve our brothers and sisters. In each lifetime, Spirit guides us through learning experiences, preparing us along the
way for our individual missions. Sometimes we are born among our
own kind, and in other instances we must seek out our spiritual family. Many of us do not remember our chosen path until we reach
adulthood, but others know instinctively of their heritage from the
time they form their own thoughts.

We are the Witches, the representation of the growth of wisdom
on our planet. We are the Hidden Children, back from the dead. We
are the people, the power, the change, and we have incarnated in
every race and every culture. We are the angels of Earth.

HOGMANAY: THE SCOTTISH NEW YEAR

BY JON KEEYES

Hogmanay is the Scottish celebration of New Year's Day, a holiday that traces its roots to the Pagan celebrations of Samhain and Yule. Celebrated at the beginning of January, many rituals and customs are associated with Hogmanay, for it is believed that the events of this day will foretell the events and luck of the coming year.

On Hogmanay, the house must be completely clean, for if it is not, the home will be untidy all year long, and bad luck will come to the household. It is also believed that a fire must be kept burning throughout the day and night, for should the fire die during this day, bad luck would follow during the year.

At midnight beginning Hogmanay, the head of the house goes to the front door and swings it open, and, with arms outstretched, invites the New Year in with a welcoming call. It is here, at midnight, that the most important ritual of "first footing" begins. The custom of first footing surrounds the belief that the first person to cross the threshold of the home bears with them the gifts of the New Year. Ideally, the first person should be a dark-haired man bringing the gifts of salt, a bit of bread, charcoal, and whiskey. He will enter the home, place the gifts on a table, and be given a glass of whiskey and a bite of bread or fruitcake. This is how the household gives thanks for what is being given. When done, the man will gift the house with salt that the home be filled with luck, bread that they may never go

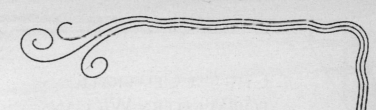

hungry, whiskey that they may never go thirsty, and charcoal that their fire may always bring warmth to the home. Groups of people will often travel the countryside first footing to ensure the gifts of the New Year are delivered to every home.

On Hogmanay, the clouds will also foretell the coming year. A sky without clouds is seen as a bad sign. Clouds from the east carry with them a decent year, and northern clouds bring with them a great year.

Another Hogmanay custom is special for ladies. On the morning of Hogmanay, young women will go to a nearby well and collect water from it. During the day, the idea is for the young woman to get the man she longs for to drink the water and thus enhance his desire for her.

Some areas of Scotland also do "thigging," which is when people sing in the streets begging for food and money. When they are done thigging, what they've collected is given to the poor and needy. This heralds back to a Samhain custom in which food was collected for the poor to help them get through the winter.

In modern times, where New Year's celebrations provide little more than drunken follies, the Scots can be looked to for ways to bring spirituality and community closer.

CHINESE CELEBRATIONS
FOR WESTERN WICCANS

BY EDAIN MCCOY

C hinese festivals with clearly Pagan roots are numerous, and a growing number of Western Pagans have discovered that learning about and incorporating some of these festivals gives their seasonal celebrations a fresh twist. Here is a list of the popular festivals from which to choose.

THE CHINESE NEW YEAR: The new year begins on the eve of the first New Moon after the Sun has entered the sign of Aquarius. Before the holiday, people try to clear their debts so that they can carry the energy of prosperity into the new year. The festival itself is celebrated with parades, especially those honoring the reigning animal of the Chinese zodiac, who will preside over the new year.

THE HERB FESTIVALS: The Chinese, who have long used herbs and plants in their healing, have several festivals honoring herbs they feel are especially important. One of the major festivals honors mugwort, an herb with a long history of healing and magical uses. Modern Wiccans often use mugwort in spells to aid in astral projection. A general herb festival that honors all of the beneficial herbs takes place on the New Moon of the fifth month of the Chinese calendar, around late July.

THE HOMAGE TO CHUNG K'UI: The Full Moon of the fifth month (Chinese calendar)—late July or early August—is set aside to honor the God Chung K'ui, a deity of protection. His image and name are used to banish negativity and evil spirits from homes and temples.

THE HOMAGE TO CHANG-O: Chang-o is a Chinese Moon Goddess who was given a festival date on a Full Moon in what is usually late September. Her sacred number is thirteen, which figures heavily in both the symbolism and feasting associated with her day.

THE ANCESTOR MOON: The festival takes place on the New Moon of the tenth month of the Chinese lunar calendar in what is our late fall or early winter. This is a time to honor the beloved ancestor spirits with picnics and processions in the family burial ground. Extra food for the spirits is always taken along.

THE FESTIVAL OF KWAN YIN: Many women seeking their own gender-specific spiritual roots have adopted Kwan Yin as a patron. She is a goddess of fertility and healing who takes on the pain of the world to ease us. Her image—seat-

ed on a lotus blossom cradling children and young animals—is still found in many Chinese homes, where she has been adopted into the Buddhist faith. Kwan Yin's festival date is at the start of the last quarter of the eleventh lunar month, usually in December.

THE LANTERN FESTIVAL: This festival, which celebrates the light of the newly waxing Sun, takes place on the last Full Moon before the new year, usually in December or January. On this night, brightly colored paper lanterns are hung everywhere, both in and out of the home.

THE HOMAGE TO THE WEALTH GODS: In the week before the new year the Chinese make pilgrimages to the shrines of their gods of prosperity to ensure a prosperous new year for themselves, their families, and their businesses. Debt is also settled as much as possible and prosperity talismans are created before the eve of the new year.

CHICKEN GINGER PASTA

Many people are aware also that the pasta we think of as being inherently Italian was actually brought to Italy from China in the fifteenth century, presumably by the famous explorer Marco Polo. Instead of the usual Chinese fare, try the following pasta recipe, which has a unique Chinese flavor to enhance your eclectic East-meets-West celebrations.

4 tablespoons soy sauce
½ teaspoon ground ginger
1 teaspoon vegetable oil
⅛ teaspoon pepper
½ cup pineapple juice
1 tablespoon vinegar
2 tablespoons brown sugar
1 teaspoon dry mustard
 Cornstarch (as needed to thicken)
1 cooked chicken breast, cut into small cubes
1 (6-ounce) can sliced water chestnuts, drained
1 cup fresh mushrooms, sliced thin
1 (4-ounce) can sliced bamboo shoots, drained
1 (8-ounce) package of linguine pasta, cooked and drained

Combine soy sauce, ginger, oil, pepper, pineapple juice, vinegar, brown sugar, and mustard. Mix well over low heat, then slowly add small amounts of cornstarch to thicken. Use no more than ¼ teaspoon at a time until you see how thick the mixture is becoming. Remove sauce from heat. In another bowl mix chicken, water chestnuts, mushrooms, and bamboo shoots. Put the pasta on plates and garnish with the chicken mixture. Spoon the sauce over the pasta mix and serve.

Garlic: The Magical Person's Best Friend

By Silver RavenWolf

O ne of the most versatile tools of any magical person is garlic. Often called the "wonder drug" by herbalists, it serves a variety of medicinal as well as magical functions.

Medicinally

Garlic is used for cold prevention, as an expectorant, for treatment of bald spots (three times daily), in aromatherapy for colds, flu, and pneumonia, a poultice for pneumonia, a treatment for a toothache and infected wounds, reducing blood pressure, decreasing cholesterol, reducing the likelihood of internal blood clots that may trigger heart attacks and some strokes, reducing blood sugar levels, assisting in draining sinus cavities, as a general antibiotic, and even in the treatment of animal mange (along with goldenseal and olive oil as a base). It can be planted around your roses to discourage Japanese beetles, and placed around the home as a fly repellent. European studies show that garlic helps to eliminate lead and other toxic heavy metals from the body. As with all herbs, if you plan to use garlic in medicinal amounts, contact your physician.

Magically

Magical correspondences for garlic are as follows: Planet: Mars; element: fire; deities: Hecate, the Morrigan, Kali, Sekhmet, and Calliech; day: Tuesday; and astrological sign: Aries. Garlic is as universal in magical applications as it appears to be in medicinal uses. Use garlic to ward off negativity and dispel nightmares; for protection in a moving vehicle or on a boat; to guard against evil, gossip, thieves, and jealousy; to put in a bridal bouquet for good luck; to sprinkle on the doorstep to keep unsavory individuals away; to wear around the neck to dispel disease; to rub into pots and pans to remove negative vibrations; and to hang over windows to absorb negativity. It can be placed in spell bottles to defeat enemies, and empowered during the dark Moon to shield and protect abused wives and children.

Psychic First Aid

By Therese Francis

We've all had days when psychic first aid would have been nice because of nightmares, numerous physical injuries, chronic illness, sudden psychological shock, or working in a stress-filled environment.

Essential Items

The basic psychic first aid kit contains the following items:

Rescue Remedy or equivalent

Blessing herbs, such as rosemary, peppermint, thyme, bergamot, sage, cinnamon, or sweetgrass

Drawing herbs, such as Indian tobacco and American tobacco (do not use standard cigarettes, which have too many additives)

Your athame

Salt or sea salt

Censer or other item to safely burn charcoal and herbs

Matches, lighter, or flint to light the charcoal

Small bowl for water and salt

You might also want to include:

Feather or fan to move the herb smoke

Broom (cinnamon brooms are a favorite)

Rattle or bell

Magical cords from your initiation

Divination equipment (pendulum, tarot, runes, etc.)

Stones, crystals, or pieces of metal that help you focus and direct power

Grounding stones, such as hematite or sodalite

Uses for Your Psychic First Aid Kit

Use your kit whenever you or someone in your family experiences a sudden injury, a chronic illness, a series of bad dreams, or when feeling "not right." Be sure to address the physical issues as well as the psychic, in the appropriate order. For example, a bleeding knee first needs physical attention. Later, soothe the psyche.

Performing Psychic First Aid

Performing psychic first aid is simple. The following is based on the idea that you will do this for someone else; if you are working on yourself, follow the same order.

Protect yourself to make sure you are not influenced by the situation. Do this by wearing your initiation cords, centering, or meditating.

Step One

Seal the area to protect others and to prevent outside influences from affecting the situation further. If you cannot do a full circle, visualize the area in bright light.

Step Two

Stabilize the person. Help them ground and center. Use a grounding stone if you have one (such as hematite). If a person is crying uncontrollably, let him. Crying is cleansing. Just be there and give him your (quiet) attention. If it's cool, get a blanket to help him stay warm.

Step Three

Review the situation. Now that everyone involved is centered and the area is protected from outside influence, look at the situation. This is a good time to do divination work to determine the root cause.

Step Four

Raise energy. This can be as simple as humming or briskly rubbing your hands together.

Step Five

Perform a cut-away between the person and the outside influence. Use your athame or visualize a bright light separating the person from the outside influence. If the problem appears to be internal, use a drawing herb to bring the influence out, and then do a cut-away. If the problem started as a physical injury, do a cut-away as a symbolic act to prevent the injury from happening again.

Step Six

Seal holes and balance the aura. My favorite is to have the person imagine a

paint can filled with all the colors of the rainbow. As this wonderful, warm paint pours out of the can, the aura absorbs whatever color is needed.

STEP SEVEN

Banish any lingering influence. Rattles and bells are good banishers/sealers. This step can be combined with the previous step through smudging with an herbal smoke, such as sage.

STEP EIGHT

Perform any other healing that's necessary.

STEP NINE

Protect the person from any returning influences. Teach her to set up her own shields and to clean her aura (sample below).

SIMPLE AURA CLEANSING/SEALING

Briskly rub your hands together until they start to tingle. If you pull your hands apart slightly, you will feel a pull bringing your hands back together. Starting at your crown, clean your aura in a sweeping motion down and away from your body. You can lightly touch your skin or hold your hands two to three inches away from your body. Do your head, neck, each arm, chest, stomach, upper back, lower back, and each leg and foot. Then do a sweeping motion from the top of your head to the ground, first on your front and then on your back. Repeat as needed. Shake your hands out when finished. The whole process takes about thirty seconds.

IF THE PROBLEM CONTINUES

If the problem continues, such as continual nightmares or hauntings, place vinegar in small bowls in each of the room's quarters. Do a circle around the room (or house) at sundown and again at sunrise. Be sure everyone involved seals their aura frequently.

For continual nightmares, place a cup of hot water near the bed. Add a few drops of the essential oil of a blessing herb like rosemary to the water. This is very good for children. If the problem still continues, you may wish to consult with a more experienced practitioner.

FOR MORE INFORMATION

Fortune, Dion. *Psychic Self Defense,* Weiser, 1992 reprint.

Reed, Anderson. *Shouting at the Wolf: A Guide to Identifying and Warding Off Evil in Everday Life,* Carol Group, 1990.

INCREASING OUR ENERGIES WITH HERBS

BY CARLY WALL, C.A.

Having good, strong physical energy is important if you are performing rituals and magical rites, but sometimes life is just too stressful to keep our energy levels up. We become depressed, or we experience headaches, backaches, digestion problems, and sleep problems. If the stress is unrelenting, negative energies leach out the positive and our balance is lost. That's when physical illness can strike!

How can we reverse the process? Well, when we feel that change, social obligations, disappointments, or responsibilities are getting us down, we can use herbal tonics to boost us up. The healing energies of the plants, as well as the supporting vibrations that plants lend to us can do the trick. Here are some herbs you can try (remember to drink no more than three cups of herbal tea per day).

BORAGE: Called the herb of gladness by the Welsh, borage restores vitality and makes one calm. Dry the leaves and flowers. Use 1 teaspoon in 1 cup of boiling water. Cover, steep for 10 minutes, and strain.

CHAMOMILE: Egyptians believed chamomile prevented aging because of its ability to ease stress. Also good for easing digestion. For tea, use 2 teaspoons dried or 1 tablespoon fresh to 1 cup of boiling water.

CLOVER: High in antioxidants, clover has been traditionally used as a spring tonic in North America. A mild sedative; it is a detoxifier; rebuilding and cleansing. Use 2 teaspoons of dried chopped flowers or 1 tablespoon fresh in 1 cup of water.

LAVENDER: Lavender is an all-around healing, tonic, sedative herb. Mentally relaxes and raises the spirits. Use 1 teaspoon dried or 3 teaspoons fresh leaves and flower buds in 1 cup boiling water.

VALERIAN: Although it isn't pleasant tasting or smelling, valerian is wonderfully renewing and gives courage and energy. Take this at bedtime to get lots of sleep and wake up full of zip! Mix this with a sweet tea herb to get it down. Make a tea by pouring 1 pint of boiling water over 1 teaspoon of powdered root. Cover, steep 15 minutes, strain. Place two teabags of a sweet herb in while steeping. Add honey too. Drink only 1 cup per day.

Red Clover

Hygeian Healing

By Marguerite Elsbeth

I n ancient Greece, true healers, those who sought to cure the whole person, body, mind, and soul, were followers of Hygeia, the goddess of health and healing.

Nature and a healthy mind are powerful healers because the entire healing process exists within the body. When you use external treatments to attain wellness, you are activating natural, inner resources that normally serve to make you well without any outside help at all! The body can magically heal itself, provided you know what to do to keep it running at maximum efficiency.

Hygeian healing uses preventive measures to enhance internal resistance to disease. You can promote healing by getting appropriate exercise and rest, holding good thoughts and mental images, fostering positive spiritual beliefs and practices, and eating less fat and protein and more grains, fresh fruits, and veggies. Hygeian tonics are especially effective for enhancing and toning the natural healing system and neutralizing harmful influences in the body.

GARLIC lowers blood pressure and cholesterol, is a powerful antiseptic, antibiotic, and anticancer agent, and protects liver and brain cells. Add fresh garlic in any form to your food daily.

GINGER, known in ancient China and India, tones, uplifts, and warms the system, stimulates digestion and circulation, calms upset stomach, and relieves nausea, aches, and pains. Ginger can be eaten in candied slices, honey-based syrups, encapsulated, or drunk as a tea.

GREEN TEA, the national beverage of Japan, protects the body against heart disease and cancer. It offers a benign form of caffeine along with great benefits as a general tonic. Try green tea instead of the usual coffee, black tea, or cola for a healthy pick-me-up.

MILK THISTLE, an old European folk remedy, detoxifies and enhances liver function. Alcohol, pharmaceutical and/or recreational drug users, or those who have suffered exposure to toxic substances should take this herb regularly.

ASTRAGALUS is a popular Chinese herb used to treat colds, flu, and chronic infections, such as bronchitis, sinusitis, and AIDS. It restores immunity, and increases vitality and resistance to disease. Take encapsulated astragalus if you lack energy or feel stressed.

GINSENG, usually recommended for men, is stimulating, sexually energizing, can improve the appetite, aid digestion, tone the skin and muscles, and balance hormones in women. It is a great rejuvenator for the tired, the elderly, and the chronically ill. Ginseng comes in candies, teas, wines, and elixirs.

DONG QUAI is a Chinese herb, used predominantly by women to build blood, increase circulation, and regulate menstrual and reproductive disorders. Try dong quai in tincture or capsule form to restore balance.

MAITAKE MUSHROOMS are highly esteemed for their healing properties. Add maitake tablets or capsules to your diet to protect your body against cancer, AIDS, chronic fatigue, hepatitis, allergies, and environmental illness.

Hygeian healing is spontaneous and natural. Be whole now!

Ginseng

Dealing with Depression

By Cerridwen Iris Shea

Depression has become a way of life in modern society. It hits people regardless of age, race, or gender. It contributes to heart disease, stroke, and numerous other illnesses. It prolongs almost any ailment, making it more difficult to recover, which in turn can feed the depression.

A friend of mine once said, "You can't be a woman in this society and not be depressed." I happen to think that's a cop-out. As people living a magical life, we have a few extra options at our disposal. Part of the commitment to living a magical life is to take responsibility for our lives and take action to change what does not work. Part of the downward spiral inherent in depression is feeling unable to do anything to change it. Use your magical will to change it.

First of all, check with your doctor to see if there is a medical or chemical reason for the depression and heed the doctor's advice. I am not a fan of surviving on pills, but if you need to be on medication, take it while you sort out the cause of the depression and ways to cure it. There is no shame involved in going to a medical or psychological professional. It is the first step toward reclaiming control of your life.

Once the medical options are handled or ruled out, it is time to turn to your magic. Here are some simple ideas to get your life moving. Once it starts moving on the astral, you can start taking action on the physical to manifest change. These ideas have all worked well for me. Use them as a starting point, and, as you get stronger and stronger, experiment on your own. Listen to your instincts.

When You Wake Up

As soon as you are able to formulate a sentence upon awakening, say to yourself, "Today will be a good day." Repeat it several times, until it feels true. Go to your altar and light a candle and some incense. Greet the elements, saying something like:

> *Good morning, earth, my sustainer; good morning, air, my inspiration; good morning, fire, my warmth; good morning, water, my creativity; good morning, spirit, my protector.*

In the book *To Stir a Magick Cauldron*, Silver RavenWolf talks about daily devotionals. I find them very helpful, but, in the darkest recesses of depression, I couldn't sustain them, so I did the above greeting instead. It is simple and uplifting, and a pleasant way to start the day.

Before Bed

Light your altar candle and some incense. Thank the elements, much as you did in the greeting, thanking each one for something specific that happened in the day. In your journal, make a list of the day's blessings. I start by listing my cats, my home, my family, my friends, my creativity, my job, and any special little pleasure I experienced during the day. I'm always surprised at the length of my list! Then say, "Today was a good day and tomorrow will be even better" until it feels true.

Eat Carefully

Watch what you put into your body even more closely than usual. Add more fresh fruits and vegetables. If you are feeling particularly run down, add more protein. Cut down or completely out of your diet processed sugar, alcohol, and drugs. Consult your doctor or a nutritionist for the best type of diet specifically for you.

Reprogram Negative Patterns

Every time you say to yourself, "I can't cope with this "immediately follow it with "Yes, I can." Cut negative phrases such as "to die for" out of your vocabulary completely. Think about it: are you really willing to die for that beaded dress? I don't think so. If you are, please see a psychological professional right away, because you need more help than can be found in books or articles.

Rearrange Your Home

Do things need cleaning? Is your head in the wrong direction when you sleep? Cleaning an entire house during a bout with depression can be overwhelming, so do it slowly. Just the couch one day, just a shelf the next, just one drawer a third day. Slowly but surely, the difference will be seen and felt. Read up on furniture arrangement and energy flow, crystals, candles, and scents to perk up a room. It doesn't have to be expensive to be cheerful and completely yours. Light a candle to Silkie, the Scottish goddess of housecleaning, while you work.

Scent

Use aromatherapy to help you feel better. What scents make you feel safe and happy? All winter, whenever I am home, I keep a cauldron simmering on the stove with a cut-up apple, cinnamon stick, nutmeg, and clove. It smells like there is an apple pie perpetually baking, which brings back happy memories and lifts my mood. Use scented candles, scented bath water, scented floor wash, and incense. Experiment with different scents to see what works for you. I find rosemary, sage, jasmine, lavender, and anything in the citrus family particularly helpful.

Look at Your World Mindfully

Take a walk around your neighborhood. Smell the

coffee from the coffee bar, the pastry from the bakery. Look at the one lone tree bravely standing against the concrete. Take pleasure in the Sun warming the street, the rain washing it clean, snowflakes dancing in the wind, and moonlight creating connection. Watch birds, cats, dogs, and children. Take joy in the thousands of tiny pleasures offered to us each day in our lives. The little pleasures add up to big pleasures.

SEARCH FOR THE CAUSE
OF THE DEPRESSION

Why are you depressed? Lack of money? Being single? Being in a bad relationship? Unhappy at work? Home life rough? Write all the possible causes out in your journal and explore them in depth, even if it is painful. Yes, you can deal with it. You must. Do this in a cast circle if you're worried about your ability to cope. Once you've explored the root of the depression, make a list of steps to change the situation. You can always change your situation. Change is a frightening prospect. Often, it is easier to stay in a harmful situation because the pain is familiar, rather than taking a leap into the unknown.

ASK YOUR PATRON DEITY FOR HELP

Cast a full ritual circle, or, if you don't have the energy to cast, simply light a candle and some incense. Ask your patron deity for help. Meditate on the information. This technique can also be used with angels, power animals, trees, and elemental companions. They will help, but you need to ask.

MEDITATE

Take the Fool card out of the tarot deck, or look at a picture of it in a book. Light a candle and some incense, either in or out of a fully cast circle. Find out how the Fool can help you take the action you need to change your situation.

ASK FOR HELP

If you work with a coven or circle, request a working circle done for and with you to help heal the depression. Ask that you be remembered when your coven-mates work on their own. In each of our working circles, we have a "requests" section, where we request work for each other in between the working circles. If you are a solitary, you can work online, or, through webweaving, set up a time where several of your correspondents will sit down and work at the same time to help you.

If you are feeling suicidal, call a hotline: ;ook in the phone book for a suicide hotline and call. These people know what they are doing and they care. Reach out to them, and they will help you.

WHAT ABOUT ST. JOHN'S WORT?

Editor's note: Many people use St. John's wort as a natural treatment for depression. As with anything, check with your doctor or holistic professional before starting any new treatment. Personally, I can only take St. John's Wort during the waning Moon, starting the third or fourth day after the Full Moon, and stopping the day before dark Moon. Technically, it is supposed to take six weeks before one sees a result, but, for me, it kicks in a few hours after I take it. I find it helpful occasionally because it keeps me from sinking so low I feel I can't cope. I feel as though I've landed in a safety net and can look at things a bit more objectively and take action. I do, however, find it interferes with my magical workings. The same safety net I can snuggle into also serves as a membrane, making it more difficult to direct raised energy.

WHAT TO DO IF YOU KNOW SOMEONE WHO IS DEPRESSED

If you know someone who is going through a depression, encourage that person to seek help. Listen as much as possible. With the person's permission, light a candle at your altar and ask for healing. Suggest a healing in a working circle. Be careful, however, that the person does not try to make you "fix" the situation, or rely on you so heavily that no effort is made on his or her own part. You can be a support, but not a savior. If the person is not willing to put personal effort and action into recovery, there is a limit to what you can do.

If someone you know does succeed in committing suicide, don't be afraid to grieve, but try to filter out the guilt. We are each responsible for our own actions. Suicide is often an act of hostility as much as it is a cry for help. Light a candle at your altar and wish the person well on the next phase of the journey. If you are angry, don't be afraid to state your anger. Anger can be positive. There are plenty of believers in reincarnation who believe if one commits suicide, one will be reborn into the same circumstances over and over until one learns the lessons necessary. Celebrate the person at the next Samhain. Acknowledge and honor your own feelings so that you don't slip into a depression yourself.

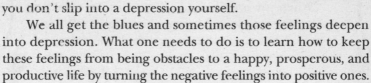

We all get the blues and sometimes those feelings deepen into depression. What one needs to do is to learn how to keep these feelings from being obstacles to a happy, prosperous, and productive life by turning the negative feelings into positive ones.

HELPFUL BOOKS

Cunningham, Scott. *The Complete Book of Incenses, Oils and Brews*. St. Paul, MN: Llewellyn Publications.

Cunningham, Scott, and David Harrington. *The Magical Household*. St. Paul, MN: Llewellyn Publications.

RavenWolf, Silver. *To Stir a Magick Cauldron*. St. Paul, MN: Llewellyn Publications.

Thompson, Janet. *Magical Hearth: Home for the Modern Pagan*. New York: Samuel Weiser, Inc.

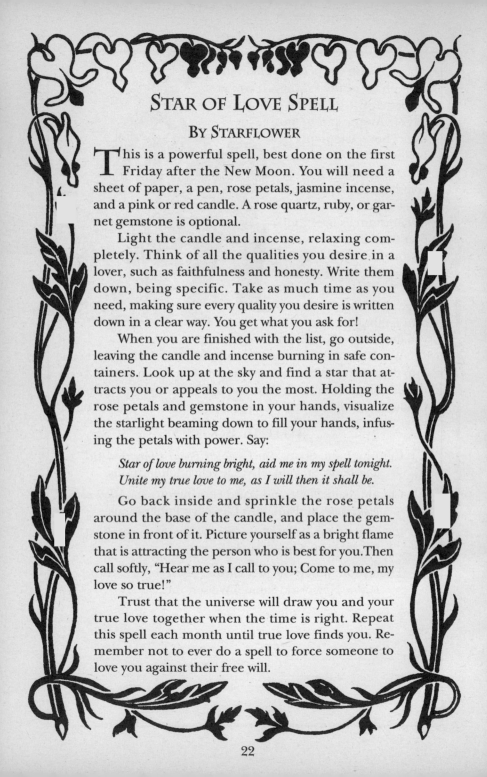

Star of Love Spell

By Starflower

This is a powerful spell, best done on the first Friday after the New Moon. You will need a sheet of paper, a pen, rose petals, jasmine incense, and a pink or red candle. A rose quartz, ruby, or garnet gemstone is optional.

Light the candle and incense, relaxing completely. Think of all the qualities you desire in a lover, such as faithfulness and honesty. Write them down, being specific. Take as much time as you need, making sure every quality you desire is written down in a clear way. You get what you ask for!

When you are finished with the list, go outside, leaving the candle and incense burning in safe containers. Look up at the sky and find a star that attracts you or appeals to you the most. Holding the rose petals and gemstone in your hands, visualize the starlight beaming down to fill your hands, infusing the petals with power. Say:

Star of love burning bright, aid me in my spell tonight.
Unite my true love to me, as I will then it shall be.

Go back inside and sprinkle the rose petals around the base of the candle, and place the gemstone in front of it. Picture yourself as a bright flame that is attracting the person who is best for you. Then call softly, "Hear me as I call to you; Come to me, my love so true!"

Trust that the universe will draw you and your true love together when the time is right. Repeat this spell each month until true love finds you. Remember not to ever do a spell to force someone to love you against their free will.

HEART MAGIC

BY RACHEL RAYMOND

Perhaps no internal organ has received as much magical attention as the heart. It is such a commonplace symbol for love that it is difficult to separate the two. The familiar heart symbol is, of course, grossly inaccurate. However it has engraved itself indelibly on our collective consciousness. The suit of hearts in a deck of playing cards replaced the original suit of cups common to tarot decks. Both suits represent emotions, interpersonal relationships, and matters of the heart.

The custom of exchanging paper hearts on Valentine's Day comes from the Ancient Roman orgiastic festival Lupercalia (wolf party). All the women at a gathering would write their names on little pieces of paper and put them in a bowl. Then the men would draw names to determine their partner for the night's festivities. The entire month of February was sacred to the goddess Februs (fever) who inflamed mortals with the fever of passion. Later, the Catholic church instituted St. Valentine's Day to replace the more hedonistic Pagan celebrations.

The heart of an issue is always the center—the deepest core. To the Buddhists the diamond heart is the indestructibility of the inner core of wisdom. In Judaism, the Temple of God is said to be located in the heart, and according to Hindu lore, the heart is the seat of Atman (Bhrama) and is symbolized by a lotus. In the chakra system the heart is located in the center of the seven chakras.

The heart figured prominently in the Ancient Egyptian judgment of the dead. After death each soul appeared before the scales of the Goddess Maat and offered her the heart for weighing. On one side of the scale was placed the petitioner's heart and on the other side was placed a feather. Then the deceased recited the Negative Confession. The Confession contained twenty-one negative affirmations of good conduct that began with "I have not been a man/woman of anger, I have done no evil to humankind," and ended with "I have not taken milk from the mouths of babes."

This worked on the same principle as a lie detector test. If the heart was heavy with deceit, then it would upset the balance and tip the scales. However, if the heart was light then it would stay balanced with Maat's feather, and this would increase the desirability of the afterlife granted the deceased. In cases where the heart was unusually heavy with misdeeds, the deceased would be devoured on the spot by a crocodile. Most people found their hearts to be slightly weighted and were designated accordingly to a middle class afterlife.

During the Ancient Egyptian embalming process the hearts were removed and replaced with amulets carved from red stone. Thousands of years later it was still common to give the heart its own private burial ceremony in Medieval funerary customs.

The Ancient Egyptian word for heart was *ab*. Its hieroglyph was a dancer, and it was thought to be the seat of intelligence, emotion, and will power. The Aztecs offered up the still beating heart, or *yollotli,* of their sacrificial victims for the gods to consume. In Ancient Egyptian the word for heart meant the same thing as "offering," so it is possible that sometime in Egypt's dim dark past that hearts were offered in a ritual of human sacrifice. In rites that recall the bloody sacrificial offerings of the Aztecs, the beating hearts of (temporarily) live animals have been used in assorted magic rituals. The most commonly noted were various love spells that called for a dove to be killed by having its heart cut out. Personally, I have found the timely administering of charm and chocolate to be an amply effective love spell.

Because the heart was considered the seat of intelligence it was also thought to be the repository of memory, which is why when we memorize something we "learn it by heart." In addition to intelligence, the heart was also considered to be the source of courage. The you-are-what-you-eat theory of magic has encouraged many people to consume the hearts of lions, tigers, and other courageous creatures in order to impart some of those same qualities to the diner. The heart of a worthy slain human opponent has also been considered good eating in many cultures.

Cardiovascular disease is the leading cause of death. Indeed all deaths are ultimately the result of heart failure. Without our pumping hearts, our exalted brains are just so much gray pudding. Even though the mind has replaced the heart as the seat of intelligence, it is still our hearts that we look to for happiness. A heartless or cold-hearted person is one without a trace of kindness or compassion. It is good to have a heart of gold, to be big-hearted, open-hearted and warm-hearted.

The true magic of the heart lies in its tireless dance. It is the only muscle of the body that never rests. It is the sacred drum that makes our blood pound and sets our passions a-fire. Follow your heart where it leads, dance to its pulsing rhythms, and you will possess heart magic in abundance.

Aphrodite's Mirror

By Marguerite Elsbeth

Have you looked into Aphrodite's mirror lately? Venus-Aphrodite, Greco-Roman goddess of love and romance, is sensual and appreciative of beauty, especially her own. She can be a seeker of self-perfection and a prisoner of passion, filled with insatiable longing to possess or be possessed by her chosen target of affection. Perhaps it seems frivolous to think of cosmetics, clothing, and flirtation in these times of global chaos, but some girls just want to have fun!

Begin on Friday (Venus' day), at 7:00 PM (Venus' hour). *Editor's Note: Check the planetary hours section on pages 122–127 to determine exact time of the Venus hour.* If the Sun and/or Moon is in the Venus-ruled signs Taurus or Libra, and the Moon is waxing, better still.

First, try this facial on for size. Warm some honey (Venus is fond of bees), mix it with mashed avocado (green is Venus' color) and a dollop of plain yogurt, and smear it over your face, neck, and chest (tastes great too!).

Next, draw a romantic bath for one. Decorate your bathroom with pale green candles and a single red rose for atmosphere. Run the bath, preferably as hot as you can comfortably stand it. Add to the bath water a mixture of myrtle and clover oil to honor Venus, one cup of sugar for sweetness, one cup of pink wine for heady intoxication, and a generous splash of sandalwood perfume for luxury. Get sky-clad, turn down the light, enter the tub, and let your imagination run wild.

After you have bathed and washed off the avocado facial, dry your hair, and give the old hundred strokes hair-brushing routine a magical twist. Let your hair hang down before you.

Sweep a natural boar-bristle brush from your scalp to the ends of your hair. Have your hand follow the brush as it works its way through. Focus your attention on your hand and imagine that you are impregnating your hair with power. Think, feel, and exude magnetic attraction into your hair with every stroke.

Now, make yourself comfortable and take several deep, relaxing breaths. Surround yourself with vibrant green light and picture yourself beautiful. Really get into the image. This is who you are—your magical self—and if you can visualize it, you can become it. Note what you might do to make the astral you a reality and affirm to do it!

Finally, if you want, don some make-up (Aphrodite wouldn't be caught dead without it), and dress to kill in your favorite come-hither fashions, including luscious lingerie. Wear emerald or turquoise jewelry, or an amulet made with these Venus stones for extra luck in love. Then head out for a night on the town and reflect Aphrodite's beauty right back at 'em!

WILD HAIR

BY RACHEL RAYMOND

Over the last few millennia, hair has acquired an impressive body of lore. In cultures where the use of magic is prized, usually the more hair one has the better. In cultures where magic is considered to be evil or irrational, hair is often correspondingly shorter.

Hair was once thought to contain so much magical power that just brushing it could cause the seas to storm and the cosmos to tremble. Highland lasses would abstain from combing their hair out at night if their brothers were at sea lest they create a storm that drowned them. "Good" women always kept their heads covered so people would know they weren't trying to cause a hurricane. The *Malleus Maleficarium*, the definitive guide to the recognition and persecution of Witches, maintained that Witches could control wind, rain, hail, and lightning with their hair.

According to Tantric tradition, the universe is created and destroyed by the letting down and binding up of the hair of the great goddess Kali. Comets were once thought to be stray hairs of the Great Mother Goddess. Disheveled hair signifies raw power and is often depicted on demons and deities of the underworld. Basilisks (a cross between a rooster and a snake) were said to sprout from the discarded pubic hairs of a menstruating woman. Snakes were used to represent the extra-powerful hair of sorceresses like Medusa.

Long hair is supposed to denote a woman of lustful wanton disposition, drive men to think impure thoughts, and to incite demons with supernatural desire. In Bavaria during the eighth century a "Lewd loosing of hair" was a heinous crime.

Ancient Egyptians and Greeks would unbraid and unbind their hair while attending a birthing woman, hoping that loosening their hair would encourage the birth goddess to allow the babe to be born more easily.

When the Egyptian god Osiris was murdered and dismembered, the goddess Isis found the pieces and reassembled them, and then brought Him back to life by covering Him with Her long black hair. They conceived a son, the falcon god Horus. When She nursed the infant Horus She protected Him by sheltering Him under Her hair. In imitation of Isis, Egyptian widows used to put a lock of their hair in their husband's coffins in order to protect them on their journey to the underworld.

Hair as a repository of the soul was often used as a sacrificial offering in place of the person's life. It might be placed on an altar or hung from the branches of a sacred tree. Teutonic women used to sacrifice their braids to the goddess Berchta, but then substituted braided bread instead.

Berenice, the wife of Ptolemy III, sacrificed locks of her hair on Aphrodite's altar in order to protect her husband on his campaigns. The hair miraculously disappeared and was placed in the stars as the constellation *Coma Berenices,* Berenice's hair.

The deliberate removal of hair for spiritual purposes signifies a rejection of worldly aims and passions. Catholic priests shaved their tonsures while Catholic nuns, Orthodox Jewish wives, and Buddhists shaved their whole heads.

During the Inquisition, the accused were shaved of all their hair. According to the Inquisitors, Satan's followers couldn't be harmed as long as they had their hair. The saying "To make a clean breast of it," meaning to confess, comes from this practice. Later Hitler, who modeled many of his methods on the Inquisition, also shaved his prisoners.

Hair color also has significance. Long dark hair is credited with the powers of sorcery and seduction. Fair hair is stereotypically used

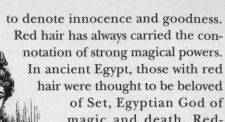

to denote innocence and goodness. Red hair has always carried the connotation of strong magical powers. In ancient Egypt, those with red hair were thought to be beloved of Set, Egyptian God of magic and death. Redheaded children were given amulets to ward Him off from taking them too early. In Russia red hair was a sign of great magical power. According to medieval inquisitors, red hair was a sign of the devil's favor and a sure indicator of a Witch. However, should you be on good terms with a redhead, it will bring you good luck if you run your fingers through his or her hair.

Because hair is so powerful it is said to be of the utmost importance how you dispose of it. Deliberately burning a lock of hair is supposed to inflict pain and possibly death on its original owner. I only know that it is certain to inflict a noxious odor on the person burning it. If you want somebody to come to you, boiling a lock of their hair is supposed to do the trick. If you want to prevent somebody else from doing anything with your own hair or nail trimmings then the safest thing to do is to bury them.

To exchange locks of hair was once a declaration of trust because it was believed possible to do tremendous harm to another through magic if you had some of their hair. Hence lover's exchanged locks as a way of saying, "I trust you with my life."

If you want your hair to grow back quickly, trim it on the New or waxing Moon. It is also said that cutting your own hair is unlucky, although that probably depends more on your skill with a pair of scissors than anything else.

The use of hair as a magical tool has a long and illustrious history. However, magic has no set hairstyle. The length of hair one possesses does not denote one's level of magical power or skill. The important thing is to use your intuitions and abilities to make the most of your own personal magic crop of wild hair.

The Magic of Music: The Harper's Dream

By Melissa Morgan

Alone Celtic harper plays by the fire, shadows flickering, shooting bronze sparks off the strings. His harp is polished by years of use, the dark wood of bog-willow and oak polished to a dull shine. Bard he is, and musician, and magician, and he is working his magic now, subtly weaving it into the music chiming from the small harp he cradles in his arms. The magic woven into the music is one of rest; he calls on Rhiannon of the Birds to help him. Rhiannon's birds sang sweetly to those who marched from war, even as the tired soldiers who are his friends, his family, his clan, are in need of his gentle magic now, crooning with his harp a sweet and lovely lullaby.

The music and magic he worked earlier was of a different sort, strong striking chords to rouse to war. The skirmish with the invaders was successful, this time. The bard's group has learned the value of hit and run, to use their knowledge of the terrain to raid and then seemingly disappear into the woods. Then the music spoke of rejoicing, congratulations, and laughter all around. That was before they realized the price.

They lost two friends and comrades this time, one of them a man he had known since he was a young boy and cared for and respected. As musician and singer, he had called on Arawn, Death Lord, to make a place for his fallen comrades in Annwn. The lament he sang and played that evening would last for hundreds of years, though he knew it not, and thought only of his friends. That was part of his job, too, to move beyond his own feelings and transmute the energies. He knew he had done his job well when he saw the tracks of tears down the grizzled face of the war leader, heard the sniffs around the fire and the quickly muffled sob from the son of the fallen.

It was time for rest. The melody deepened and changed, with always the high harmony for the sentries to keep them awake and aware and shielded from the power of the music to put to sleep. The musician imagined the beautiful face of Rhiannon in his mind and heart, and asked Her blessing on his world. Images of green meadows and golden sunshine, times of harvest, times of hope, the land healed and all harm gone, all pain eased—this and more flowed from his harp, from his heart.

With a sigh, the harper set down his harp gently, with a prayer of thanks to Bran the Blessed, he who carried all of the string musicians on his back when he marched to war. Humming quietly to himself, the harper turned to settle himself in his cloak. His work, for this day, was done. He began to fall asleep, with music still whispering in his mind. As he slept, he dreamed. He dreamed of his ancestors. He saw himself surrounded by great stones.

STONEHENGE

Women and men gather outside the temple to ritually cleanse themselves before entering. The cleansing has been going on all day, with water and herbs and fasting. They gather for the final preparations. Clothes are removed. Breathing is deepening. The chant that will take them to the other state of awareness is begun.

It starts low, with the deepest voices, barely audible. This is an internal process. Each individual adds their voice as they feel moved to do so. Concentration is intense. Their bodies run with sweat. The sound is increasing now; the volume begins to resonate in the stones. When the vibration has reached the perfect balance, the woman who is the Goddess' representative leads the way in. She pauses to touch each stone, to check the vibration and balance. All is perfect. It is the night of the New Moon, clear and cloudless. The woman leads the way in and up. It is a glorious night, incredibly clear. The sound begins to slow and fade. The appropriate space has been achieved. It is now time to look and commune with the stars.

The harper's dream continues. He is reaching further back in time and to another part of the world—to Egypt.

TEMPLE OF ISIS

The temple prepares for the morning hymn. The chironomist who is conducting is gathering her singers, both women and men. A young priestess is having trouble keeping her sistrum, a rattle-like percussion instrument, appropriately silent; small clanking sounds accompany the hushed voices and scurrying about that goes with all pre-performances. The statue of the goddess Isis is brought out; sudden sacred silence falls. As Isis is carried to her place in the center of the temple, all present rattle and shake their sistra to send away all negativity, to magically create a clear and serene space for the holy goddess.

As Isis is placed in her hall, the sweet voice of one young priestess sings out to begin the ritual now that the temple has been cleansed. The voice of the single sister echoes in the main hall of the temple; the troubled water on the reflecting pool in front calms. The choir begins the hymn of praise that welcomes Isis into her temple for the day, and thanks her for keeping all within safe throughout the night, especially the dark hour of Set.

The opening hymn sung, the temple gets on with its work for the day, healing the sick. Often the priestesses will call on some of the temple musicians to come and assist with the healing. It is well known that the resonance and vibrations of different instruments help drive away pain and darkness, and also help bring to the surface underlying emotions.

The bard stirs in his sleep and almost awakens, but there is yet one more journey for him in his dreams, this one into the far future.

CHILDREN'S HOSPITAL, 1997

The Neonatal Intensive Care Unit is busy. It has thirty-three beds, with thirty filled. The beds are cribs with incredible technology attached and available. Next to the units are rocking chairs, some occupied with nurses and infants, some with mothers and infants, some empty.

Baby Rachael has not slept in three days. The nurses have tried everything. Mom has tried everything. Nothing is working. Baby has been having a rough time; she desperately needs her sleep. Mom is pretty tired herself. With circles under her eyes, her attention is focused on the baby.

In comes a man with his harp. He plays at the Neonatal Intensive Care Unit at Children's Hospital regularly. Some on the staff sit up straighter, put their shoulders down; they had not realized how tense they were until they saw him. He begins to play. The music begins very softly, then swells up, then recedes. Baby Rachael goes to sleep. Mom continues to rock her, tears in her eyes, and looks up at the musician. "I don't know what you did, but thank you," she says.

The harper is done now with his dreaming. Deep sleep overtakes him. In the morning, he will wonder at some of the images in his mind. His heart will know he is a part of a long and unbroken tradition. The magic of music comforts him, in his sleeping, in his waking, in his life.

A Sachet for
the Expectant Witch

By Mario Furtado

Throughout the centuries village midwives, who later came to be known as Witches, have had a rich tradition of herbal lore. Their grimoires might have included a recipe for an infusion of fennel to aid an ailing stomach, or a tea made from chamomile to lull the insomniac to sleep. Unfortunately, there has been little said for the expectant Witch, who, like the Goddess, carries the seed of life within her womb. With the exception of the well-versed coven elder, most modern Witches in the course of their studies inadvertently overlook this aspect of herbal wisdom. In doing so, we lose an integral part of our heritage.

In hopes of reversing this trend I'd like to share with you one of my favorite recipes. It is for a truly wonderful and soothing sachet that I created during my wife's pregnancy. In the bath or as the special ingredient in a dream pillow, this recipe is perfect for relaxing away the common discomforts of the magical event to come. To make the sachet, mix together the following ingredients in your cauldron or a wooden bowl.

½   tablespoon lemon balm

1   teaspoon lemon verbena

3   tablespoons lavender

2   tablespoons rose petals

1   teaspoon mugwort

7   drops pure jasmine oil

After mixing all of the ingredients, cut a three-inch square piece of light blue cloth (natural works best). Then place some of the herbal mixture in the center and tie up the loose ends with matching yarn while visualizing the discomforts being soothed away. When you're ready, just toss the sachet into a warm bath and enjoy, or hide it in the batting of your favorite pillow and you've got yourself a special dream pillow.

CREATING A MAGICAL FORMULA

BY RAVEN GRIMASSI

Everyone wants to perform spells and works of magic with consistent and reliable results. There are essentially five so-called "ingredients" that comprise the art of creating successful works of magic. You can adapt them or arrange them according to your own needs as long as you employ them all. These components are personal will, timing, imagery, direction, and balance. Let's look at each one and gain an understanding of the concept.

PERSONAL WILL

Personal will can also be thought of as motivation, temptation, or persuasion. In order to establish enough power to accomplish your goal, you must be sufficiently moved to perform a work of magic. If you do not focus fully on the results, or if you invest only a small amount of energy in your desire, you are unlikely to realize any true results. The stronger your need or desire is, the more likely it is that you will raise the amount of energy required to manifest what you seek. However, desire or need is not enough by itself. Bear in mind that desire must be controlled, and the will must be focused only upon a detached view of the desired outcome of your spell or magical rite. Enflame your mind in the intent while at the same time separating yourself from the desired result. In other words, run the race mindful of the finish line but totally focused on the pace.

TIMING

In the performance of ritual magic, timing can mean success or failure. The best time to cast a spell or create a work of magic is when the target is most receptive. Receptivity is usually assured when the target is passive. People sleep, corporations close overnight and during holidays, etc. One must also take into account the phase of the Moon and the season of the year. Wiccans always work with nature and not against her. Generally speaking, 4:00 AM in the target zone is the most effective time to cast a spell of influence over a person or a situation.

IMAGERY

The success of any work also depends on images created by the mind. This is where the imagination enters into the formula.

Anything that serves to intensify the emotions will contribute to success of your spell. Any drawing, statue, photo, scent, article of clothing, sound, or situation that helps to merge you with your desire will greatly add to your success. Imagery is a constant reminder of what you wish to attract or accomplish. It acts as a homing device in its role as a representation of the object, person, or situation for which the spell is intended. Imagery can be shaped and directed all according to the will of the Wiccan without detracting from focusing the mind on the spell's intent. This becomes the pattern or formula that leads to realization of desire. Surround yourself with images of your desire and you will resonate the vibrations that will attract the thing you desire.

DIRECTION

Once enough energy has been raised, you must direct it toward your desire. Do not be anxious concerning the results, because anxiety will act to draw the energy back to you before it can take effect. Perform your spell casting with the expectation that the magic will work, accept that it has, and simply await its manifestation. Reflecting back on the spell tends to ground the energy because it draws the images and concepts back to you. Once the spell is cast, mentally detach yourself and try to give the matter no more thought so as not to deplete its effectiveness. Mark a seven-day period off on your calendar and evaluate the situation seven days later. It usually takes about seven days (one lunar quarter) for magic to manifest.

BALANCE

The last aspect of magic one has to take into account is personal balance. This means that one must consider the need for the work of magic and the consequences on both the spell caster and the target. If anger motivates your magical work, then wait a few hours or sleep on it overnight. While anger can be a useful propellant for a spell, it can also cloud the thinking. If possible, make sure you have exhausted the normal means of dealing with something before you move to a magical solution. Make sure you are feeling well enough to work magic and plan to rest afterward. Magic requires a portion of your vital essence drawn from your aura. Replenish this with rest even if you do not feel tired. Health problems begin in the aura long before the body is aware of them.

THE RITE OF BALANCE

BY JIM GARRISON

The Lesser Banishing Ritual of the Pentagram (LBRP) is probably one of the most common techniques for preparing sacred space that you'll encounter. Often in the course of magical working or day-to-day life we have use for methods of grounding and centering. While many of us learn the LBRP as a traditional technique for this, as well as many other purposes, the LBRP is not exactly the most obvious expression of Wiccan theology or philosophy. It is compatible, but why not use something that is derived directly from a Wiccan outlook and expresses a distinctly Wiccan philosophy? Here is one alternative technique that is based on a Wiccan approach to the same task. Below is the basic form of this rite, which can easily be adapted to suit your particular tradition or style.

THE RITE OF BALANCE (BASIC FORM)

Face north. Reach upward and feel yourself making contact with a powerful, brilliant source of light beyond the Sun, Moon, and stars. Say:

> From the heavens above I call down the light. Cleanse me and purify my soul that I might enter the circle.

Pause. Feel. Reach down to the Earth below and extend yourself into the core of the world to touch the heart of the planet. Say:

> From the depths below I call upon the spirit of the land. Fill me with vitality and strength that I might serve the old gods.

Close your eyes and look deep within. Extend your right hand toward the east. Say:

> With my right hand I reach out to the new dawn and welcome the wind to walk with me, that I might know the Mysteries.

Extend your left hand toward the west. Say:

> And on the left, I reach out to the crashing waves of the sea, mother of all life, that I might dare to dance with life's tides.

Pause. Feel. Breathe. Say:

> *Behind me, I acknowledge the flames of my passions and drives, the forces of ecstasy and creativity, of rage and chaos that have shaped my life. Now I begin to shape their influence upon me, as I will.*

Pause. Feel. Breathe. Say:

> *Before me is the dark, fertile soil of my future. I stand upon a foundation built by my ancestry. I am a child of the ancient ones, and I would bring life, light, and love into the world whether through my words, my deeds, or my silence.*

Pausc. Feel. Breathe. Say:

> *I stand between wisdom and understanding, that I might pursue truth. I share the gifts of compassion and discipline, that I might respect myself and others. I embrace sensuality even as I pursue knowledge, that I might truly taste and partake of life in its fullest. In my heart I seek beauty and glory, that I might create balance and harmony in all that I do.*

Pause. Feel. Breathe. Open your eyes and proceed.

Simple, yet effective, the Rite of Balance is useful for grounding and centering in a group context, preparing for ritual work, or even after driving home in rush-hour traffic. The words can easily be replaced with others of similar intent. Ideally, you should modify this rite to be more appropriate to the way you do magic. Think of it as a framework on which to create your own, unique structure.

Once this basic form has been mastered, you might consider adjusting and elaborating on it to create a wide range of special versions specifically for self-purification, consecrating tools, performing spell-work, or in healing. Use your intuition and imagination. More advanced forms of this Rite could be used in initiations and special observances such as eldering. Again, take what works and run with it—an it harm none; do as you will!

Magical Stones and Your Sun Sign

By Kim Rogers-Gallagher

O ver many years of being an astrologer, I've found that certain stones possess energies that seem tailor-made for use by each of the Sun signs. So if you're feeling the need to increase your personal power or bring out the most positive qualities of your sign, take a look at this list, and try the stones I've mentioned. No matter what you use, keep in mind that carrying or wearing any stone on the right means you're projecting or sending out that energy, while using it on the left means you're filtering what you receive or attract from your environment.

Aries

Red belongs to Mars, your ruling planet, so you'll love bloodstones, rubies, and garnets, which are all good fiery choices. When you'd like to tamp your fire down a bit, try carnelian. It promotes peace, harmony, and patience, but holds fire and lends warrior-energy to the wearer. Now, your traditional birthstone is the diamond—not a bad fit, since diamonds are known for purity, and Aries energy is pure, too—clean and uncluttered by hidden motives. If your budget doesn't allow for jeweler's diamonds, substitute Herkimer diamonds, long used as a stand-in.

Taurus

There's nothing you like more than a great big chunk of polished, perfect rock—of any kind. The stones that are best for you are lapis, that gorgeous blue stone that's laced with flecks of gold, and rich, fertile jade. The emerald is your traditional birthstone. Emeralds are the charming representative of both the earth element and the planet Venus—the building blocks you're made of. Its soothing color suits you since you're spring-born. This stone is most powerful when set in copper, the metal that corresponds with Venus.

GEMINI

Since you so love variety, it's no wonder your birth stone is the agate. The agate is also associated with Mercury, your ruling planet. It's an aid to truth-telling and good to carry when you want your words to be accurate. Although flourite is not traditionally associated with Gemini, it's a natural match. Fluorite is connected to the air element, as it keeps the mind keen. Stick it on the computer and pick it up when you get stuck between paragraphs.

CANCER

Your planet is the Moon, so the moonstone is naturally connected to you. Its gentle energy protects against absorbing the emotions of others. Sapphires have an affinity with the Moon, too, and will magnify your natural instinct and psychic powers. Chalcedony (a translucent, milky quartz) calms the emotions, and, like moonstones, will keep away depression and sadness—quite a boon for an emotional creature like you. Any pink stone with soothing properties, like rose quartz or rhodochrosite, is also a good talisman for Cancer. Carry or wear any stone on your left (the "incoming" side) as a filter for the emotions.

LEO

Like Aries, a kindred fire sign, you love red, so when it comes to gems and stones, the royal ruby springs to mind. Speaking of royalty, have whatever you wear set in that most royal of all metals—gold. Nothing suits a legend more, and gold has a long-standing link with the Sun, your ruling planet. To increase your natural courage and help you speak eloquently, a trait any performer appreciates, wear carnelian. Amber is also a good match for you, as it holds the life force your sign is famous for.

VIRGO

Although the agate is one of your birthstones, the type that seems to correspond best with your sign is the moss agate, a lovely clear stone

41

with feathery green threads running through it that look like ferns. This stone is best worn while gardening, one of your very favorite pastimes. Agates also promote good physical health, and health is your business, after all. Your other birthstone, the aventurine, increases the perceptive powers, sharpens the intellectual faculties, and helps to fine-tune the eyesight—something any craftsperson can use.

LIBRA

Your traditional birth stone is the opal, but there are other stones that can be worn or carried to help you achieve your goal of finding and keeping that one special other. Any stone associated with Venus, your ruling planet, will do nicely, such as lapis lazuli. This lovely blue stone with golden flecks of pyrite mystically blends the energies of Venus and Mars (the planets in charge of relationships), and is worn to soothe, heal, and calm the wearer. Another good stone for Libra is kunzite, since its specialty is attracting love.

SCORPIO

Black is Pluto's color, and red belongs to Mars, the planet that ruled Scorpio before Pluto was discovered. These are the traditional power colors, and power is your specialty—so these stones will attract you most. Red stones like carnelian, jasper, and red garnets appeal to your warrior side, and black stones fascinate you—like apache tears, black tourmaline, or hematite. To ground and protect yourself, use Pluto's favorite stones, spinel, kunzite, or rutilated quartz, which is perfect for Scorpio since it's a stone within a stone, and, like you, is full of buried treasure.

SAGITTARIUS

Sagittarius' most important goal is to truly be a "wise one," so sodalite is wonderful for you. It helps to gain wisdom and to pass that wisdom back out into the world. Sodalite (and sugilite) also calms the mind, and may help even Sagittarians settle down long enough to meditate. Amethyst, ruled by Sag's planet, Jupiter, is another good match. It

clears the mind and quickens the wit. You'll love both blue and amber topaz, too, said to bring wealth and happiness to all December-born.

CAPRICORN

Rock endures, and permanence is a quality Capricorn finds all too rare, so you're quite fond of all stones. Most books say darker stones are your favorites, like onyx, hematite, and obsidian, because they're affiliated with Saturn, your planet, but try malachite. It operates like a magnet when it comes to attracting a good deal, and if you carry this stone on your left, you'll draw business success. Malachite also helps heal broken bones, and since your sign rules the skeleton of the body, this stone is a kindred spirit.

AQUARIUS

Although your birthstone is the gentle, peace-loving amethyst, your energies seem to blend better with stones that conduct ideas, since you're an air sign, and communication is your business. Aventurine is carried to enhance mental clarity and keenness, and sphere, a greenish stone, is reputed to help with processing information. The best conductor of all is clear quartz, however, so it's not surprising to find clusters placed strategically throughout an Aquarian's home—especially around the computer.

PISCES

The color of any stone you carry directly affects your disposition. So if you're feeling like you need to put out a little more energy than you've got, toss a couple of red stones into your right (or "outgoing" side) pocket. Red carried there gives our personal presentation a fiery "lift." As far as birthstones go, the amethyst has always been yours, and appropriately so: these gentle lavender crystals lift the spirits, protect you from addictions, and aid in good judgment. Sugilite has also been used, just lately, as a birthstone for Pisces. It's a relatively new stone, but it seems to bestow psychic awareness and is said to make the wearer wise.

READING THE ROCKS

BY KEN JOHNSON

Everyone's heard stories like this one: The hero or heroine is wandering through a dark and lonely mountain range on some kind of a quest. The mountain opens up, a light shines from within the earth, and the hero or heroine walks inside—into the world of dwarves and gnomes and hidden treasure.

According to the village sorcerers of Eastern Europe, this opening in the rocks is quite real, and we can learn how to find it for ourselves.

Start with a rock, any rock. Choose one that you like. If need be, you can work with a small one, the kind that will fit in your hand. Personally, I like to hike out to where I can find large rock outcroppings and escarpments—real serious stone people.

Once you have chosen a rock, enter into a state of meditation. Relax. Let your thoughts float away and disappear. When your mind is no longer clouded with mental chatter, shift your awareness to your body. This is important: your attention must rest in your body instead of your mind.

When you have entered fully into your body, examine your rock. Are you a visual person? Then gaze at your rock. Are you a feeling person? Run your hands over your rock, touch it, place your cheek against it and feel its warmth and coolness.

Better still, use your eyes and your sense of touch at the same time.

Whether you're working with a pebble or Mt. Everest, you will eventually notice that there's a part of the rock that looks and feels different. Different in what way? Well, this part of the rock will just seem...softer. It's like the soft spot on a baby's head. This spot is the rock's inner doorway.

Now focus all your attention on that part of the rock. Breathe deeply. Close your eyes. Imagine that you are entering the rock through its doorway.

What comes next? That depends on you and your rock. Everyone's experience is individual. Some people simply feel an incredible sense of calm; their whole being slows down and moves on geological time, which is restful indeed. Other people see visions—pictures and images floating vividly through their minds. These images are part of the imprint of everything that's ever happened here on planet Earth, encoded in the stones. Rocks are very slow and retentive, and they remember everything. They store the imprint of the planet's history in their crystalline grid. If you tap into that endless stream, you have found hidden treasure indeed. Some people see the recent past, like Indian tribes wandering the land. Others see a past more distant. I know of Californians who have practiced this technique and seen echoes of lost Lemuria appear before their inner eyes, and I know of other people who have calmly observed the dinosaurs at their prehistoric pastimes. Like I said, it all depends on you and your rock.

But whatever you see, enjoy.

Brujería Beliefs of
Northern New Mexico

By Marguerite Elsbeth

Back in the 1600s, rumors of witchcraft, or *brujería*, ran rampant in the pinon-spotted hills of northern New Mexico. Many of the locals say that it still does. Here are some modern beliefs about brujería from the Southwest.

Malevolent Witches, called *brujas*, bury carved idols representing their intended victims under the hearthfire, or hang clay likenesses from a tree to let someone know that he or she is marked for mischief.

Tuesdays and Fridays are special days for spell-casting. According to New Mexican folklore, these days are best for making rag dolls, wax figures, magic charms, amulets, and recipes of enchantment.

Rings of salt are sometimes placed around a suspected bruja's house to stop an enchantment. Or one may throw salt at an owl (the bruja's familiar spirit) while making the sign of the cross.

Salves, massage, and medicinal herbs and plants are some of the healing remedies used by *arbularias* (Witches who heal) to help patients recover their self-esteem, confidence, and good health.

To cure the fright of being enchanted, a healer takes dust from the four corners of a graveyard, places it on a piece of red flannel, and boils it with the victim's mother's wedding ring. The healer then makes the sign of the cross over the brew. The patient takes three swallows, repeating a quick prayer between each sip, and is cured.

High Magic
in Colonial America

By John Michael Greer

The images of America's colonial past that show up during the Thanksgiving season each year may seem to have little relevance to modern magicians and Pagans beyond their relation to the grim memories of Salem Village. Most of the time, accordingly, when we think of the spiritual lives of people in the American colonies, what comes to mind is the sort of dour Puritan grimness found in works like Jonathan Edwards' *Sinners in the Hands of an Angry God*. Still, the reality was a good deal more complex, and there were plenty of other currents at work in colonial society. One of them, an important one, was the tradition of Renaissance high magic, which continued to be practiced in the colonies through the eighteenth century and beyond.

It's impossible to say just how early the first ceremonial magicians arrived on this continent. Well before 1700, though, Pennsylvania boasted several groups of German Rosicrucians, who had immigrated in search of religious freedom. The most significant of these groups, founded by the mystic Johann Kelpius, set up a community near what is now Ephrata, Pennsylvania, where they performed rituals, practiced alchemy, and studied the writings of Jacob Boehme and other mystical occultists. The Ephrata community took in very few new members and gradually died out in the mid-eighteenth century, but not before leaving a

legacy of occult traditions that many later magicians would follow.

The presence of these Rosicrucian groups was not the only factor in bringing high magic to the colonies, however. It's also clear that some of the most important texts of the English magical revival underway in those same years were crossing the Atlantic as well. In 1696, for example, a young Quaker named Robert Roman was formally censured by the Concord Monthly Meeting for practicing "astrology, geomancy, chiromancy, and necromancy." Disowned by the meeting a short time later for refusing to renounce his belief in astrology, Roman was hauled into court for "practicing geomancy according to Hidden (Heydon) and divining with a stick." Court records indicate that Roman owned copies of John Heydon's *Temple of Wisdom,* an important manual of geomancy, and Cornelius Agrippa's *Three Books of Occult Philosophy,* the most complete of all the handbooks of Renaissance high magic.

The remarkable Christopher Witt had a more successful career as a colonial magician. Witt was one of the few English students of Johann Kelpius, and he continued to study and practice Kelpius' teachings long after the original community had disappeared. The botanist John Bartram, a friend of Witt's, described a visit in 1743 in terms that leave no question of Witt's involvements: "We went into his study, which was furnished with books containing different kinds of learning; as Philosophy, Natural Magic, Divinity, nay even Mystical Divinity; all of which were the subject of our discourse within doors." Witt was apparently the author of several volumes of "Rosecution (Rosicrucian) philosophy," now unfortunately lost.

Witt had several students whose names survive, and their histories point up an important factor in the social status of magic during this time. A Mr. Fraily, more commonly known as "Old Shrunk," went on to become a successful "cunning man" in parts of Pennsylvania and New Jersey. His professional repertoire included cures for bewitchment, methods for finding lost treasure, and all the rest of the stock-in-trade of American folk magic. Another of Witt's students, Anthony Larry, followed much the same course in another part of New Jersey. As the new learning of the Scientific Revolution won over the upper classes, the social standing of the magician slid accordingly. Much of Renaissance magical theory and practice, though, stayed intact all through this process of downward mobility, and as a result, material straight out of high magic became mingled with every level of American folk tradition. It's because of this that a remarkable amount of the hoodoo and conjure magic still practiced in America can trace its roots back to the great magical theorists and practitioners of Renaissance Europe.

It's important for us to remember that the history of magic in America goes back to the beginnings of American history itself, and that modern magicians on this continent are part of a long and living tradition. As you pass by pictures of men and women in Pilgrim outfits this Thanksgiving, take a moment to recall that some of the people they represent spent a good deal of their time casting spells and studying forbidden books by firelight.

SOURCES

Hyatt, Harry Middleton. *Hoodoo-Conjuration-Witchcraft-Rootwork*. 1970.

Leventhal, Herbert. *In the Shadow of the Enlightenment: Occultism and Renaissance Science in Eighteenth-Century America*. 1976.

Sachse, Julius F. *The German Pietists of Provincial Pennsylvania*. 1895.

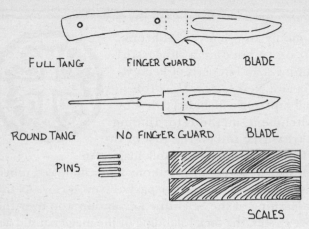

Knife-Making Terms

Assembling Your Own Athame

By Breid Foxsong

Most books of shadows recommend that you make your own tools. This gives you a closer tie to them, as well as a great deal of respect for those who do this commercially. One of the most essential tools of the Witch is the athame, or black-handled knife.

The simplest way to make a knife is to glue two scales on the tang of a blade to form a handle. This is called a basic scale handle. Before going into the actual process of attaching the hilt to the blade, we need to define a few terms and discuss the process of finding the blade you want.

Knife-Making Terms

BLANK: The metal section of the knife, usually a blade with a tang.

KNIFE: The completed blank with a handle.

SCALE: This is the wood (or other material) that makes the handle. It comes pre-split and in the proper size for handle-making.

TANG: This is the part of the knife that the handle goes on. The blank we will use is called a *full scale tang*.

BLADE: The sharp end of the knife.

PINS: Most commonly available in brass or German silver (nickel), the pins are what hold the scales to the tang. Uncoated brazing rods make good inexpensive pins, and work as well as commercial pins. They are available in several different sizes (¼₆, ³⁄₃₂, ⅛, and ³⁄₁₆ inches are the most common diameters), so be sure to get the right size (usually ³⁄₃₂ inch).

FINDING PARTS

To find the proper blank, you have two choices—buying locally or buying through the mail. By buying locally, you are also purchasing expertise, or at least meeting face to face with someone whom you can ask questions. You also have a chance to see the blades close-up and can decide clearly which blades you like. The disadvantages include a limited supply and sometimes higher prices. Mail order often has a wide supply of blades, but you never quite know what you are getting until you have already spent the money.

Now, how do you go about exercising these options? First, you can locate a knife-making supply store near you. This will take time and a good telephone directory. Start by looking under cutlery, black powder supplies, gun shops, hunting supplies, or sporting goods (in that order of likelihood) in the phone book, and just keep going until you find someone with blanks for sale. If you cannot find a local supplier, you can move on from there to option number two, mail order. You can find supplies and suppliers listed in any knife or weaponry magazine such as *Blade*.

It's probably better to obtain the scales and pins when you get the blank, but any place that does braising or welding should have bits of rod lying around, and any fancy wood store can make scales. Traditional woods for a black-handled knife are ebony, rosewood, or walnut.

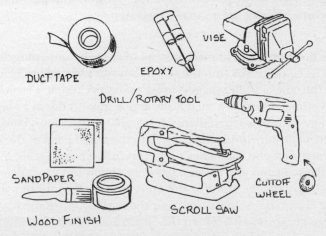

DUCT TAPE   EPOXY   VISE

DRILL/ROTARY TOOL

SANDPAPER   CUTOFF WHEEL

WOOD FINISH   SCROLL SAW

What You'll Need to Assemble an Athame

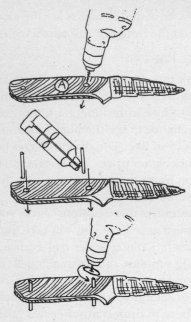

The Assembly Process

After you've bought the blank, the scales, and the supplies, you can start the assembling process. Be sure to read the article through before beginning so you know what to expect.

Step One

Wrap tape around the sharp end of the blade. Duct tape or something similar is necessary so that you can grasp the blade without cutting yourself or accidentally damaging the blade. If you are concerned about damaging the surface, wrap a piece of paper around the knife before you tape it, but you must be sure it will not come off as you handle the blade.

Setting the Pins

Step Two

If you are going to etch or draw runes or symbols on the tang, do so. By drawing the symbols on the tang rather than on the blade, you can conceal the symbols. Many people prefer to write just a simple rune for protection or power. If you are not going to put runes or symbols on your tang, go on to the next step.

Step Three

Pins will hold the scales in place instead of rivets because pins do not need to be countersunk into the scales, but you will need to glue the scale to the tang as well. I suggest using epoxy because it is watertight and very strong. Epoxy is a chemically drying glue (it doesn't need air to set) mixed from two ingredients. It is available from most hardware or department stores and adheres well to the metal parts of the knife (and everything else it touches so be careful). Epoxy a scale to one side of the tang and place it in a pressure clamp or tape it firmly so that it will dry tightly. Wait for the epoxy to dry. Be sure to pad the pressure clamp so that it does not mar the new handle of the blade. A thin piece of cardboard between the clamp and the scale is sufficient.

Step Four

Drill holes through the tang and scale from the tang side (most knives have pre-drilled holes to guide you). Your drill bit should be exactly the same size as the hole in the tang (usually $\frac{3}{32}$ inch). This will ensure that the holes are perpendicular to the tang.

Step Five

Epoxy the second scale to the other side of the tang. Place it in a pressure clamp or tape it firmly so that it will dry tightly and wait for it to completely dry. Make sure that the ends of the scales are even on the blade end of the blank. They are hard to cut, polish, or grind when they are already glued on.

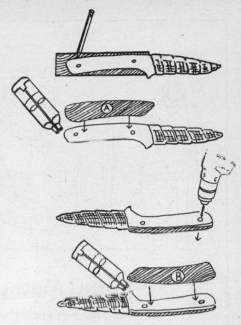

Shaping and Fixing the Handle

Step Six

Drill holes through the handle (through the second scale), then glue the pins in the holes.

Step Seven

Clip or grind the pins down to level with the handle. Then sand and polish the handle to shape. Most tangs come in a finished shape. On a first knife it is best to match the scale to that shape. If you want to put runes on the handle, then carve, burn, or paint them on at this time. Finish the handle using varnish, tung oil, or some other sealer to waterproof the wood.

Step Eight

Remove the tape on the blade. If any residue is left from the tape, it can easily be removed with acetone or rubbing alcohol. Don't cut yourself. Take your time and be careful and you will create your own functional and highly personalized magical tool.

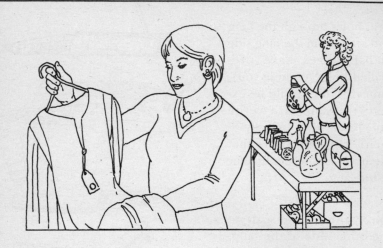

FINDING MAGICAL TOOLS

BY ESTELLE DANIELS

Hello once again, all you magical practitioners, this is Honest Roj of Honest Roj's Occult Emporium and Discount Supply Shoppe. We just got in a new shipment direct from the manufacturers to you. We cut out the middle man to bring you the best prices in this continuum! Browse our shop on the astral before coming into the store to buy. That's Honest Roj's Occult Emporium and Discount Supply Shoppe. Thirteen convenient locations to serve you!

Wouldn't it be wonderful if there were really an "Honest Roj's," where a person could get whatever they needed in the way of magical supplies, all for discount store prices? Well, it just isn't that way, so magical people are stuck with more conventional means when looking for magical goodies.

There are, however, resources that you might not have considered when going to get that new athame or jewelry. Let Auntie Estelle the magical bargain hunter give you a few of her time-honored tips.

First and foremost, the best place to get magical goodies is your plain old-fashioned garage sale. The trick here is to go to a lot of sales. One or two won't get you the big bargains, but if you take a day and plan your route you can hit twenty or more, and you are almost guaranteed to find something that others have overlooked. Make a magical shopping list, but keep an open mind as well for those unexpected treasures. Having change helps lots, and don't be afraid to bargain, as long as it's done with a noble intent and respect for the other person. Always remember to thank your deity when you do get a good bargain. It helps in getting more. Flea markets and rummage sales are another resource for interesting items. They are just more concentrated versions of garage sales.

Mall shows, craft fairs, and gem, mineral, and rock shows are also interesting places to find things. You may end up buying materials and then doing the assembly work, but that makes the item more personalized. Jewelry is an especially good find at gem, mineral, and rock shows. You can get one-of-a-kind pieces and possibly even commission that perfect piece. Many of the vendors at these larger shows come from great distances and some will also do mail-order business once you have hooked up with them.

Going-out-of-business sales sometimes have remarkable things. This is when the store owner has everything on sale, even that stuff that has been in the back closet for a couple of years and never sold. Liquidator or dollar stores that end up with a lot of last season's or slow-selling merchandise are another resource the enterprising magician should know about. With these stores it's definitely buy it when you see it, for it may be gone next time you come in.

A great source for athames and swords is a gun show. Along with firearms, many dealers also sell knives. There is a wonderful variety available, and you have it there in front of you to see and handle. The prices are also usually better than you can find in the catalogs. You can learn a bit about the different kinds and qualities of materials and understand why two swords may look similar yet be priced very differently. You can also subtly run energy through the piece before you buy it, to see if it will be good for you. There may also be people there who make custom knives.

Catalogs are another source, but they aren't universally great. Many "New Age" catalogs seem to tack an extra zero onto all of their prices. Some people prefer to see the item and actually handle it before making a commitment to buy. Using catalogs and shows together is definitely helpful because you get an idea of what's available from the catalog and then when you see it at the show (or wherever) you know what the catalog price was, and how much of a bargain it really is in person.

Museum replicas are a good source of statues and jewelry. There are stores that specialize in these items, and most museums have a gift shop attached. Shop their sales and you can really get some good bargains. They may also publish a catalog, and you can get good stuff there also. Understand though that many museum shops are there to generate revenue for the museum, so prices may be higher than in a catalog or other place. Natural product and nature stores are another place to go for rocks and other interesting jewelry items.

Food co-ops are a great resource for spices and loose incense. Bring your own baggies and containers. They may have imported dishware and other items that can be adapted for magical use. Some places do mail-order herbs and spices, and that is where you might find those hard-to-find items like asafoetedia. Don't forget the ethnic grocery store. If you live in a place where there are various ethnic stores, go in and take a look. Most carry way more than just food and spices (though those can be really neat also), and looking for magical type goodies is certainly possible in those crowded shelves. Places like that become a treasure hunt, as you never really know just what you might find. You might be able to get god and goddess pictures, statues, and the like there as well. Books are also sometimes available, usually imported directly.

Be flexible, be open to things where you might not ordinarily expect them, and keep your eyes open.

56

Swords of Magic and Myth

By deTraci Regula

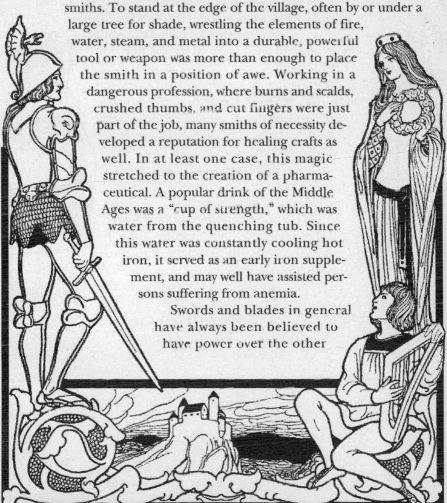

Shrieking through the air, glinting in the sunlight, pulled flame-red out of the forge, defending against demons and daughters of darkness, casting power or protection; swords, magical or otherwise, fascinate us. From a pile of metallic rocks to this gleaming tapered triangle of steel, the process alone of creating one seems almost magical. Smiths were known and feared as potent wizards. A historical priestly charm begs for protection from the magic arts of women and smiths. To stand at the edge of the village, often by or under a large tree for shade, wrestling the elements of fire, water, steam, and metal into a durable, powerful tool or weapon was more than enough to place the smith in a position of awe. Working in a dangerous profession, where burns and scalds, crushed thumbs, and cut fingers were just part of the job, many smiths of necessity developed a reputation for healing crafts as well. In at least one case, this magic stretched to the creation of a pharmaceutical. A popular drink of the Middle Ages was a "cup of strength," which was water from the quenching tub. Since this water was constantly cooling hot iron, it served as an early iron supplement, and may well have assisted persons suffering from anemia.

Swords and blades in general have always been believed to have power over the other races of beings that inhabit this Earth. Iron and steel were thought to be potent against faeries, and blades were not to be left edge-up, as it was believed that the faerie beings would cut themselves and then seek retribution. In magic, swords and knives are used to direct power, erect magical protection, and, if necessary, remind a turbulent spirit that the magician is armed physically as well as magically.

By the nature of the processes that form them, swords are considered to possess a kind of purity. All the dross, the impurities of the metal, has been burned away. From early times, this was used as a metaphor for human spiritual development as well, though some religions took the "burning away" portion of it a bit too literally.

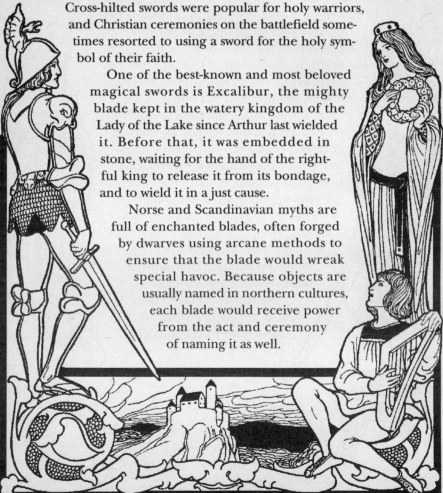

Cross-hilted swords were popular for holy warriors, and Christian ceremonies on the battlefield sometimes resorted to using a sword for the holy symbol of their faith.

One of the best-known and most beloved magical swords is Excalibur, the mighty blade kept in the watery kingdom of the Lady of the Lake since Arthur last wielded it. Before that, it was embedded in stone, waiting for the hand of the rightful king to release it from its bondage, and to wield it in a just cause.

Norse and Scandinavian myths are full of enchanted blades, often forged by dwarves using arcane methods to ensure that the blade would wreak special havoc. Because objects are usually named in northern cultures, each blade would receive power from the act and ceremony of naming it as well.

Dwarves are renowned as metal-workers, and tales of their weapons and other adornments are abundant. They were associated with the "knocking" heard by miners. It was natural to believe that these sounds represented a hidden forge where metals were worked and pounded to tempered strength. There are many named swords in Northern European myth. Here are a few of them.

BALMUNG: The blade of Siegfried, forged by dwarves and given to him to defend the Nibelungs, who betrayed him. Balmung was resistant to magic spells, and aided him in his battle against twelve giants.

ECKESAX: Gold-hilted, inlaid blade also made by Wieland, and borne by the giant Ecke. He fought with Dietrich for the hand of Seburg, a beautiful princess. They fought by the light created from the swords sparking against stones. Only by seizing the giant's fine sword and using it against him was Dietrich able to prevail against his huge foe.

MIMUNG: Forged by Wieland, the famous smith, and given to his son Witege.

SWORD OF VICTORY: A rare blade believed to be more powerful than Thor's hammer, it was forged by Thjasse-Volund, whose family turned against the gods and allied themselves with the frost giants. He intended to conquer Asgard with it. There was nothing that it could not slice through. However, before the smith could put his plan into action, the sword was seized by Mimer-Nidhad and kept in a treasure cave. Eventually, this blade was wielded by

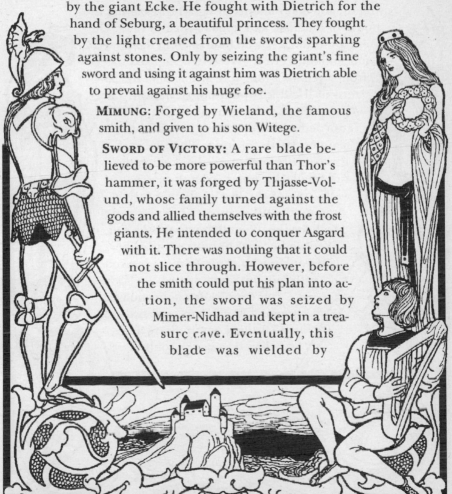

Svipdag the Brave, who ultimately prevailed over Thor himself, as Thjasse-Volund had hoped.

In China, both men and women were sometimes involved in the forging of a sword. Taoist adepts, similar to Western alchemists, were masters of the secrets of metal-making and of swords. Since many of the Taoist deities are believed to be star gods, placing star-patterns on the blade brings in the cosmic force from that region of the sky. Constellation designs, represented by a pattern of dots or stars, are often engraved on blades, particularly those of the Longquan style, a popular martial arts sword even today. One of the most potent of these designs is the Big Dipper, often placed in combination with dragon and phoenix designs representing the power of the male and female, yin and yang. Ou Yezi, a swordmaker who flourished in the Spring and Autumn Period (770–476 BCE), used water from seven wells that were arranged in the pattern of the Big Dipper constellation. The first pair of swords he made that were adorned with these designs did not remain on Earth for long. When he cast this pair of swords into the quenching tub filled with water from these seven wells, one of the blades turned into a dragon, the other into a phoenix, and both flew away together into the sky. Ou Yezi worked with another swordmaker, a woman who is sometimes pictured with him but rarely named.

There is a close connection between dragons, stars, and swords in Chinese myth. Stars are believed to be the souls of

60

dragon swords, and dragons can appear in the shape of swords. By this logic, the star-gods are really dragons, which are swords, which are stars. Japanese swords share some similar traditions.

At the Tokyo National Museum, a recent exhibition brought together hundreds of the nation's most renowned swords in one exhibit. Displayed in cases one after the other, the gleaming, slightly curved, and very yang blades looked like slivers of the Moon, bringing together the power of male and female. Regrettably, many of the scabbards were not displayed with the blades. They are lost to time, since they are less durable than the steel they protect. The designs on them ranged from the magical strength of swirling dragons to delicate images of tri-color cats playing against a delicate gold lacquer background.

Japanese sword makers traditionally chant while taking the blade through the various processes. Modern observers believe that these chants serve a purely practical function, that of timing the various stages in the making of the blade. But each piece of steel created against this vibratory background contains the magic of countless years from the first moment a stone, tossed in a very hot fire, emitted a stream of shining metal, creating an object of havoc, power, and beauty.

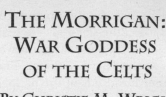

THE MORRIGAN: WAR GODDESS OF THE CELTS

BY CHRISTIE M. WRIGHT

In Celtic society, women played a very important role. Equal to men, they could own land, obtain a divorce and not be left penniless, and fight in battles. They were mothers, lovers, warriors, hunters, politicians, leaders, and much, much more.

It seems natural that their goddess of war should be a feminine entity. I should say goddesses, for the Morrigan is a triple-figure composed of Macha, Badb, and Nemain. Collectively, their name means "the phantom queen," probably due to their uncanny powers of shapeshifting.

In looking at the three goddesses of the Morrigan, one can see the Mother in Macha, whose name means "battle." While pregnant with twins, she was forced to run a race against the two fastest horses in Ireland, incidentally mares. She won the race, but died while giving birth afterward. With her last breath, she cursed the men of Ulster to have great labor pains whenever danger threatened.

Macha may also be equated to Brighid, another triple entity. Macha, like Brighid, possessed a sacred shrine in which an eternal flame was tended by temple maidens; both shrines were eventually taken over by nuns who kept the flame living, yet changed the name of the deity to whom the shrines were devoted.

Badb, on the other hand, is an extremely powerful goddess whose name means "one who boils," linking her to the Otherworld cauldron over which she is said to preside. In Celtic belief, it is Badb who will bring about the end world destruction by causing the great cauldron to boil over, drowning the planet and all creatures upon it.

Badb belongs to two triplicities: The Fury and the Morrigan, playing the part of the hag in each. She is linked with the *Beansidhe* (English: banshee), a faery of death who was often seen at a ford, washing the armor of those who would die in the battle ahead. It is said that on Samhain Badb can tell you the time of your death, should you wish it!

Little is said of Nemain, save that her name means "venemous one," and that she is a crone goddess.

When battle ensued, the Morrigan would sometimes fly over the field in the form of a crow or raven, watching eagerly for carrion, and screeching to cause the slain to move about in a grotesque dance. Her harvest consisted of trophies of slain warriors.

There might even be a link between the Greek goddess of war, Athena, and the Celtic Morrigan. Each can be seen as a personification of the culture in which she existed. The Greeks were philosophical by nature, so it stands to reason that their goddess of war would not run into battle screeching and calling for blood. As it is, Athena is often depicted wearing a long white tunic with hardly any armor, and a snow white owl perched upon her shoulder. The Morrigan likely entered the battle naked, as did her warriors, screaming like a banshee and killing any enemy that dared to move. The Celts were a wild people, governed by the natural world with all its dangers, while the Greeks appeared to live in a kingdom of clouds. Both goddesses were a product of their society and each served their purposes for the people.

It is best to work with the goddesses of the Morrigan one at a time as their collective energies are powerfully dangerous. One may call on Them for passing over rituals, or to aid in overcoming an enemy. Servicemen and women may call on Them when entering battle. Symbols of the Morrigan include the raven, crow, obsidian, and rubies, the waning and dark Moons, nighshade, henbane, and black dogs.

The Morrigan has much to teach, and like any teacher, commands respect. Remember, the Morrigan is a potent force that must be treated with care and caution.

Spic 'n' Span

By Therese Francis

All Natural Super Cleaner

½   ounce rosemary leaves
1   quart hot water
2   tablespoons borax
1   teaspoon liquid vegetable oil-based soap (such as castile)

Steep rosemary leaves in hot water for at least 10 minutes. Strain into spray bottle. Add borax and soap. Spray on and wipe off counter tops, bath tubs, etc. For really tough spots, let soak for 10 minutes. Good for windows and mirrors, too.

Wood Furniture Polish

1   part lemon juice
2   parts olive oil
1–2   drops vitamin E oil (preservative)

Mix and apply to wood furniture. Rub in. This will also take care of minor scratches for most wood finishes. (I keep the mixture in the refrigerator between uses.)

Mildew Away

1   cup vinegar or ½ cup lemon juice
    Pinch of salt

Mix together and use to clean the hard-to-get-rid-of mildew from anywhere.

Drain Cleaner

½   cup baking soda
½   cup vinegar

Pour baking soda down drain. Add vinegar. Stand back because the chemical reaction causes lots of bubbles.

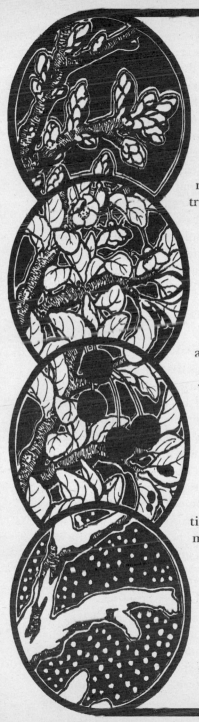

Celebrating The Eight Seasons

By Kim Rogers-Gallagher

It's inarguable that modern life affords us with many wonderful conveniences the ancients never had, like electricity, telephones, and heating. With the planet Uranus, the computer genius, now in Aquarius, there's a lot more to come.

Unfortunately, although these advances in communication and technology have pulled us closer together intellectually, they've drawn us farther away from our spiritual selves, and we've lost a great deal of the connection the ancients had with our mother, the Earth.

One of the most important traditions we've lost is the concept of the eight seasons. Yes, eight. Ancient peoples realized that the earth was alive, and therefore in a constant state of change. They knew that those changes occurred far more often than four times a year, and that, in fact, the Earth made a transition that was quite noticeable about eight times a year, or every forty-five days. It makes sense, too, if you think about it. Take summer, for example. The Sun is at its brightest and hottest in the Northern Hemisphere during this season, but the Earth doesn't stay the same for all ninety days. Summer has a beginning, a peak, and a waning. So although the beginning of each of the four seasons— the Equinoxes and Solstices—were times of celebration, the peaks of these three-month periods were, too. In short, the ancients renewed their relationship with our Earth Mother every forty-five days.

No matter how technologically advanced we become, we're still guests on this planet—and the least we can do to thank the Earth for her hospitality is to honor her on each of her eight seasons.

There are all kinds of books that outline the beliefs and customs of the wise folks who came centuries before us. Two of the best I've found are *Wicca: A Guide for the Solitary Practitioner,* by the late, great Scott Cunningham, and *The Wheel of the Year* by Pauline and Dan Campanelli. For those of you who can't wait to get started on your path toward bonding with the Earth, here's a nutshell listing of each season, its meaning, and some simple celebrations to help you begin.

MARCH 20
EOSTAR/SPRING EQUINOX

This is one of the seasons that reminds us that we're mammals like our animal brothers and sisters. We share the joy of the Earth in spring as we tilt back our heads, sniff the air, and notice that everything smells new. We feel the life force stirring beneath our feet. In ancient times, this day when light and darkness were equal was called Eostar or Ostara. This season of rebirth was the predecessor of the Christian holy day Easter, which children now celebrate by decorating eggs. Back then, these eggs were eaten to promote prosperity and fertility. Celebrate spring by venturing out for a walk and saying good morning to the earth as she awakens from her long winter nap. Decorate your home with fresh spring flowers, and shake off the winter blues. Daylight is overtaking darkness, and life is returning.

MAY 1
BELTANE/MAY DAY

Spring is at her peak now. That good green smell is everywhere. Waterfalls burst over familiar paths, and the Earth is wet and fertile. Flowers of every color fill the meadows, and the promise of new life made to us at Ostara is fulfilled. Just as the passions of the Earth Mother are obvious now, so too are our own. Traditionally, this was the time of year when the ancients danced and wove ribbons around the Maypole, made love in the cornfields, and leaped the bonfires. Do homage to the Earth at this time by sipping a cup of wine or spreading out a blanket and enjoying a picnic beneath a special tree with a lover. Creating a May bowl is another way to connect with the season. Fill a bowl with fruits and wine, and float white flowers and green leaves on top. Rejoice in the warmth of spring at her fullest.

JUNE 20
MIDSUMMER/LITHA/SUMMER SOLSTICE

This first day of summer is also the longest day of light in the Northern Hemisphere. The breeze is balmy and pleasant, and flowers are in full bloom. The ancients celebrated Midsummer because the fruits (literally) of their hard work were now obvious in their gardens and fields, and even in the fruit-laden trees. They also considered this the most potent time of year to work magic of any kind, and the best month to be married. Decorate your home with roses and other summer flowers. Gather herbs and look for feathers on the ground to weave into magical charms and talismans. The Earth Mother welcomes us outdoors to share her wonders in warmth and comfort. Celebrate summer by walking barefoot whenever you can.

AUGUST 1
LAMMAS

As summer peaked, it was time for the ancients to take in their first harvests. This was a time of both joy and sadness, for although the light was waning and the growing season was winding down, the cupboards were full of the products of their hard labor. Corn dollies that symbolized the goddess of grain were created by weaving wheat stalks, and corn breads in the shape of the god of grain were baked in honor of his sacrifice. Celebrate this time of first harvest by baking corn bread, visiting wineries, and sprouting seeds to symbolize the resurrection of the Corn King. Decorate with sheafs of wheat and grain, and spend the warmest of evenings on a porch swing.

SEPTEMBER 20
MABON/FALL EQUINOX

Once again, day and night are in perfect balance. The ancients thought of this month's Full Moon as the Wine Moon (now our Harvest Moon), and they celebrated accordingly. The second harvest was taken in, and it was time to take stock of how well they had prepared for the coming winter. In European countries, fruits for wine are still harvested at this time. Celebrate this time of balance and preparation by taking stock of yourself. What can you harvest now? Which of your labors has yielded fruit? What's unfinished that must still be done? Gather seeds of knowledge by taking classes. Hang Indian corn on your door, decorate with gourds, pumpkins, and cornstalks, and gather dried plants and roots for medicines.

OCTOBER 31
SAMHAIN/HALLOWEEN

As autumn peaks and the Earth Mother draws in her resources to prepare for the coming cold of winter, we think fondly of those living creatures, both human and animal, who have left us over the year. In many ways, the harvest is over, and it's time to accept what's gone. Samhain, or Halloween, was a time to celebrate those passages—even the passage of the living to the Underworld. One of the most charming traditions involves burying an apple at the foot of your favorite tree at midnight as food for the dead on their journey to the Underworld, and leaving a candle lit in the window to guide them along their way. This is also a time of recognition, and as such, it is thought that if you look into a mirror by candlelight at midnight, you'll see the face of your true love. The veil between the worlds is at its thinnest now, as any good magic book will tell you, so it's a wonderful time to use your predictive tools (tarot cards, pendulums, runes, or crystal balls) to see the future. Celebrate the season by filling a clay pot with autumn flowers. Drink warm cider, and gather in foodstuffs for the winter.

December 21
Yule/Winter Solstice

On the longest night of the year, the Winter Solstice, the Sun God symbolically begins his journey back to the light. It's a time of silence and rest for all of us—another season when we realize how much like the animals we really are. We turn in earlier and seem to have less energy during the dark evenings as the Earth Mother rests, gathering her strength for the coming spring. Celebrate this season by decorating with mistletoe, holly, and evergreen boughs. If you celebrate Christmas, buy a "living tree" or Norfolk Island Pine to keep the spirit of the season alive all year in your tree, rather than destroying one needlessly. Burn wood from a felled oak tree in your fireplace—the roots, if you can find them. Decorate a yule log (also of oak) with greens and a red bow or ribbon—a symbol of the Sun God who is symbolically born at this time. Kiss someone you love under the mistletoe (an old Druid custom).

February 2
Imbolc/Candlemas

Even as winter peaks, the days gradually grow longer, and it seems that spring may come after all. In warmer climates, bulbs begin to peek up through the warming earth. This is the feast of the waxing light, as the Sun God grows and strengthens. It is called Candlemas (and corresponds with our modern Groundhog Day) because the ancients traditionally lit candles just after sunset throughout their homes, sometimes in the shape of a star, to welcome the Son of the Goddess—the Star Child. It is a time of inspiration to prepare for spring. Celebrate by creating a Corn Bride from grain or corn. Dress her in a white dress, and set her in her bride's bed—a basket. Imbolc also means first milk, and was named as such to celebrate the return of milk to the homes of those who kept animals. Have a cup of warm milk or a glass of spring water during the evenings, light white candles and invite the Earth Mother to wake gradually and peacefully from her slumber.

Birthday Rite for Sun Sign and Spirit

By Janina Renee

Birthdays were big family affairs in ancient Rome because the Romans celebrated them religiously. One of the main features of a Roman birthday feast was a rite in honor of the individual's special tutelary spirit (known as a man's "genius" or a woman's "juno") that corresponded to what we might think of as a guardian angel or a personal spirit of good luck. Until the emperor Theodosius banned birthday parties in AD 392, Roman celebrants wore white for luck, placed flowers on an altar made of turf, burned candles and incense, and made offerings of wine and honey cakes to the birthday person's guardian spirit. They made wishes for happiness, well-being, prosperity, good health, and long life, and the genius or juno was asked to "return often to his festival" (Thomas 55–57).

The Romans thought that the luck and well-being of the individual was bound up with this spirit, and perhaps they felt that honoring one's genius or juno had an energizing effect. Philosophically, we could relate this regeneration of the personal spirit to the solar return. This astrological event occurs on or very near your birthday, when the Sun returns to its original position in your chart, in the same degrees it occupied on the day of your birth. Your Sun, which represents your core creative and energetic self, is re-energized, so birthdays are also auspicious astrologically.

To take advantage of this added good energy and to reaffirm both your solar core and your connection to the spiritual world, you can take inspiration from the ancient Romans. Following is a simple birthday rite to refresh the "numen" (the psychic energy store) of your personal Sun and your guardian spirit. Select three candles: a white candle representing the guardian spirit, a gold candle representing the vitality of the Sun, and an "astral" candle, which is a candle in one of the colors associated with your Sun sign (see last paragraph).

Upon rising on the morning of your birthday, prepare a focus area with the candles, as well as flowers and incense. Then, light the white candle and say:

> *On this day of self-renewal, I light this candle in honor of the spirit of light within me.*

Light the golden candle and say:

> *On this day of my Sun's anniversary, I light this golden candle, and honor the energizing power of the Sun within me.*

Finally, light the colored astral candle and say:

> *With this candle, I honor the qualities and the needs of my core self, the expression of the creativity within me.*

You can leave the candles burning for as long as is convenient. Then go about your day, mindful of the many spiritually auspicious meanings of your birthday, a day when you can really shine.

Following are some colors attributed to the signs of the zodiac. However, if there is some other color that resonates for you, use that instead. Aries: red, white, and yellow; Taurus: green, brown, and pink; Gemini: yellow, blue, and orange; Cancer: white, silver, and light blue; Leo: gold, yellow, and red; Virgo: yellow, green, and orange; Libra: rose, blue, and white; Scorpio: red, black, and dark blue; Sagittarius: purple, indigo, and turquoise; Capricorn: black, brown, and dark green; Aquarius: blue-green, metallic blue, and white; and Pisces: foam green, blue-green, and salmon pink.

SOURCES

Adkins, Lesley and Roy A. *Handbook to Life in Ancient Rome.* NY: Facts on File, 1994.

Balsdon, J.P.V.D. *Life and Leisure in Ancient Rome.* NY: McGraw-Hill, 1969.

Thomas, Ruth Edith. *The Sacred Meal in the Older Religion.* diss. U of Chicago, 1935. Chicago: U of Chicago Libraries, private edition. 1937.

Cat Tales

By D. J. Conway

Down through the centuries there have been many tales and superstitions about cats, some of them positive, but even more of them negative. The cat was considered to be an animal of the Great Goddess. When the patriarchal cultures replaced the Goddess with their God, they needed to discredit any creature that was connected with Her. What happened to the cat also happened to the owl, the bat, and the raven. Unfortunately, constant propaganda turned the tide against the Goddess' creatures, especially the cat.

The following beliefs are given for the sake of interest alone. Common sense will tell any intelligent person that the negative beliefs about cats are not true. Cats are loving but independent animals who share our homes and fill our lives with joy and happiness. It is amazing that the belief that black cats bring bad luck exists primarily in the United States. In many European countries, a cat of this color is considered to bring the very best of luck into a household.

- In ancient Egypt, women wore amulets of cats so they would be fortunate in love and all things feminine. A woman who wanted children would wear an amulet of a cat and kittens. The number of kittens indicated the number of children she wished to have.

- Wives were once made to drink milk with a cat's eye stone in it to prevent them from conceiving children while their husbands were gone on a journey.

- If a black cat crosses your path and/or enters your house, it will bring good luck. This superstition may have come from ancient Egypt where the sacred cats (and especially the black ones) were said to bring blessings on any house that took care of them.

- You will be extremely rich or lucky in love if you pull off a white hair from a black cat without getting scratched (Lowlands of Brittany).

- If a cat crosses your path and does you no harm, you will be very lucky. This superstition comes from medieval times, during the very era when the "devil-cat" was so hated. Because the orthodox church could not peacefully separate the people from Goddess worship and the veneration of Her cats, they linked the cat with their devil. Obviously, this superstition is a twisted version of the older, less negative one.

- If a black cat crosses your path, you will have good luck. The black cat is also considered to be an omen of money (England).

- If a cat comes into your house, be kind to it, and the devil will not bother you. Another medieval twist of the superstition, this also assumes that the cat and the devil are in league. By inference, if you have the devil on your side, he will go torment someone else.

- Whenever the cat of the house is black, the lasses of lovers will have no lack.

- Keep an old cat collared and chained in a shop, and prosperity will be yours. If the cat escapes, the prosperity is believed to go with it (China).

- In parts of Yorkshire the wives of fishermen keep black cats at home to ensure their husbands' safety at sea.

- In southern England if a black cat crosses the path of a bride as she leaves church, it will be a fortunate marriage. This is still a popular English belief. Like hiring a chimney sweep to give her a good luck kiss when she exits the church, the bride may also make arrangements to have a black cat led across her path.

- An ancient Buddhist superstition states that if you have a white cat, silver will always be in the house. If you have a dark-colored cat, there will always be gold.

- A tortoise-shell cat brings good fortune. (Ireland and Scotland)

- People who dislike cats will be carried to the cemetery through rain. (Holland)

- If you treat a cat badly or neglect it, carry an umbrella to your wedding. (Holland)

- Cats who have three colors (red, white, and black) are able to predict the approach of storms. (Japan)

- To decide whether to say yes or no to a marriage proposal, take three hairs from a cat's tail. Wrap them in white paper and put this under the doorstep overnight. In the morning, carefully open the paper. If the hairs are in a Y-shape, it is yes; if in an N-shape, it is no. (Ozarks)

- Cats will deliberately suffocate babies in their cribs. They will suck away the breath of any sleeping or ill person, leaving them weak or even killing them. This erroneous idea was developed during the witch-frenzy and, unfortunately, is still widely held by otherwise intelligent people. Some cats will sit on your chest and get close to your face because they want attention, but they have absolutely no need or ability to suck away your breath.

- Cats carry the souls of the dead to the afterworld. (Finland)

- If a cat jumps over a coffin, the soul of the deceased will not be able to find its way to heaven. (Scotland)

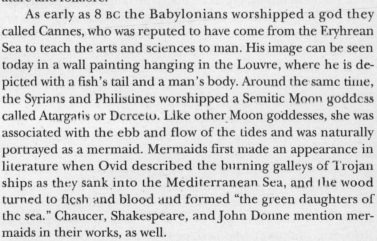

Can You Hear the Mermaids Singing?

By Chandra Moira Beal

The beautiful half-woman, half-fish creatures that we call mermaids have captivated our imaginations for thousands of years. For centuries sailors have returned to land with wild tales of mermaid sightings, and legends of water spirits abound in world literature and folklore.

As early as 8 BC the Babylonians worshipped a god they called Cannes, who was reputed to have come from the Eryhrean Sea to teach the arts and sciences to man. His image can be seen today in a wall painting hanging in the Louvre, where he is depicted with a fish's tail and a man's body. Around the same time, the Syrians and Philistines worshipped a Semitic Moon goddess called Atargatis or Derceto. Like other Moon goddesses, she was associated with the ebb and flow of the tides and was naturally portrayed as a mermaid. Mermaids first made an appearance in literature when Ovid described the burning galleys of Trojan ships as they sank into the Mediterranean Sea, and the wood turned to flesh and blood and formed "the green daughters of the sea." Chaucer, Shakespeare, and John Donne mention mermaids in their works, as well.

During the rise of Christianity, the mermaid goddesses, along with many other Pagan deities, were seen as a threat to the Church. To subvert Pagan beliefs, the Christians used the mermaid as a symbol of sin, particularly feminine vanity and beauty, because they feared those qualities would cause the downfall of men. This is probably the origin of the image of the mermaid holding her comb and mirror. Much to the Christians' dismay, the mermaid's forbidden qualities only made her more popular.

While most people are familiar with the beautiful water nymph, mermen are legendary, too. In Celtic lore, the merman is thought to have green teeth and hair, pig-like eyes, a red nose, webbed fingers, and a weakness for brandy. It is no wonder, then, that mermaids prefer handsome sailors and fishermen as lovers.

Other water spirits are often mistaken for true mermaids. Naiads were water creatures who lived in the world's ancient fresh waters but took human form. Other water spirits, such as water nymphs, are often musically talented and strikingly beautiful. Sirens, which are actually half-bird, half-woman creatures, are also sometimes confused with mermaids.

Mermaids are occasionally sighted on the wild, uninhabited coasts of Northern Europe, sunning themselves on the rocks, but water spirits can dwell in any body of water, such as ponds, lakes, streams and rivers, water wells, and the world's oceans. Some sources say that water pixies live on a patch of dry land beneath the ocean and can magically pass through the water to the Earth's surface. Wearing the skin of a water animal such as a seal or fish enables them to move from the ocean to land. There they discard and hide the skin to take human form, retrieving it later to re-enter the water when they wish. A mermaid may also possess these magic powers while wearing a special red cap covered in feathers. To steal a mermaid's cap or skin is to disempower her.

Mermaids have varied reputations. Some lure men to their deaths on rocky coasts with their beautiful songs or drown swimmers while bathing, while others rescue sailors from shipwrecks and protect ships on the high seas. A few consider it unlucky to catch sight of a mermaid. Mermaids seem to have a penchant for dry land and human companionship, but they are not allowed to forget their aquatic origins.They are sometimes thought to be the spirits of drowned women, or else the protectors of women drowned before their time. Some accounts tell of men who have fallen in love with and married mermaids, even borne children with them, but the mermaid can never fully reveal her true identity or live as a normal human.

Most fables involving mermaids have common elements. The ending is rarely a happy one, as the mermaid must always hide her true identity, but is eventually discovered, leaving everyone heartbroken. The mermaid will trade her oceanic life for a human soul, but she will never completely leave her Neptunian world. Melusine is the name of one such double-tailed mermaid who married a knight and gained a soul. When the knight fell in love with another woman, Melusine's soul was lost and she had to return to the sea. This story is nearly identical to that

of Undine, a German water sprite who also marries a knight.

European sailors believed that a mermaid sighting foretold the coming of windy gales on their voyage, and the wind storm's howls were said to be Melusine crying. The Indians worshipped a flute-playing water nymph called Asparas, while Japanese and Chinese legends tell of Ningyo, a woman with a fish's body and a human head, and sea-dragons who take human wives. Polynesian mythology includes a creator god named Vatea who was half-human and half-porpoise. Greek and Roman water gods Neptune and Poseidon were also thought to be half-man and half-fish carrying tritons, or three-pronged forks associated with sea gods. Africans, too, believed that water Witches dwelled in their rivers.

There have been numerous claims of mermaid sightings, some outlandish and some by well-educated and well-respected professionals. There have also been frauds, such as P. T. Barnum's freak show attraction, the "Fiji Mermaid," which turned out to be the torso of a monkey stitched together with a fish tail. Whether mermaids truly exist or not remains a fascinating mystery. Graceful, exotic and mysterious, half-woman and half-animal, the mermaid continues to enchant us with her spell.

ENCHANTING HENNA TATTOOING

BY deTRACI REGULA

You've seen it everywhere—celebrities holding up their hands in front of their faces, or exposing a shoulder, revealing an intricate, rust-colored mark. Another tattoo patron? Not exactly. Somewhere between temporary tattoos and full needling lies the magical land of henna tattooing, the art and craft of Mehndi.

Henna is a fragrant plant that grows throughout the Middle East and India. Its gray-green leaves hold a powerful secret: properly prepared, they release an orange-brown dye, the secret weapon of generations of graying matrons. Used another way, this same plant can tint the skin in delightful patterns believed to confer protection and act as an aphrodisiac.

In folklore, the ritual henna painting is a part of marriage ceremonies. It is believed to adorn enticingly, protect ritually, and smell and feel good on the skin. More practically, a bride who is henna painted is protected from the drudgery of housework in her mother-in-law's home until her henna painting has completely worn off. Drastic measures have developed to assure the long delay, with some rare recipes said to last up to a year before losing the last of the pigment. Modern practice and frenzied Western bathing habits usually keep the henna intact for only a couple of weeks, though this is dependent on skin type, the freshness of the henna, the other ingredients in the recipe, where the design is placed (palms of hands and soles of feet will last longest) and how long the henna paste is allowed to rest on the skin. Ideally, the henna "mud" should stay intact and in place for at least twenty-four hours.

MEHNDI MAGIC

Henna tattooing is a wonderful addition to ritual. Temporary marks can be tailored to the need of the rite. Like its fellow body art, the woad painting of the Celts, the images can be as varied as the individual. The henna used can be magically charged with a specific purpose. Prior to use, simply cup your hands around the henna, raise energy into your hands, and fill the henna paste mentally with your intent. This can be used to augment healing rites, particularly where the affliction is to a specific part of the body that can be henna painted. Or, a symbol of a current bad habit can be placed on the skin, and then banished away as the design fades.

Receiving a henna tattoo is a euphoric experience. First the skin is cleaned and then rubbed with oil. The painting of mud doesn't hurt and is calming and relaxing. Many henna artists use essential oils that help to darken the design and have the secondary effect of soothing the human canvas. Lying still to let the henna dry is wonderfully relaxing. Once the henna is dry, most artists soak it with a mixture of lemon or lime juice, water, and sugar, which acts as a kind of developer to bring out and fix the color.

APHRODISIAC DESIGNS

Henna painting is simple, but like most things, only a few will have the stamina to really master the art. In the Middle East and India, techniques and recipes are passed through the women in the family for the extensive pre-marital henna painting. The reddish color symbolizes fertility, and the intricate designs stimulate the close interest of the new husband. However, the art is not just limited to women. While men generally eschew the delicate designs favored by women, in many places men are also henna painted prior to the wedding night. Henna is also used by men in a medicinal ritual to improve virility. During the time of the waxing Moon, each morning when the Sun rises, they anoint themselves with henna and say a prayer for virility. By the time the Moon is Full, they are supposed to be restored to full potency—their maleness will be enhanced in color, if nothing else!

Other medicinal uses for henna are to prevent sore feet and to treat

rheumatism. It is still used in modern Egypt today, where the elderly will have their feet painted with henna to keep them warm and relieve arthritis. Some people believe it helps skin disorders as well.

INTRODUCTION TO MEHNDI

If you want to try your hand (or foot, or wherever!) at henna tattooing, here is a simple recipe that will work with most henna.

Note: Do not use henna meant for hair coloring. Do not use so-called "black henna," which is filled with chemical additives. Also, most bulk henna sold at herb and health food shops is henna for hair coloring, which uses a coarser, older leaf from the plant. It won't work well, or at all, on the skin. The best sources for henna for hand painting are Middle Eastern and Indian grocery stores, which will have packages of henna showing painted hands. They may also have "henna oil," which helps the henna last longer. Ask for it if you can't find it. These items are often kept behind the counter. Also be on the outlook for henna stencils, plastic cut-outs that are taped to the skin and then covered with henna. These are good sources for design ideas, but can be hard to work with as they tend to slip and blur the henna.

While allergic reactions are rare, they do occur. Sometimes the reaction is not to the henna itself, but to other ingredients used in the process, such as the essential oils, the henna oil, or the acidic lemon juice. Certain parts of the body may be more sensitive than others. Though this varies between individuals, the underside of the forearm usually is resistant to reactions.

Also, don't be disappointed if the color is not as dark as you see in photographs of henna art. Those photos, like the one here, are shot while the henna paste is still covering the design. The actual color of the tattoo will range from a rusty orange to a deep brown, depending on the henna, the recipe, and the part of the body where it is used. The palms of the hands and the soles of the feet will give the darkest color.

Basic Henna Recipe

⅛ cup powdered top grade henna for hand painting

⅛ cup very hot but not boiling water

4-6 drops amber oil or other fragrant but non-irritating essential oil (both benzoin and clove oil will tend to darken the ultimate design; however, some people are sensitive to these oils)

Mix together the henna, water, and oil thoroughly until you have a paste about the consistency of a good chocolate cake icing. Then resist the temptation to use it immediately! Set it aside for at least one hour, stirring it occasionally.

On cold days, wait longer or place the henna in a plastic bag and knead it, keeping it warm until a slightly orange liquid appears against the dark green paste. Place the henna in a baggie, small plastic squeeze bottle, or pastry cone. Oil the skin first, using "henna oil" if you can find it, or a small amount of room-temperature pure coconut oil or high-grade virgin olive oil. Apply the henna by squeezing it out slowly. Make sure the paste stays in contact with the skin, with no gaps or bridging.

Let the henna dry, then dab thoroughly with a mixture of one part lemon juice, one part sugar, and one part water. Let dry again, and then repeat the dabbing process. Ideally, wrap with gauze bandages and let it stay on for at least twenty-four hours. In reality, do the best you can! The longer the henna stays on the skin, the stronger the design will be. It's preferable to let the mud fall off naturally, instead of washing it off. If your first attempt henna painting doesn't work, try again with another brand of henna. Old henna loses its potency.

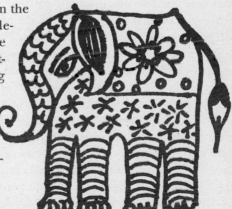

BODY MODIFICATION: THE MAGICAL ART OF TRANSFORMATION

BY DAVID HARRINGTON

A middle-aged reformed hippie couple walking along the street encounters a clean-cut young man—very clean-cut, with a shaved head and a row of lethal-looking stainless steel spikes embedded in his scalp. "How disgusting! How can they do that to their bodies?" one says to the other. They walk on, mortified by this latest expression of youth's foolishness.

Ironically, in the cultures that have practiced body modification for millennia, such blatant marks of changed soul-status are usually designed to promote unity within a tribe as a method of showing conformity with the norms of the group, and even of compliance, not rebellion. In modern Western culture, body modification has enhanced the ritual meaning of these experiences for many.

Probably the most basic form of body "modification" is the temporary art of body painting. Pigments and clays, and today, prepared body paints, are applied to the flesh. Animal patterns are believed to convey some of the power of that animal to the human, and in the past were used as a form of sympathetic magic. In tattooing, similar images are permanently etched on the body and also convey the protective power of the animal depicted. This is the reason even today, dragons, tigers, lions, eagles, and other animals perceived as potent and powerful are still the most common tattoo images. In tattooing in the Indian Subcontinent, images of gods and goddesses are used in a similar way, though tattoo artists will sometimes refuse to draw a deity that is too powerful. It is considered to be very bad luck, a form of sacrilege, if a weak individual chooses to wear the image of a powerful god. The god, displeased by an unworthy devotee seeking to benefit from the divine image, will create turmoil in that person's life instead of conferring blessing or protection.

The recent "tribal" style of tattooing, popularized by artist Leo Zulueta and others and employing bold organic or geometric lines, generally black, seeks to transform the skin to a pelt of power. By breaking up the lines of what we perceive as the normal human form, the body becomes more liminal, less attached to ordinary reality, apparently more able to slip between the dimensions.

Many cultures believe that tattoos make permanent marks in the aura, and that these pictures are tokens for entry into a positive afterlife. Other groups believe that these auric marks can be bartered in the afterlife to gain benefits in the underworld or admission to a better class of heaven.

The harshest criticism these days is reserved for body piercing, cutting, scarification, and other drastic modifications. The usual question is why anyone would choose to endure the pain associated with these changes, often in sensitive areas of the body. Some people attracted to this form of body modification state that it is precisely the fact that they can choose to undergo these procedures that makes them so powerful and necessary to their own sense of well-being. The modification of the body under their own control helps these individuals to take back their own flesh, and can compensate, at least for some, for past emotional or sexual abuses that were inflicted on them by others. Others simply choose to mark themselves in a way that they perceive to be beautiful. How better to claim one's body as one's own, than to "redecorate" it?

For many, however, the physical act of piercing releases powerful euphoric chemicals into the bloodstream. These endorphins act as a potent, pleasurable shock to the body. Some individuals find that deep spiritual or emotional insights or cleansing can be released by the flow of these natural substances, allowing us to survive and even grow through the experience of pain. Like almost any strong, chemical-based stimulus, some people can become addicted to post-piercing euphoria, and piercing may become a habit rather than a transformative experience. Others begin to relate differently to a pierced individual. It demands a reaction or a response, though this is fading as these arts become more common.

The more extreme methods of body adornment are not for everyone, but the marks on the bodies of many individuals have acted as windows to greater spiritual understanding and exploration.

CHIRON, TEACHER AND MENTOR

BY ESTELLE DANIELS

In 1977, astronomer Charles Kowal discovered a new planetary body orbiting between Saturn and Uranus. It was the first body discovered in that orbit. It was named Chiron, after the mythological being known as "King of the Centaurs."

What is Chiron? Its orbit in cosmological terms is unstable. It got to where it is roughly 250 million years ago and will leave that orbit in about 100 million years. Chiron ended up in that orbit after a gravitational encounter with another planet. Astronomers are still debating about what kind of body Chiron is. Some theorize that it is a burned-out comet, an asteroid pulled "off course," a planetoid, or escaped moon.

Astrologically, there is also controversy about Chiron. Soon after it was discovered, ephemerides (tables that show planets' placement) were calculated for it and it was retroactively put into charts. Astrologers started getting ideas about the nature and influence of Chiron. Other bodies in similar orbits have been found, and so Chiron isn't such a big deal anymore. Only about twenty-five percent of practicing astrologers use Chiron in charts.

Astrologers start with the mythology of the character the body is named after. Chiron's discoverer named it, and he had no astrological interests, but the Cosmos takes care of its own, and the name for each new body discovered in modern times has been "correct" for its influence as it was determined by astrologers.

Mythologically, Chiron was a centaur, half man, half horse. He was the son of Chronos (Roman Saturn) who visited his mother Philyra in the form of a horse, so he was not of the breed of the rest of the centaurs. This made his nature more serious and noble, and less wild and erratic than the other centaurs. He was half-brother to Zeus (Jupiter). He ran a school that taught all the arts: martial arts, medical arts, political arts, and also general knowledge and education. His medical school and hospital were world renowned, and Chiron himself was trained by Apollo, the god of healing. Chiron's most famous medical student was Asclepius (Roman Aesculapius), the father of medicine.

Chiron's medicine was a blend of standard medicine and alternative healing methods, including spiritual healing. One famous tale describes how sick people would come to Chiron's hospital and would spend their first night in a special chamber in the cave. In the morning they would tell the doctor/priests their dreams, and supposedly in those dreams would be their diagnosis and suggested remedies for a complete cure. Chiron also taught herbs, diet, and other forms of healing, similar to chiropractic, homeopathy, and energy healing.

Chiron's school for heroes was a blend of a university education, martial arts school, and finishing school where the heroes learned statecraft, manners, and diplomacy. To the Greeks, a person was supposed to be well-rounded. Even a "mere warrior" was expected to have a good education, and to be ethical and well-mannered. The kings were expected to be the best educated.

When Heracles visited Chiron's school, he had poisoned arrows that had been dipped in Hydra's blood. Heracles got drunk (as he was prone to), and was fooling around while practicing archery. One of his arrows went wild and hit Chiron in the knee.

Being an immortal, Chiron could not die, but the arrow was poisoned, so the wound never healed. Chiron was doomed to live an immortal life in unending pain. Because of this Chiron, became a more gifted healer, as now he could empathize with his patients because he too suffered. The unending pain eventually became too much to bear, and Chiron asked Zeus to withdraw his immortality so Chiron could die and end his torment. Zeus refused, for immortality was an attribute of the gods and not something to be discarded.

Prometheus had given fire to humankind, defying Zeus, and had been given the eternal punishment of being chained to a rock and having his liver eaten out each day by an eagle, only to have it grow back again each night so the torment could start anew each dawn. After centuries of this, Heracles petitioned Zeus to end Prometheus' torment, and free him. Zeus agreed, provided Heracles could find an immortal willing to die for him. Zeus had forgotten about Chiron and upon hearing this, Chiron decided to offer his life. Zeus was displeased, but honored his promise. Prometheus was freed and Chiron's immortality taken, and he finally died from the poison. In recognition of his contributions and accomplishments Chiron was immortalized in the heavens as the constellation Centaurus the Centaur.

Chiron has many attributes. He is a teacher who teaches more than one subject, and strives for a well-rounded person. He is a healer, but one who is not immune to disease or injury, who can transmute his own pain into a greater level of healing skill. Chiron also deals with the issues of quality of life and death and dying. Chiron is a wise guide and mentor, someone who makes a good counselor to those in power, someone who is busy and works hard at many different things simultaneously. Chiron is also a maverick. Though he was immortal, he dwelt apart from the gods and interacted more with mortals than gods.

Some astrologers consider Chiron an inconvenient benefic. He brings good things, but not without trouble or upset first. His symbol is a key that opens new doors of knowledge, experience, and opportunity. Old doors must be closed, though, and there comes the pain that Chiron can bring. Chiron's key will only work after your old options have gone and you are in the dark. To take the key and open Chiron's doors takes faith in the future.

Traditional and Eclectic Witchcraft

By Silver RavenWolf

There's been an ongoing debate in our community for the past fifteen years about who is more "Witchie" than whom, Traditional Witches or Eclectic Witches. Are the lines drawn securely in the purified salt?

Twenty-five years ago, to be a Witch in the United States you had to be initiated by another Witch, and normally you belonged to a coven environment (usually Gardnerian or Alexandrian) where through study and community service, you worked your way through the levels of training until you achieved the honor of clergy status. In most cases, this process took from five to eight years of training, sometimes more. As a result of this rigorous training process, few made it to the "top." Once you had this training you could branch off and develop a system of your own.

There were, scattered among these groups, a few Fam Trad (Family Traditional) witches—those individuals whose families practiced a folk-flavor of witchcraft and passed their techniques from one generation to another. With Puritan pressure many of these family lineage lines were lost or broken as families moved into mainstream Christianity to avoid persecution. Most Fam Trad Witches remaining had no desire to mingle with the Euro-Americanized flavor of ceremonial Craft, but preferred the folk customs and techniques handed down through their own family history. Vestiges of these systems, specifically the German Pow-Wow, Cajun Hoodoo, the Italian Strega, and the Scotch-Irish Appalachian Faith Healers (sometimes called Grannies) remained. These countrified magicians gained respect from their clients, but fell short of acceptance from the Euro-American hierarchy of Witches, as well as the general public.

A few of the lesser-trained Fam Trad descendants strove to ingratiate themselves with the Euro-American Craft community, claiming the energies passed to them by family had more power because of the length of lineage and blood ties. It was at this point that the desire of Euro-American Witches to have lineage became important. And so, perhaps twenty-five years ago, the main argument of validity raged between the Euro-American Witch and the Fam Trad, and little else. Any other arguments centered on whose lineage was better, or whose lineage could be considered "more" valid. These two types of Witches did have one thing in common—initiation by someone already initiated either formally in ceremony or by passing the power in Grandma's kitchen—meaning it always took a Witch to make a Witch, whether you were Fam Trad, Euro-American, or an offshoot of either system. Of course, people on both sides fibbed on occasion.

Enter now please, from off-stage right, the New Generation of Witches, Sybil Leek, Herman Slater, Lady Sabrina, Z. Budapest, StarHawk, Doreen Valiente, Raymond Buckland, Scott Cunningham, and Marion Weinstein, to name a few, who produced with their writing and private practices a revolution in the religion of Craft, moving the belief system into the realms of Wicca—the New Generation Craft that most of you practice today. These authors shoveled information into the needy arms of the average populace. Note, however, that all of the afore-mentioned authors were, in one way or another, traditionally trained. The problem with this explosion of information was not, at first, apparent. More people were having their personal spiritual needs fulfilled by practicing what they read, which was the idea in the first place, so where was the difficulty? The popular authors sought (either consciously or subconsciously) to destroy Craft elitism. The speed bump emerged when many readers started looking additional training from qualified sources. It became quickly apparent that there weren't enough traditional teachers to go around.

Witness, then, the birth of eclecticism, otherwise known as good old American do-it-yourself methodology. With their wide-eyed zest for knowledge and their unending energy, the Eclectic Witches pulled the Traditional Witches into the twenty-first century by increasing the number of Wiccan practitioners exponentially. By their sheer numbers, Eclectic Wiccans demanded to know "more," and slowly, some Traditional Witches have relented.

The second problem faced was that "more" in Traditionalist jargon really meant learning advanced techniques in a group environment, not necessarily fun magical activities. Whether you are a Traditionalist or Eclectic, the spiritual growth that Wicca (Witchcraft) requires falls in the realm of solitary achievement—meaning that not everything can be or should be done in a group format, and some of your most outstanding achievements will be done all by your lonesome.

The issue that some Traditionalists have heart failure over (and deservedly so) is those Eclectics who decide to begin a "tradition," yet they have had no traditional training. I think here we are dealing with the meaning of the word "tradition" as it relates to Craft history in this country. In effect, an Eclectic tradition that is not supported by Traditional training is not Traditional in the eyes of a Traditionalist.

Does it matter in the eyes of Spirit if you are a Traditional Witch or an Eclectic one? I don't think so. I think it matters more how you behave in your day-to-day life, and whether or not you have fulfilled your oath of service (whether that oath was taken in a Traditional setting or in an Eclectic one). Either way, Witches have had a profound impact on the total religious philosophies of this century, and I don't think in fifty years anyone is going to care who was a Traditionalist and who was an Eclectic in 1998. If they do, they'll be missing the point entirely. By that time, hopefully, they'll have something else to fight about—or better yet—something to agree on.

Music Magic: A Solitary Ritual

By Melissa Morgan

S ince the dawn of time, women and men have used music and sound to create the sacred. The power of the human voice and the strength of percussion have the ability to take one to another space entirely. The sounding of the Om is used now by many to bring in the sacred and focus the mind. Our ancestors had instruments and the ability to create percussion with them at all times, as we do now. Anyone can make magic with music with the tools at hand. It is done as magic is always done, with intent, will, and focus.

Imagine a problem or difficulty, or something you have negative feelings about. When the picture is clear in your head, clap your hands and watch the negatives dissipate. Keep clapping until you feel the negatives are gone. If you wish, beat a drum or hit a stick on something that will not be harmed, or shake a rattle. Use the sound to chase the negatives away.

Relax. Breathe deeply and slowly. See yourself cleansed and surrounded in light. Focus on the light. Let your voice fill with light. Make a sound with your voice that fits with you in the light. You could make the Om or other sacred sounds if you wish. Let the light sink deeper into you. Let your voice reflect that. For some, this may mean deepening the voice, for others an ascent or descant may emerge. Your voice does not have to be the only source. Give yourself permission to have the tones go higher or lower than your vocal range. Please allow your voice to just be the way that it is, without judgment. Opera this is not!

Let it last as long as you want. Then open your eyes and lighten your breathing. How do you feel? What has changed? Recognize and acknowledge any changes. You can simply go about your day or evening afterward, or this ritual can be used as an opening way to help achieve the proper state for other ritual work. Enjoy this simple process and use it whenever you wish or feel the need to. It is simple, yet can have dramatic results.

When I first experimented with this, I had a severe pain in my neck. I closed my eyes to take stock of my body. I could see the area where the pain was throbbing red. As I clapped my hands, I imagined the red of the pain being chased away. For me, it worked to clap faster and faster for just twenty seconds or so. I felt a shift, so I stopped. Also, my hands were beginning to complain about how hard I was clapping them.

I started the next phase, seeing myself surrounded in light. I felt very calm and allowed my breathing to deepen. I found myself staying with some mid-range tones, which quickly turned into descending slides with my voice. As the descending patterns continued, I got past the range of my voice. I kept going anyway. I felt this very strong vibration when I was very deep; it felt as if the vibration itself separated the pain from my neck, like my whole body was vibrating at this deep tone and no pain could stay with that. I found myself singing a mid-range tone for a long time, then a very high one at an odd interval to the first. It felt very freeing and relaxing.

Then I felt done. I checked my breathing; it was light, so I opened my eyes. The pain in my neck was gone. I found the results startling; I'd had the pain for most of the day and was beginning to wonder what I was going to do.

Sound is a potent tool that can be used anywhere. Customize this ritual to have it suit your own needs, and have fun!

TRANCE

BY KEN JOHNSON

Trance has become a big word in the occult world. One of the biggest. People go into trance when they open to channeling. Shamans all over the world go into trance when they visit the spirit world, and the journeys of guided imagination that pass for shamanic work in our culture are sometimes referred to as trance. Mediums who work in a trance are simply called "trance mediums." Even your aunt, who knows nothing and cares even less about your wacky metaphysics, claims that her husband, your redneck uncle, goes into a trance whenever he's out fishing.

A trance is quite simply an altered state of consciousness, one in which the spiritual world (or perhaps even the world of the spirits!) or one in which the astral world (which is perhaps the same as the world of imagination) comes close to our own. In trance, we leave our ordinary reality and our ordinary thoughts behind. In its mildest form (as with your redneck uncle), we simply drift through the dreamworld of our own thoughts. In a more formal or shamanic trance, we actually leave our own consciousness behind and enter the Otherworld, where we may receive information of great value.

Here is an easy method of trance, well known among traditional magicians and sorcerers from Eastern Europe whose arts extend back into Pagan times. However, even such a simple technique as this can leave us open to unwanted (translate: weird) influences from the Otherworld, and it is always best to have a well-trained, sympathetic friend at hand before you attempt this exercise.

First, light a candle. A candle is a doorway to the Otherworld—Russian mystics often see angels poised upon the flames of the candles in their churches. Sit comfortably, relax all the muscles of your body, and release all those pesky thoughts and ideas from your mind. Stare at the candle while at the same time allowing your eyes to drift out of focus. Try to keep your consciousness or awareness centered behind you. Why? Because this is where your second body, your "astral double" or "follower," is positioned. The influence that chooses to speak through you will need to merge itself with this part of you. If you've ever heard trance mediums ask you to please not step behind them while they're working, then now you know the reason.

In time, you will feel another presence. In old European tradition, this is usually the spirit of a relative or ancestor. Be sure that the new influence is kindly and well disposed toward you (this is where the presence of your well-trained friend comes in) Then go ahead and try to hear what it has to say to you.

In the beginning, you will probably need a tool to elicit information. For simple yes and no questions, you can use a pendulum or write down the words "yes" and "no" on some surface, then either a) turn a shot glass upside down, or b) turn a plate upside down, and allow the item to slide to the "yes" or "no."

For answers that go beyond yes and no, you can use the whole alphabet, which is the same as using an ouija board.

After practice, you will begin to hear the "voice" of the ancestral spirit adding information to the original "yes" or "no." This information will simply come through, unconsciously. After even more practice, you may be able to dispense with all tools, even the candle flame, and work with the ancestral voice directly as a channel.

ALICE AND HER MAGIC BROOM

BY EDAIN MCCOY

O nce upon a time there was a well-to-do Irish lass named Alice who owned a magic broom, and that broom got her into big trouble. It is hard to believe that a humble cleaning tool, used for centuries, could embody so much folklore and magical potential; yet it's no accident that brooms are intimately associated with the popular image of the Halloween Witch who rides hers across the face of the Moon with her familiar black cat in tow.

The broom itself functions as a symbol of the sexual union or sacred marriage of the God and Goddess, a rite that has been symbolically reenacted each spring by followers of the world's Earth religions for thousands of years. The staff or pole portion represents the phallus of the God, and the bristles symbolize the mound of Venus that guards the opening to the Goddess' reproductive organs. When both parts are united in a completed broom they form a potent magical symbol of wholeness and creative potential.

This sexual imagery naturally makes the broom the perfect choice for a magical tool to use in fertility rites of all sorts. Even today it is used at the conclusion of many Pagan marriages (called handfastings) as the couple "jumps the broom" after exchanging their final vows. This is similar to the fertility custom of tossing rice at a newly married couple today.

In the distant past women would ride their brooms hobby-horse-style over newly tilled fields to encourage growth, and through barns and pasture land to encourage the reproduction of animals. On festival days, livestock animals were often swatted with the business end of the broom to keep them healthy and fertile.

Because brooms represent the totality of the deity—both male and female aspects—they have been used as talismans of protection. They have been placed under beds, across thresholds and windows, at the entrances to sacred space, and they have stood sentinel at hearth sides.

The sweeping action of the broom itself—its ability to cleanse any area through which it is taken and to take whatever debris it collects to someplace else—is so obvious that the magical potency of this simple action is sometimes overlooked. A seventeenth-century Irish widow woman named Dame Alice Kyteler knew this secret of the broom, and was apparently adept at using it to good effect until she was caught in the act and condemned to death for practicing Witchcraft.

Alice loved her children and was willing to use magic to help them succeed. She would take her broom out into the streets of her native Kilkenny late at night and begin a methodical sweeping action that was aimed toward her home. While doing this she would chant a magical rhyme in which she bid all the wealth in town to come to her eldest son William who lived with her.

No one knows just how long the very prosperous Alice had been working at this spell when she was discovered by a neighbor and reported as a Witch, but we do know that she was able to escape her persecutors and flee to England with most of her considerable wealth intact. No one is sure just how it is she managed to elude her captors—and many rumors still abound—but whenever I think I see something flitting across the face of a full moon, I like to think maybe Alice merely mounted her faithful broom and just flew away.

Editor's note: for a historical account of the trial of Dame Alice Kyteler see the following sources.

Sources

Cohn, Norman. *Europe's Inner Demons.* New York: Basic Books, 1975.

Hole, Christina. *Witchcraft in England.* New York: Charles Scribner's Sons, 1947.

Robbins, Rossel Hope. *Encyclopedia of Witchcraft and Demonology.* New York: Crown Publishers, 1959.

DISCOVER YOUR PAGAN ROOTS

BY MARGUERITE ELSBETH

E uropean and Native American shamans say that the roots of the World Tree, a universal symbol of creation, are dying. They say this is so because the founders of our people or culture, the ghosts of our past, all of our relations—our deceased cousins, aunts, uncles, sisters, brothers, mothers, fathers, grandmothers, and grandfathers—are neglected, ignored, or forgotten.

We aren't just associated with our relatives—we are our relatives! The genetics that form our beings fashioned us from the spirits, souls, and flesh of all our ancestors combined. Consequently, our ancestors are alive within us, and some still talk with us, usually through our dreams. They want us to know their hopes, thoughts, and desires, so that we can honor them. It is up to us to assist our relations in the here and now, because this ensures a better future for ourselves, our clans, and the world.

All our relations were Pagan at one time or another! Did you know that seventy-five percent of all Americans may have Native American ancestors? Though you will have to prove that your ancestors once shared relations in Indian Country, there are some tribes who are actively looking for members. If you have Native ancestry, you may be entitled to reservation rights or educational grants, or be authorized to receive free treatment at special medical facilities. It is far better, however, to hunt up evidence of your Indianness for more spiritual reasons.

If your heritage is Indian, European, Asian, or African, or a little of everything, your purpose is to improve the standing, further the ideals, and relieve the distress of your relations, whoever they may be. The whole point of being alive is to know who you are, because if you don't know where you've been, how can you know where to go?

To Discover Your Pagan Roots

※ Speak with your relatives and family friends. They can tell you stories and names.

※ Contact all necessary bureaucratic agencies—the Mormon Church, genealogical societies, and local libraries are good places to start.

※ Research the geography and history of your relatives, paying close attention to the specific time periods in which they lived.

※ Generate a paper trail back to at least one Pagan relation.

※ Make contact with your Pagan group or tribe to request information and an application for membership.

※ Be patient with those who are trying to help you in your search.

※ Enclose a stamped, self-addressed envelope (SASE) when inquiring about your ancestors.

※ It is important to authenticate all data with certified documentation!

※ Save your descendants the trouble of researching their Pagan roots all over again. Record all information on tape or in writing.

※ If all else fails and proof is hard to come by, join a revival group anyway. Strive to learn the spiritual tradition, language, history, lifestyle, and crafts of your ancestors, so that you can walk your talk with pride in your Pagan roots.

TEEN WITCH:
GENERATION Y

BY SILVER RAVENWOLF

In the December 22, 1997 edition of *USA Today*, a statistical analysis for the entertainment business showed that we will have more teens per capita by 2010 than in any other era in American history. To date, teenage influence in movie-ticket purchases spawned such sleeper hits as *The Craft* and *Scream*. In the coming years cinema conglomerates plan to throw billions of dollars at this ballooning generation like confetti at a Christmas parade, and the tastes of old fogies like me will drift into the cracks and crevices of film noire. Throw in the availability of information on the internet, where parental control falls to minimal or nonexistent, and the surge of young minds questing for "the meaning of it all" or "unlimited power" will exponentially increase.

What does all this have to do with the religion of the Craft? Plenty, and we'd better be prepared.

If you are winded from the fast rate of growth that Wicca has experienced from the original baby boomers in the last ten years, then you'd better hold on for the broom booster of the new millennium. In other words, you ain't seen nothin' yet. The Wiccan groups of the 50s, 60s, and 70s never dreamed that the religion of Wicca would become a spiritual explosion in the 80s, and therefore weren't prepared for the onslaught of new practitioners. We now have more flavors than an ice cream parlor—a few of which are missing a standard ingredient (like the ice cream). Let's not let this happen again.

Is this an elitist position? No, but it is one of practicality.

A surge of young, vigorous minds means the need for compassionate, moral teachers. It also means (oh dear) the necessity for some type of structure. You can't teach well without a lesson plan. Although many in our community parry and joust on such rules, these parameters are exactly what any new student seeks when embarking on a course of study. And I'm sorry, the rule of three just isn't enough. We need more—rather, we need to make a concerted effort to get the spiritual, practical, and moral rules out there for our fledgling Witches to see and to understand. We already have these, but often dance around them in an attempt to be "universal," "mysterious," or downright snooty.

Wicca, as you practice the religion today, is a new religion, barely fifty years old. The techniques you use at present are not entirely what your elders practiced even thirty years ago. Of course, threads of "what was" weave through the tapestry of "what is now." Times have changed and with that movement, the Craft has developed into a religion to meet the needs of the mind existing in the technological age. Although folklore exploration may produce mind invigorating results, in no way can we replicate to perfection the precise circumstances of environment, society, culture, religion, and magic a hundred years ago, or a thousand. Why would we want to? The idea is to go forward with the knowledge of the past, tempered by the tools of our own age. We are one of the few religions that delight in ancient truths, rather than attempt to cover them up to support our own doctrines. If we teach these new practitioners of the Craft anything at all, we should encourage them to seek and understand ancient traditions for what they were, rather than what we would like them to be.

As of 1999, Generation Y is already here, the last of them bursting into this world in December 1997. Their desire to find spirituality will influence the world in unique and amazing ways, just as you have. The original baby boomers rocked the world of religion and magic with their development of New Generation Wicca and other alternative paths. What will these children do? What legacy are you prepared to hand them?

This article was prompted by Silver RavenWolf's new book for teens, entitled Teen Witch: Wicca for a New Generation. *Check out Silver's Teen Wicca page on the World Wide Web at http://www.magusbooks.com/silver.*

Thirteen Pagan Parenting Tips

By Jim Garrison

1. First and foremost, love your child. Self-esteem is a valuable commodity. A few kind words or a simple hug from you as your children are growing up could save thousands of dollars in therapy bills down the road.

2. It is essential to the continued good health and well-being of any parent to cultivate a positive outlook as much as possible. No, I don't mean running out and joining the Barney fan club. What I mean is that it is important to welcome every good thing that comes into your life, so that as you show gratitude, your child learns to likewise develop gratitude. You can't expect your child to develop such things without first learning them from you.

3. As a parent, you have incredible power and influence in shaping the life and attitudes of your child. It's a big responsibility. Being a parent is a task and obligation that defines us, our role, and our community from that point onward. Parents shape the future through their children. Think about what you teach your child, the words you use around them, and the way you respond to their needs and demands.

4. Be fair, honest, and open in how you treat your child. No good comes from lying to your children. Attempting to teach your child the concepts of honor, integrity, and honesty will force you to adhere to these same things. If that doesn't teach you some humility, nothing will.

5. The best thing about being a parent is that you get to do all the things you wish you could have done as a kid, and in this way you can heal your own inner child.

6. I do not preach to my child. I dislike proselytizing, and will not condone it in my home. I raise my child to be tolerant of other religions. I encourage my child to think for herself, to make up her own mind, and to feel free to discuss or question anything. If I can't explain to her that I need to get some sleep so I can go to work in the morning, how am I going to explain such things as manners, boundaries, spirituality, or (eventually) sexuality to her? I see my child developing in leaps and bounds and going places I could never have gone at her age. Watching her grow has given me a renewed and deepened respect and reverence for the way life works.

7. Laugh and play with your children. Be part of their fun. It will strengthen your bond and it can heal a lot of the grimness and hardness we all accumulate over the years. Your kids can teach you a lot about how to be happy, to reconnect with the child-self within all of us and how to make life special again.

8. Act responsibly and show some respect to your children. If they want to follow in your footsteps, there's plenty of time to do things right. Your children don't have to be initiated to grow up within the Craft. When and where it's appropriate, include your children. Create your own rituals together, traditions that the whole family can share and take pride and pleasure in. Provide them with suitable activities, like seasonal crafts and decorating the house. Take this special time to teach your children the stories and myths, the reasons you do what you do. Give them the chance to participate in the fun Pagan stuff and don't make a big deal about what goes on in the circle—leave that for another day, when they are more mature and ready to deal with it in a spiritual context.

9. Always let your kids know that you love them and take pride in them, no matter what. The three most powerful magic words in the English language are "I love you." Don't be afraid to use them on your kids frequently.

10. You're human and make mistakes. We all know this. Make sure that your children know this, too. That way they'll know it's okay for them to make mistakes, and they won't have to watch as you fall off of that pedestal they might have built for you. Their expectations are shaped in response to your own. Cut them a little more slack than you do yourself. They haven't made all the same choices you have, and they may see things differently than you do.

11. Empower your kids. Teach them how to get things done. As they get a little older, show them how to do things for themselves. Learning how to cook or help to do laundry can cultivate problem-solving skills better than practically anything else. After a few domestic training sessions, you'll find the shared context useful in explaining all manner of things to them down the road.

12. Encourage your children to read, first by reading to them, then by having them read to you. One of the most powerful and important acts of magic is literacy. This is a very important gift to give to your child, and one that will enrich and enhance their life.

13. Listen to your children. They can sometimes teach you a great deal about things you probably have been taking for granted for a long time. Just remember that you're the parent and it's up to you to set the limits and boundaries for your children, not the other way around. Give them their say, but the final decision is yours.

NIGHT VISION

BY KEN JOHNSON

A wizard can see in the dark. Not just the darkness of night, but the inner darkness where both danger and wisdom lie.

In Eastern Europe, the *Kolduny*, or traditional village sorcerers, have a way of training their apprentices to see in the dark. It's an easy exercise, but it requires the help of a friend so you won't go crashing into things.

First, find yourself a good hiking trail. Go there after dark, and have your friend carry a flashlight.

Now, close your eyes. Breathe deeply, and try to sense everything around you. Since you can't use your eyes, you'll have to rely on your other senses. Try to feel the wind, listen to the night sounds, and smell the air.

Now start to walk. Your objective is simple: to stay on the trail. A path or trail of any kind sets up its own energy flow, and that's what you're trying to feel. If you can find a path that leads downhill, so much the better—as the Chinese geomancers will tell you, earth energies, like water, flow naturally downhill, so the energy stream is simpler to identify if you point yourself downhill.

Of course, your friend will be walking nearby with a flashlight to make sure that you don't tumble into a cluster of poison ivy or trip over a big rock. After a while, you won't make many mistakes. You will begin to feel the flow of the energy all around you. You will walk the path with complete confidence, even with your eyes closed.

Once you've mastered the basic exercise, you can open your eyes and use them along with your other senses. The Kolduny say that by so doing you will always be able to find your way, even in the darkest places. For example: a forest can be utterly and completely dark at night, but if you practice this exercise long enough you will be able to navigate through the deepest woods even on a moonless night. You will be able to see and feel the faintest trail by connecting with the subtle paths of energy all around you.

In time, you will be able to see through other kinds of darkness as well—the darkness of ignorance and deception. Because, as everyone knows, a wizard sees through every kind of darkness.

SOUTHWEST INDIAN WITCHCRAFT

BY MARGUERITE ELSBETH

American Indians have their own ideas regarding witchcraft. Among the Apache, Navajo, and Pueblo tribes of the Southwest, there are many stories about healing and bewitchment, and especially about certain illnesses and castastrophes thought to be brought on by magical means.

Many Southwest Indians believe that anyone at all can be a Witch, and one never knows when a Witch will retaliate for a supposed slight! The Indians are always careful, alert, and aware of how they interact with others.

Eagle feathers, turquoise beads, and cattail pollen are common protective amulets among Apaches. Lightning, bear, and snake ceremonies are performed to cure victims of harmful magic.

Apache Witches claim to embody the power of birds, animals, or even primal forces. A healer or Witch usually stays one step ahead of his or her enemies by keeping this power a secret. This is necessary, because even when a healer has the power to do good deeds, he or she may turn it around and cause wickedness.

Apache healers enjoy an afterlife ripe with corn, wild crops, and plentiful game, while practitioners of evil magic go to a place where there is little air or light.

Among the Navajo Indians, wealthy and powerful or old and senile folk are thought to be Witches. Pointing at a person, at someone's property, or looking directly into someone's eyes can also cause suspicion of witchcraft.

Evil Navajo Witches draw sand paintings of their enemies in caves, or "shoot" spells into their victims with magical bows.

It is said that Navajos greatly fear "skinwalkers," human wolves who live unrecognized in the villages, drop enchanted powders through the smoke-holes of houses, and, once inside the dwelling, stab their victims with sharpened sticks.

The Navajo use various home remedies to guard against evil magic, such as talking prayer sticks, medicines made from eagle, bear, skunk, or mountain lion gall, corn pollen, and a variety of herbs. Navajo medicine men perform curing ceremonies, called "sings," to "pray the evil back" to the person who sent it.

Pueblo magicians can magically shoot clay figurines, bone splinters, thorns, pebbles, or even small animals into a person's body. Earthen dolls stuffed with hair and nail clippings of the intended victim are also popular items of bewitchment.

The Witches of Cochiti Pueblo are said to shape-shift into owls, crows, snakes, frogs and toads. Sometimes they dance along the ground at night disguised as brilliant red fireballs with black centers.

The Bear Societies of Santa Clara Pueblo gaze into bowls filled with water from a sacred Southwest lake in order to divine the identity of an evil Witch. If someone is badly afflicted by magic, bear or mountain lion hairs are placed in a bowl and mixed with hot coals. The vapors are inhaled by the victim while the medicine men pray; the ash is removed, and water is added to the bowl. The victim is washed with the liquid, drinks what remains, and a charm or fetish is tied about his waist for protection.

BIBLIOGRAPHY

Perrone, Bobette H., Henrietta Stockel, and Victoria Krueger. *Medicine Women, Curanderas, and Women Doctors.* Oklahoma: University of Oklahoma Press, Norman and London, 1989.

Fortuna Redux

By Janina Renee

If you travel often, there is a goddess whose favor you are sure to appreciate: Fortuna Redux, the goddess of safe and happy homecomings.

The Goddess was honored in this aspect in ancient Rome. In fact, the emperor Augustus established a shrine to honor Fortuna Redux for his own successful journeys home after his campaigns. October 12 was set as her special date because that was the anniversary of her shrine's dedication.

Travel is seldom without problems and anxieties, both for travelers and the loved ones who await their return, so consider honoring Fortuna Redux as part of a special devotion on October 12. If you wish, you can invoke her along with Hermes (Mercury), the Orisha Esu, and other gods, goddesses, and spirits associated with protection of the traveler. You can also perform this devotion at any other time that you are concerned about safety in travel—for example, to bless your family's local errands and commutes. Those who live in high-traffic neighborhoods or who have teenage children drivers are familiar with how even a trip to the grocery store can be cause for concern. You can give thanks for all your family's successful homecomings and respectfully request continued protection with the following devotion.

Prepare a large candle to be used and reused for this purpose, or use individual votives as the need arises. You can use any color you think appropriate, but yellow is a good choice because it has magical associations with travel as well as with luck and happiness. Anoint the candle with fragrant oil. Some oils that are considered to be especially good for luck in travel are lavender, lemon grass, lemon verbena, peppermint, benzoin, and mace.

Now, light the candle and hold your hands over it in an attitude of blessing while saying:

I honor and acknowledge you,
all you gods and goddesses,
guardian angels, and all good spirits
who look after the well-being of travelers.
As Fortuna Redux of the happy returns,
Mercury-Hermes, the traveler,
Esu, the Orisha of the roads,
and in all of your other names, forms, and manifestations,
I give thanks for the safety and luck,
and all of the homecomings that I and my loved ones
have enjoyed throughout this year!
Gracious ones,
I also ask your continued blessings and protection
for my loved ones and me on this occasion,
and in the years to come.
Blessed Be!

If you are awaiting the homecoming of a special person, you can modify this devotion by adding words of petition such as "Please extend your special protection to my dear one, (insert name), now, as I await his/her safe arrival."

You can also use the wording in the devotion above as part of a spell for protection in car travel: simply recite the same words while annointing the midpoint of your steering wheel and your four hubcaps with fragrant oil.

REFERENCE

Roscher, W. H., ed. *AusFührliches Lexikon Der Griechischen Und Römiscen Mythologie.* Leipzig: Teubner, 1889.

PENTAGRAM, HEXAGRAM, AND CROSS: SACRED GEOMETRY IN MAGICAL RITUAL

BY JOHN MICHAEL GREER

M ost magicians today use geometrical figures such as pentagrams, hexagrams, and crosses in their ritual workings. Very few realize, though, that behind these useful symbols lies an almost forgotten branch of magical lore: the art and science of sacred geometry. Once a core element of high magic, with connections to astrology, music, architecture, and Western martial arts, sacred geometry has dropped out of the standard curriculum of magic so completely that many magicians have never even heard of it.

One of the major keys to sacred geometry is found in a set of proportions that, to drop briefly into mathematical jargon, are irrational—that is, they can't be expressed exactly in numbers. The most famous irrational proportion in geometry is the one between the diameter and the circumference of a circle, which is called *pi* and written π; for a circle with a diameter equal to 1, it works out in numbers to 3.1415927... and so on for an infinite number of digits. Whenever an irrational proportion appears in sacred geometry, it represents the presence of the spiritual side of things—the side that can't be understood by ordinary reasoning—and the ways that each irrational proportion works in geometry has a good deal to teach about the ways that spirit works in the universe of our experience.

While π is important in sacred geometry, three other proportions of the same kind are more central to our present purpose. These are based on the square roots of 2, 3 and 5—in mathematical shorthand, $\sqrt{2}$, $\sqrt{3}$, and $\sqrt{5}$—and they are central to the geometries underlying the cross, the hexagram, and the pentagram respectively.

THE CROSS

Most people in the magical community these days think of the cross as a purely Christian symbol, but various kinds of crosses have been used in magic and spirituality for thousands of years and in many different cultures. Crosses, especially the equal-armed kind, are used in modern magic to represent the four elements in balance. They appear much more often than many people realize; whenever you face the four directions in turn to invoke the elemental powers, for example, you're formulating a cross of this kind.

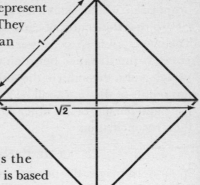

The geometry that gives the equal-armed cross its meaning is based on √2, as shown in the cross diagram. If you draw a square, put in a diagonal line that connects opposite corners, and then

The Cross

use the diagonal line as the side of a new, larger square, the second square will contain exactly twice the area of the first one. If the side of the first square is equal to 1, the side of the second square will be √2—and if you repeat the process again using the diagonal of the second square, the side of the third square will be 2. This process of increase echoes growth and reproduction in living things, and for this reason the √2 proportion is the geometrical expression of generation and the natural world. It's for this reason that the equal-armed cross, which is based on √2 geometries, is a standard symbol of the four elements of nature.

THE HEXAGRAM

The hexagram, or star of David, is made up of two triangles pointing in different directions. In modern magical practice, it's used to summon and banish the energies of the planets, bringing celestial forces into contact with terrestrial ones.

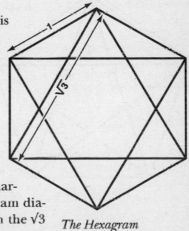

There's a good geometric reason the hexagram should be used to bring two worlds into harmony. As shown in the hexagram diagram, the hexagram is based on the √3

The Hexagram

proportion, which is modeled geometrically by drawing two circles so that the center of each one is on the edge of the other. The overlapping space between makes a shape called the *vesica piscis*. If the distance between the centers of the two circles (which is also the width of the vesica) is 1, the length between the two points of the vesica will be √3. The two circles can represent male and female, or any other pair of polarized powers; the √3 is their reconciliation.

THE PENTAGRAM

In modern magic, the pentagram is used to represent the presence of spirit working through the four elements of matter. The pentagram's geometry is more complex than those we've already examined because, although based on √5, it relates to this proportion indirectly. The proportion directly governing the pentagram is the crown jewel and supreme mystery of sacred geometry: the Golden Proportion.

The Golden Proportion, symbolized by the Greek letter phi, Φ, is half of √5 + 1, which shows its connection to the √5 proportion. Entire books could be written about the Golden Proportion and its philosophical and magical properties—in fact, entire books were written on the subject in the Renaissance—but the factors that concern us here are first that any pattern based on Φ reproduces Φ and a handful of closely related proportions over and over again on every level, and second, that Φ occurs constantly throughout the world of nature, governing such things as the positions of leaves on a branch and the curve of snail shells. Φ and the related √5 thus represent hidden unity rising out of seeming confusion, making Φ a perfect symbol of spirit as a hidden factor of balance and unity within the dance of the elements.

The Pentagram

110

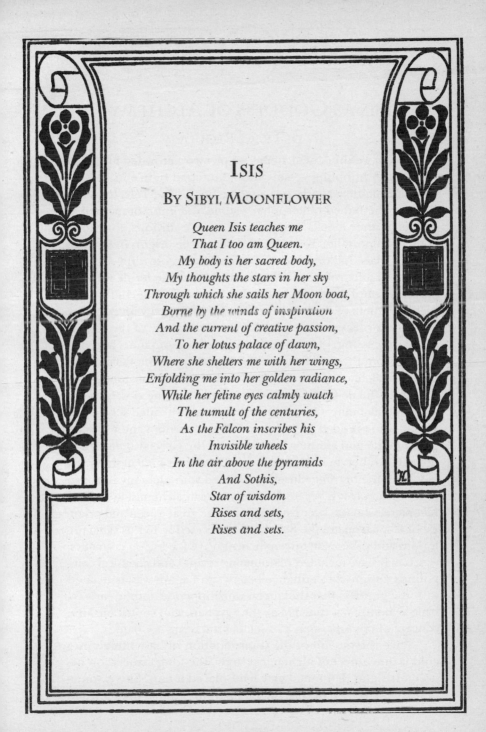

ISIS

BY SIBYL MOONFLOWER

Queen Isis teaches me
That I too am Queen.
My body is her sacred body,
My thoughts the stars in her sky
Through which she sails her Moon boat,
Borne by the winds of inspiration
And the current of creative passion,
To her lotus palace of dawn,
Where she shelters me with her wings,
Enfolding me into her golden radiance,
While her feline eyes calmly watch
The tumult of the centuries,
As the Falcon inscribes his
Invisible wheels
In the air above the pyramids
And Sothis,
Star of wisdom
Rises and sets,
Rises and sets.

ISIS AS GODDESS OF ALCHEMY

By deTraci Regula

When we think of alchemy, we picture a crowded loft filled with bubbling vessels and a hunched figure in Renaissance or medieval garb, peering at a book of secrets, trying to discover the famed philosopher's stone, the lump of metal that will turn other metals into gold. In some traditions, this stone confers immortality. Yet, alchemy had its true origins in Egypt, a timeless place full of ancient mystery. The Arabic term *Al-Khem,* the Black Land, referred to Egypt, the land made fertile with the dark, rich mud deposited by the flooding of the Nile. In the temples, members of the priestly class experimented with complex chemical processes necessary for the technology of the time—metal processing, glassmaking, and creation of paints and pigments. From these crafts came the beginnings of modern chemistry (like alchemy, a word derived from the old name for Egypt).

Of all the deities of ancient Egypt, two became closely associated with alchemy. One of these was the ibis-headed scribe god Thoth, who presided over the recording of wisdom and was compared to the god Hermes or Mercury in the Greco-Roman traditions. The other, in this case often referred to as his daughter, was Isis. Why she became closely associated with alchemy is not so clear. Some say it is because an early woman alchemist was called Kleopatra, who was later confused with the great queen and priestess of Isis, Cleopatra the Seventh. Others ascribe to this same notorious and passionate queen the writing of a book on cosmetics, which may have included rejuvenating recipes and chemical compounds designed to enhance beauty, and again was associated with the goddess that the queen worshipped. Another early female alchemist was called Mary the Egyptian, who contributed the concept of the *bain-marie,* a vessel that still bears her name.

Since the pursuit of the transmutation of base metals into gold is one aspect of alchemical study, the long association between Isis and that metal may have played a part. She is sometimes depicted perched on the hieroglyphic symbol for gold, and

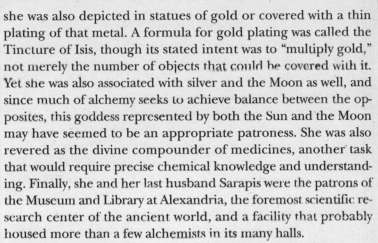

she was also depicted in statues of gold or covered with a thin plating of that metal. A formula for gold plating was called the Tincture of Isis, though its stated intent was to "multiply gold," not merely the number of objects that could be covered with it. Yet she was also associated with silver and the Moon as well, and since much of alchemy seeks to achieve balance between the opposites, this goddess represented by both the Sun and the Moon may have seemed to be an appropriate patroness. She was also revered as the divine compounder of medicines, another task that would require precise chemical knowledge and understanding. Finally, she and her last husband Sarapis were the patrons of the Museum and Library at Alexandria, the foremost scientific research center of the ancient world, and a facility that probably housed more than a few alchemists in its many halls.

What we do know is that by late classical times, Isis was the key player in a book of alchemical recipes called *The Prophetess Isis to Her Son Horus,* in which Isis receives secrets of alchemy from an angel, Amnael. In this story, Isis is observed by Amnael, who desires her. She knows he possesses alchemical secrets, and refuses to yield herself until he agrees to share them with her for her benefit and that of her son, Horus. Like most alchemical manuscripts, the text can be read symbolically or as practical (if obscure) instructions on the creation of rare compounds. Another text called *The Virgin of the World* recounts some of what the angel may have revealed to Isis, which she passes on to Horus.

For alchemists obsessed with discovering the secret of immortality, Isis was also a revered patroness. Most of the alchemical texts related to Isis portray her as a more mortal woman, who is fortunate to discover the secrets of immortality, which she then uses to revive Osiris and to pass on to her son, Horus.

Isis is still invoked as a patroness of the compounding arts today, through the creation of herbal medicines, and in perfumes and incenses. One pharmaceutical company named after her produces life-extending drugs for AIDS patients; surely, the goddess believed to have granted immortality to Osiris will not be displeased by this modern use of that powerful name.

THE WORLD TREE

BY KEN JOHNSON

We live in a cosmos based on the teachings of science. It is an infinite cosmos, one that began with a big bang that expands in an elliptical shape into infinity, and that will someday contract back upon us again, like some gigantic being breathing in and breathing out.

But there is another, much older vision of the cosmos that still resonates deep within our souls. This is the cosmos of shamanism. It exists all over the world. The same teachings about the universe can be found among the Pagan Vikings of Scandinavia and the Classic Maya of Central America. Ours is a truly universal universe.

According to the shamanic world view, a great tree stands at the center of all things. It is the pivot around which the Three Worlds revolve—Heaven, Earth, and the Underworld.

The World Tree's mighty roots reach down into the Underworld. There, at the bottom of all things, is a dark pool of water in which some great reptile lives (the Vikings said it was a snake; the Maya said it was an alligator). This primordial dragon lies coiled at the source of the cosmos.

Above it, the World Tree stretches on and on. In the very center of its trunk lies the circle of Middle Earth, the greening world in which we move and have our being.

The Tree stretches far above our own Earthly domain, its branches soaring into Heaven, the world of the Gods. Each great branch leads to another Heaven, another divine realm.

At the top of all, above the highest Heaven, a great bird soars. Siberian and Norse shamans claimed it was an eagle; the Maya spoke of a mystical, legendary bird called the muan. Even higher, at the apex of all things, shines the North Star.

When shamans travel to other worlds, they climb up and down the World Tree. They may travel down its trunk to seek the souls of ancestors and the dead who dwell in the darkness beneath the tree. They may travel up its trunk to commune with the souls of those yet unborn, who blossom like flowers in the branches; or they may climb to the highest Heavens of all, to seek wisdom from the Goddesses and Gods.

Such was the cosmos of our ancestors. It has nothing to do with the teachings of contemporary science. Yet it is more than a simple relic of times past.

The shamanic cosmos lives on within us.

We ourselves are the tree, and our spinal column the strong trunk. Below us, deep in our bellies and sexual organs, a great serpent lies coiled—the source of our magical and sexual energy, waiting to rise, to ascend the tree.

All of yoga is based on this shamanic paradigm. When the yogini or yogi awakens the kundalini or Serpent Power within, and coaxes it up the spinal column, she or he is simply climbing the inner World Tree, like a shaman of old. Those inner centers of power that many of us call the chakras are none other than the various Heavens and Otherworlds that serve as stations on the shaman's journey.

What about the Three Worlds themselves? What about Heaven, Earth, and Underworld? These are none other than the Spirit, the Body, and the Soul.

When the Serpent Power reaches the thousand-petaled lotus in the top of the yogi's head, enlightenment occurs. When the shaman climbs to the top of the World Tree—to the place of the eagle and the North Star—the Goddesses and Gods speak their wisdom.

The cosmos of our ancestors lives on because it was founded in one of the greatest of all possible truths:

You are the cosmos!

THE WITCH'S TRISKELE

BY JIM GARRISON

With integrity I do approach the gods, that I might know perfect love and perfect trust.

With honor do I approach the gods, that I might dare to embrace the truth of responsibility that comes from doing one's true will.

With respect do I approach the gods, that I might remain silent and thus protect the sacred mysteries.

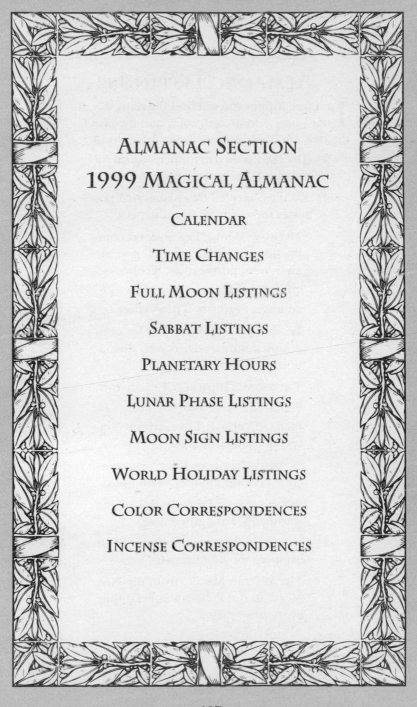

Almanac Section
1999 Magical Almanac

Calendar

Time Changes

Full Moon Listings

Sabbat Listings

Planetary Hours

Lunar Phase Listings

Moon Sign Listings

World Holiday Listings

Color Correspondences

Incense Correspondences

ALMANAC LISTINGS

I n these listings you will find the date, day, lunar phase, Moon sign, color and incense for the day, and festivals from around the world.

❖c THE DATE is used in numerological calculations that govern magical rites.

❖c EACH DAY is ruled by a planet that possesses specific magical influences:

MONDAY (Moon): Peace, sleep, compassion, healing, friends, psychic awareness, purification, fertility.

TUESDAY (Mars): Passion, sex, courage, aggression, protection.

WEDNESDAY (Mercury): The conscious mind, study, travel, divination, wisdom.

THURSDAY (Jupiter): Expansion, money, prosperity, generosity.

FRIDAY (Venus): Love, friendship, reconciliation, beauty.

SATURDAY (Saturn): Longevity, exorcism, endings, homes, and houses.

SUNDAY (Sun): Protection, healing, spirituality, strength.

❖c THE LUNAR PHASE is important in determining the best times for magic.

THE WAXING MOON (from the New Moon to the Full) is the ideal time for positive magic.

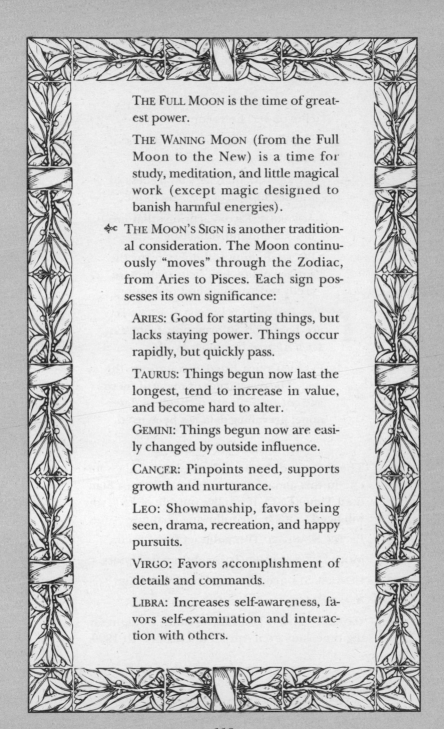

THE FULL MOON is the time of greatest power.

THE WANING MOON (from the Full Moon to the New) is a time for study, meditation, and little magical work (except magic designed to banish harmful energies).

❖ THE MOON'S SIGN is another traditional consideration. The Moon continuously "moves" through the Zodiac, from Aries to Pisces. Each sign possesses its own significance:

ARIES: Good for starting things, but lacks staying power. Things occur rapidly, but quickly pass.

TAURUS: Things begun now last the longest, tend to increase in value, and become hard to alter.

GEMINI: Things begun now are easily changed by outside influence.

CANCER: Pinpoints need, supports growth and nurturance.

LEO: Showmanship, favors being seen, drama, recreation, and happy pursuits.

VIRGO: Favors accomplishment of details and commands.

LIBRA: Increases self-awareness, favors self-examination and interaction with others.

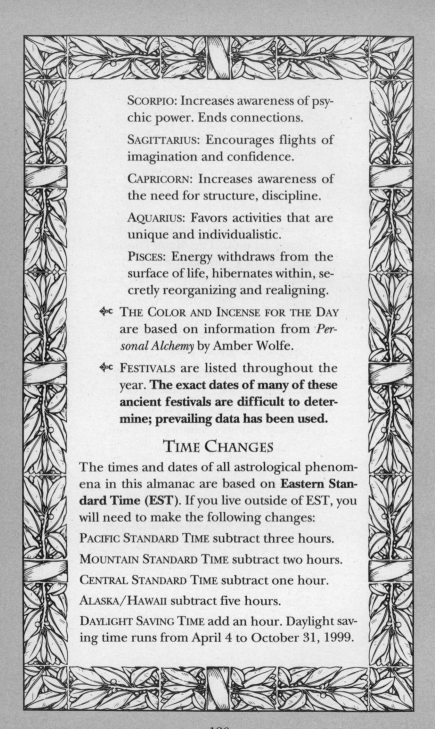

SCORPIO: Increases awareness of psychic power. Ends connections.

SAGITTARIUS: Encourages flights of imagination and confidence.

CAPRICORN: Increases awareness of the need for structure, discipline.

AQUARIUS: Favors activities that are unique and individualistic.

PISCES: Energy withdraws from the surface of life, hibernates within, secretly reorganizing and realigning.

❖c THE COLOR AND INCENSE FOR THE DAY are based on information from *Personal Alchemy* by Amber Wolfe.

❖c FESTIVALS are listed throughout the year. **The exact dates of many of these ancient festivals are difficult to determine; prevailing data has been used.**

TIME CHANGES

The times and dates of all astrological phenomena in this almanac are based on **Eastern Standard Time (EST)**. If you live outside of EST, you will need to make the following changes:

PACIFIC STANDARD TIME subtract three hours.

MOUNTAIN STANDARD TIME subtract two hours.

CENTRAL STANDARD TIME subtract one hour.

ALASKA/HAWAII subtract five hours.

DAYLIGHT SAVING TIME add an hour. Daylight saving time runs from April 4 to October 31, 1999.

1999 Sabbats and Full Moons

January 31	Full Moon 11:07 AM
February 2	Imbolc
March 2	Full Moon 1:59 AM
March 20	Ostara (Spring Equinox)
March 31	Full Moon 5:50 PM
April 30	Full Moon 9:55 AM
May 1	Beltane
May 30	Full Moon 1:40 AM
June 21	Litha (Summer Solstice)
June 28	Full Moon 4:38 PM
July 28	Full Moon 6:25 AM
August 1	Lammas
August 26	Full Moon 6:48 PM
September 23	Mabon (Fall Equinox)
September 25	Full Moon 5:51 AM
October 24	Full Moon 4:03 PM
October 31	Samhain
November 23	Full Moon 2:04 AM
December 22	Full Moon 12:31 PM
December 22	Yule (Winter Solstice)

The Planetary Hours

The selection of an auspicious time for starting any affair is an important matter. When a thing is once commenced, its existence tends to be of a nature corresponding to the conditions under which it was begun. Not only should you select the appropriate date, but when possible you should also start the affair under an appropriate planetary hour.

Each hour of the day is ruled by a planet, and so the nature of any time during the day corresponds to the nature of the planet ruling it. The nature of the planetary hours is the same as the description of each of the planets, except that you will not need to refer to the descriptions for Uranus, Neptune, and Pluto, as they are considered here as higher octaves of Mercury, Venus, and Mars, respectively. If something is ruled by Uranus, you can use the hour of Mercury.

The only other factor you need to know to use the Planetary Hours is the time of your local Sunrise and Sunset for any given day. This is given in the chart following.

Example

Planetary hours for January 2, 1999, 10 degrees latitude.

1) Find sunrise (table, page 125) and sunset (table, page 126) for January 2, 1998, at 10 degrees latitude by following the 10º latitude column down to the January 2 row. In the case of our example this is the first entry in the upper left-hand corner of both the sunrise and sunset tables. You will see that sunrise for January 2, 1999, at 10 degrees latitude is at 6 hours and 16 minutes (or 6:16 AM) and sunset is at 17 hours and 49 minutes (or 5:49 PM).

2) Subtract sunrise time (6 hours 16 minutes) from sunset time (17 hours 49 minutes) to get the number of astrological daylight hours. It is easier to do this if you convert the hours into minutes. For example, 6 hours and 16 minutes = 376 minutes (6 hours x 60 minutes each = 360 minutes + 16 minutes = 376 minutes). 17 hours and 49 minutes = 1069

minutes (17 hours x 60 minutes = 1020 minutes + 49 minutes = 1069 minutes). Now subtract: 1069 minutes - 376 minutes = 693 minutes. If we then convert this back to hours by dividing by 60, we have 11 hours and 33 minutes of daylight planetary hours. However, it is easier to calculate the next step if you leave the number in minutes.

3) Next you should determine how many minutes are in a daylight planetary hour for that particular day (January 2, 1999, 10 degrees latitude). To do this divide 693 minutes by 12 (the number of hours of daylight at the equinoxes). The answer is 58, rounded off. Therefore, a daylight planetary hour for January 2, 1999, at 10 degrees latitude has 58 minutes. Remember that except on equinoxes, there is not an even amount of daylight and night time, so you will rarely have 60 minutes in a daylight hour.

4) Now you know that each daylight planetary hour is roughly 58 minutes. You also know, from step one, that sunrise is at 6:16 AM. To determine the starting times of each planetary hour, simply add 58 minutes to the sunrise time for the first planetary hour, 58 minutes to that number for the second planetary hour, etc. So the daylight planetary hours for our example are as follows: 1st hour 6:16 AM–7:14 AM; 2nd hour 7:15 AM–8:11 AM; 3rd hour 8:12 AM–9:08 AM; 4th hour 9:09 AM–10:05 AM; 5th hour 10:06 AM–11:02 AM; 6th hour 11:03 AM–11:59 AM; 7th hour 12:00 AM–12:56 PM; 8th hour 12:57 PM–1:53 PM; 9th hour 1:54 PM–2:50 PM; 10th hour 2:51 PM–3:47 PM; 11th hour 3:48 PM–4:44 PM; 12th hour 4:45 PM–5:51 PM. Note that because you rounded up, this isn't exact to the sunset table, which says that sunset is at 5:49 PM. This is a good reason to give yourself a little "fudge space" when using planetary hours. For most accurate sunrise or sunset times, consult your local newspaper.

5) Now, to determine which sign rules which daylight planetary hour, consult your calendar pages to determine which day of the week January 2 falls on. You'll find it's a Saturday. Next, turn to page 127 to find the sunrise planetary hour chart. (It's the one on the top.) If you follow down the column for Saturday, you will see that the first planetary hour of the day is ruled by Saturn, the second by Jupiter, the third by Mars, etc.

6) Now you've determined the daytime (sunrise) planetary hours. You can use the same formula to determine the night time (sunset) planetary hours. You know you have 11 hours and 33 minutes of sunrise planetary hours. Therefore subtract 11 hours and 33 minutes of sunrise hours from the 24 hours in a day to equal the number of sunset hours. 24 hours - 11 hours 13 minutes = 12 hours 47 minutes of sunset time. Now convert this to minutes $(12 \times 60) + 47 = (720) + 47 = 767$ minutes. (This equals 12.783 hours, but remember to leave it in minutes for now.)

7) Now go to step 3 and repeat the rest of the process for the sunset hours. When you get to step 5, remember to consult the sunset table on page 126 rather than the sunrise one. When you complete these steps you should get the following answers. There are (roughly) 63 minutes in a sunset planetary hour for this example. This means that the times for the sunset planetary hours are (starting from the 17:49 sunset time rather than the 6:16 sunrise time) first hour 5:49 PM; second 6:52 PM; third 7:55 PM; fourth 8:58 PM; fifth 10:01 PM; sixth 11:04 PM; seventh 12:07 AM; eighth 1:10 AM; ninth 2:13 AM; tenth 3:16 AM; eleventh 4:19 AM; twelfth 5:21 AM. You see which signs rule the hours by consulting the sunset hours chart on page 127.

SUNRISE

UNIVERSAL TIME FOR MERIDIAN OF GREENWICH

Latitude		+10°	+20°	+30°	+40°	+42°	+46°	+50°
		h:m	h:m	h:m	h:m	h:m	h:m	h:m
JAN	2	6:16	6:34	6:57	7:21	7:28	7:42	7:59
	14	6:21	6:34	6:55	7:20	7:26	7:39	7:53
	26	6:23	6:37	6:53	7:14	7:19	7:29	7:42
FEB	7	6:22	6:33	6:46	7:03	7:06	7:15	7:24
	19	6:18	6:27	6:36	6:48	6:50	6:56	7:03
	27	6:15	6:21	6:28	6:37	6:38	6:43	6:48
MAR	7	6:11	6:15	6:19	6:24	6:26	6:28	6:31
	19	6:05	6:05	6:05	6:05	6:05	6:05	6:05
	27	6:00	5:58	5:56	5:52	5:52	5:50	5:49
APR	12	5:51	5:44	5:37	5:27	5:25	5:19	5:14
	20	5:47	5:38	5:28	5:15	5:12	5:05	4:57
	28	5:44	5:33	5:20	5:04	5:00	4:52	4:42
MAY	6	5:41	5:29	5:13	4:54	4:50	4:40	4:28
	18	5:38	5:23	5:05	4:42	4:37	4:25	4:10
	26	5:38	5:21	5:01	4:36	4:30	4:17	4:01
JUN	3	5:38	5:20	4:59	4:32	4:26	4:12	3:54
	15	5:39	5:20	4:58	4:30	4:24	4:09	3:50
	23	5:41	5:22	5:00	4:32	4:25	4:10	3:51
JUL	1	5:43	5:24	5:02	4:35	4:28	4:13	3:55
	9	5:45	5:27	5:06	4:39	4:33	4:19	4:01
	17	5:47	5:30	5:10	4:45	4:39	4:26	4:10
	25	5:48	5:33	5:15	4:52	4:46	4:34	4:20
AUG	2	5:50	5:36	5:19	4:59	4:54	4:43	4:31
	10	5:51	5:38	5:24	5:07	5:02	4:53	4:42
	18	5:51	5:41	5:29	5:14	5:11	5:03	4:54
	26	5:51	5:43	5:34	5:22	5:19	5:13	5:06
SEP	3	5:51	5:45	5:38	5:29	5:27	5:23	5:18
	11	5:50	5:46	5:42	5:37	5:36	5:33	5:30
	19	5:49	5:48	5:47	5:45	5:44	5:43	5:42
	27	5:49	5:50	5:51	5:52	5:53	5:53	5:54
OCT	13	5:48	5:54	6:01	6:08	6:10	6:14	6:19
	21	5:49	5:57	6:06	6:17	6:10	6:25	6:31
	29	5:50	6:00	6:12	6:26	6:29	6:36	6:45
NOV	6	5:52	6:04	6:18	6:35	6:39	6:48	6:58
	14	5:54	6:08	6:24	6:44	6:49	6:59	7:11
	22	5:57	6:13	6:31	6:53	6:58	7:10	7:24
	30	6:01	6:18	6:37	7:02	7:07	7:20	7:35
DEC	8	6:05	6:23	6:44	7:09	7:15	7:29	7:45
	16	6:09	6:28	6:49	7:15	7:22	7:36	7:53
	24	6:13	6:32	6:53	7:20	7:26	7:40	7:57
	30	6:17	6:35	6:56	7:22	7:28	7:42	7:59

SUNSET

UNIVERSAL TIME FOR MERIDIAN OF GREENWICH

Latitude		+10°	+20°	+30°	+40°	+42°	+46°	+50°
		h:m	h:m	h:m	h:m	h:m	h:m	h:m
JAN	2	17:49	17:30	17:09	16:43	16:37	16:23	16:06
	14	17:57	17:41	17:22	16:58	16:52	16:40	16:25
	26	18:03	17:48	17:32	17:12	17:07	16:57	16:44
FEB	7	18:07	17:55	17:42	17:26	17:23	17:14	17:05
	19	18:09	18:01	17:52	17:40	17:38	17:32	17:25
	27	18:10	18:04	17:58	17:50	17:48	17:44	17:39
MAR	7	18:11	18:07	18:03	17:58	17:57	17:55	17:52
	19	18:11	18:11	18:11	18:11	18:11	18:11	18:11
	27	18:11	18:13	18:16	18:19	18:20	18:22	18:24
APR	12	18:10	18:17	18:25	18:35	18:38	18:43	18:49
	20	18:11	18:20	18:30	18:43	18:47	18:53	19:02
	28	18:11	18:22	18:35	18:52	18:55	19:04	19:14
MAY	6	18:12	18:25	18:41	19:00	19:04	19:14	19:26
	18	18:14	18:30	18:48	19:11	19:17	19:29	19:43
	26	18:16	18:33	18:53	19:18	19:24	19:38	19:54
JUN	3	18:18	18:37	18:57	19:24	19:30	19:45	20:02
	15	18:22	18:43	19:03	19:30	19:37	19:53	20:11
	23	18:23	18:42	19:05	19:33	19:39	19:55	20:13
JUL	1	18:25	18:43	19:05	19:33	19:39	19:54	20:12
	9	18:25	18:43	19:04	19:31	19:37	19:51	20:09
	17	18:25	18:42	19:02	19:27	19:33	19:46	20:02
	25	18:24	18:42	18:58	19:21	19:26	19:38	19:53
AUG	2	18:23	18:36	18:53	19:13	19:18	19:28	19:41
	10	18:20	18:32	18:46	19:03	19:07	19:17	19:28
	18	18:16	18:27	18:38	18:53	18:56	19:04	19:13
	26	18:12	18:20	18:30	18:41	18:44	18:50	18:57
SEP	3	18:08	18:14	18:20	18:28	18:30	18:35	18:40
	11	18:03	18:06	18:10	18:16	18:17	18:19	18:23
	19	17:58	17:59	18:00	18:02	18:03	18:04	18:05
	27	17:53	17:52	17:50	17:49	17:49	17:48	17:47
OCT	13	17:44	17:38	17:32	17:24	17:22	17:18	17:13
	21	17:40	17:32	17:23	17:12	17:09	17:04	16:57
	29	17:37	17:27	17:16	17:01	16:58	16:51	16:42
NOV	6	17:36	17:23	17:09	16:52	16:48	16:39	16:29
	14	17:35	17:21	17:04	16:45	16:40	16:30	16:17
	22	17:35	17:19	17:01	16:39	16:34	16:22	16:08
	30	17:36	17:19	17:00	16:36	16:30	16:17	16:02
DEC	8	17:39	17:21	17:00	16:35	16:28	16:15	15:58
	16	17:42	17:24	17:02	16:36	16:30	16:15	15:59
	24	17:46	17:27	17:06	16:40	16:33	16:19	16:02
	30	17:50	17:32	17:11	16:45	16:39	16:25	16:09

Sunrise and Sunset Hours

Sunrise

Hour	Sun	Mon	Tue	Wed	Thu	Fri	Sat
1	☉	☽	♂	☿	♃	♀	♄
2	♀	♄	☉	☽	♂	☿	♃
3	☿	♃	♀	♄	☉	☽	♂
4	☽	♂	☿	♃	♀	♄	☉
5	♄	☉	☽	♂	☿	♃	♀
6	♃	♀	♄	☉	☽	♂	☿
7	♂	☿	♃	♀	♄	☉	☽
8	☉	☽	♂	☿	♃	♀	♄
9	♀	♄	☉	☽	♂	☿	♃
10	☿	♃	♀	♄	☉	☽	♂
11	☽	♂	☿	♃	♀	♄	☉
12	♄	☉	☽	♂	☿	♃	♀

Sunset

Hour	Sun	Mon	Tue	Wed	Thu	Fri	Sat
1	♃	♀	♄	☉	☽	♂	☿
2	♂	☿	♃	♀	♄	☉	☽
3	☉	☽	♂	☿	♃	♀	♄
4	♀	♄	☉	☽	♂	☿	♃
5	☿	♃	♀	♄	☉	☽	♂
6	☽	♂	☿	♃	♀	♄	☉
7	♄	☉	☽	♂	☿	♃	♀
8	♃	♀	♄	☉	☽	♂	☿
9	♂	☿	♃	♀	♄	☉	☽
10	☉	☽	♂	☿	♃	♀	♄
11	♀	♄	☉	☽	♂	☿	♃
12	☿	♃	♀	♄	☉	☽	♂

☉ Sun; ☿ Mercury; ♄ Saturn; ♂ Mars; ♀ Venus; ☽ Moon; ♃ Jupiter

CAPRICORN

☺ **FRIDAY** • *New Year's Day* • *Kwanzaa Ends*
Full Moon 9:50 pm   Moon Sign: Gemini
Moon Phase: Third Quarter   Moon enters Cancer 3:16 am
Color: Rose   Incense: Floral

2 SATURDAY • *Disting Moon* • *Birthday of Inanna (Sumerian)*
Waning Moon
Moon Phase: Third Quarter   Moon Sign: Cancer
Color: Indigo   Incense: Jasmine

3 SUNDAY • *Pueblo Deer Dances (Native American)*
Waning Moon   Moon Sign: Cancer
Moon Phase: Third Quarter   Moon enters Leo 5:31 am
Color: Gold   Incense: Sandalwood

4 MONDAY • *Martyrs of Independence (Zaire)*
Waning Moon
Moon Phase: Third Quarter   Moon Sign: Leo
Color: Silver   Incense: Temple

5 TUESDAY • *George Washington Carver Day* • *Feast of Befana*
Waning Moon   Moon Sign: Leo
Moon Phase: Third Quarter   Moon enters Virgo 10:49 am
Color: Red   Incense: Cinnamon

6 WEDNESDAY • *Epiphany (Three Kings' Day)*
Waning Moon
Moon Phase: Third Quarter   Moon Sign: Virgo
Color: Yellow   Incense: Sandalwood

7 THURSDAY • *Feast of Sekhmet (Egypt)*
Waning Moon   Moon Sign: Virgo
Moon Phase: Third Quarter   Moon enters Libra 7:53 pm
Color: Turquoise   Incense: Laurel

JANUARY

8 FRIDAY • *Elvis Presley's Birthday*
Waning Moon
Moon Phase: Third Quarter   Moon Sign: Libra
Color: Pink   Incense: Floral

◖ **SATURDAY** • *Festival of Janus*
Waning Moon
Moon Phase: Fourth Quarter 9:21 am   Moon Sign: Libra
Color: Blue   Incense: Thyme

10 SUNDAY • *Geraint's Day (Welsh)*
Waning Moon   Moon Sign: Libra
Moon Phase: Fourth Quarter   Moon enters Scorpio 7:48 am
Color: Orange   Incense: Orange

11 MONDAY • *Festival of Carmentalia (Roman)*•*Plough Monday*
Waning Moon
Moon Phase: Fourth Quarter   Moon Sign: Scorpio
Color: White   Incense: Frankincense

12 TUESDAY • *St. Distaff's Day* • *Nez Perce War Dances*
Waning Moon   Moon Sign: Scorpio
Moon Phase: Fourth Quarter   Moon enters Sagittarius 8:23 pm
Color: Gray   Incense: Sage

13 WEDNESDAY • *Midvintersblot (Norse)*
Waning Moon
Moon Phase: Fourth Quarter   Moon Sign: Sagittarius
Color: Peach   Incense: Fruity

14 THURSDAY • *Makar Sankrati (Hindu)*
Waning Moon
Moon Phase: Fourth Quarter   Moon Sign: Sagittarius
Color: White   Incense: Myrrh

CAPRICORN

15 FRIDAY • *Feast of Christ of Esquipulas* • *Black Christ Festival*
Waning Moon
Moon Phase: Fourth Quarter
Color: Gray

Moon Sign: Sagittarius
Moon enters Capricorn 7:29 am
Incense: Sage

16 SATURDAY • *Festival of Ganesha (Hindu)*
Waning Moon
Moon Phase: Fourth Quarter
Color: Gray

Moon Sign: Capricorn
Incense: Temple

☽ SUNDAY • *St. Anthony's Day* • *Ben Franklin's Birthday*
New Moon 10:47 am
Moon Phase: First Quarter
Color: Yellow

Moon Sign: Capricorn
Moon enters Aquarius 4:12 pm
Incense: Sandalwood

18 MONDAY • *ML King, Jr.'s Birthday (Observed)* • *Surya*
Waxing Moon
Moon Phase: First Quarter
Color: Lavender

Moon Sign: Aquarius
Incense: Lavender

19 TUESDAY • *Ramadhan Ends* • *Festival of Thor (Norse)*
Waxing Moon
Moon Phase: First Quarter
Color: White

Moon Sign: Aquarius
Moon enters Pisces 10:41 pm
Incense: Vanilla

20 WEDNESDAY • *Festival of Thorablottar (Icelandic)*
Waxing Moon
Moon Phase: First Quarter
Color: Brown

Sun enters Aquarius 7:38 am
Moon Sign: Pisces
Incense: Woodsy

21 THURSDAY • *Santa Ines' Day (Mexican)*
Waxing Moon
Moon Phase: First Quarter
Color: Violet

Moon Sign: Pisces
Incense: Lilac

JANUARY

22 FRIDAY • *St. Vincent's Day*
Waxing Moon
Moon Phase: First Quarter
Color: Peach

Moon Sign: Pisces
Moon enters Aries 3:26 am
Incense: Fruity

23 SATURDAY • *Goddess month of Bridhe commences*
Waxing Moon
Moon Phase: First Quarter
Color: Brown

Moon Sign: Aries
Incense: Cedar

◑ **SUNDAY** • *Blessing of the Happy Woman's Candle (Hungarian)*
Waxing Moon
Moon Phase: Second Quarter 2:16 pm   Enters Taurus 6:53 am
Color: Peach

Moon Sign: Aries
Incense: Fruity

25 MONDAY • *Burns' Night (Scottish)*
Waxing Moon
Moon Phase: Second Quarter
Color: Gray

Moon Sign: Taurus
Incense: Sage

26 TUESDAY • *Festival of Ekeko (Bolivian)* • *Australia Day*
Waxing Moon
Moon Phase: Second Quarter
Color: Red

Moon Sign: Taurus
Moon enters Gemini 9:30 am
Incense: Cinnamon

27 WEDNESDAY • *Sementivae Feria (Roman)*
Waxing Moon
Moon Phase: Second Quarter
Color: White

Moon Sign: Gemini
Incense: Almond

28 THURSDAY • *Upelly-Aa (Scottish)*
Waxing Moon
Moon Phase: Second Quarter
Color: Green

Moon Sign: Gemini
Moon enters Cancer 11:57 am
Incense: Evergreen

AQUARIUS

29 FRIDAY • *Martyr's Day (Nepalese)*
Waxing Moon
Moon Phase: Second Quarter   Moon Sign: Cancer
Color: Rose   Incense: Rose

30 SATURDAY • *Three Hierarchs Day (Eastern Orthodox)*
Waxing Moon   Moon Sign: Cancer
Moon Phase: Second Quarter   Moon enters Leo 3:16 pm
Color: Indigo   Incense: Jasmine

☺ **SUNDAY** • *Lunar Eclipse* • *Hecate's Feast (Greek)*
Full Moon 11:07 am
Moon Phase: Third Quarter   Moon Sign: Leo
Color: Gold   Incense: Sandalwood

FULL MOONS

January	Cold Moon, Moon after Yule
February	Snow Moon, Wolf Moon, Hunger Moon
March	Quickening Moon, Storm Moon, Sap Moon
April	Wind Moon, Grass Moon
May	Flower Moon, Planting Moon
June	Strong Sun Moon
July	Blessing Moon, Honey Moon
August	Corn Moon, Thunder Moon
September	Harvest Moon, Grain Moon, Fruit Moon
October	Blood Moon, Hunter's Moon
November	Mourning Moon, Frosty Moon
December	Moon Before Yule, Long Nights Moon

The second Full Moon of any month is called a Blue Moon.

FEBRUARY

1 MONDAY • *Tu B'Shevat (Jewish Arbor Day)*
Waning Moon
Moon Phase: Third Quarter
Color: Silver

Moon Sign: Leo
Moon enters Virgo 8:37 pm
Incense: Temple

2 TUESDAY • *Imbolc* • *Candlemas* • *Groundhog Day*
Waning Moon
Moon Phase: Third Quarter
Color: Red

Moon Sign: Virgo
Incense: Cinnamon

3 WEDNESDAY • *Powamu Festival (Hopi)*
Waning Moon
Moon Phase: Third Quarter
Color: Yellow

Moon Sign: Virgo
Incense: Sandalwood

4 THURSDAY • *King Frost Day (English)*
Waning Moon
Moon Phase: Third Quarter
Color: Green

Moon Sign: Virgo
Moon enters Libra 4:55 am
Incense: Bayberry

5 FRIDAY • *Feast of St. Agatha (Sicilian)*
Waning Moon
Moon Phase: Third Quarter
Color: Rose

Moon Sign: Libra
Incense: Floral

6 SATURDAY • *Festival of Aphrodite (Greek)*
Waning Moon
Moon Phase: Third Quarter
Color: Indigo

Moon Sign: Libra
Moon enters Scorpio 4:06 pm
Incense: Jasmine

7 SUNDAY • *Selene's Day (Greek)*
Waning Moon
Moon Phase: Third Quarter
Color: Gold

Moon Sign: Scorpio
Incense: Sandalwood

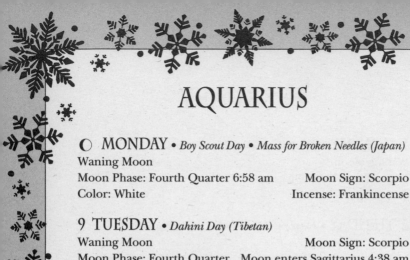

AQUARIUS

◯ MONDAY • *Boy Scout Day* • *Mass for Broken Needles (Japan)*
Waning Moon
Moon Phase: Fourth Quarter 6:58 am   Moon Sign: Scorpio
Color: White   Incense: Frankincense

9 TUESDAY • *Dahini Day (Tibetan)*
Waning Moon   Moon Sign: Scorpio
Moon Phase: Fourth Quarter Moon enters Sagittarius 4:38 am
Color: Gray   Incense: Sage

10 WEDNESDAY • *Li Chum (Chinese)*
Waning Moon
Moon Phase: Fourth Quarter   Moon Sign: Sagittarius
Color: Peach   Incense: Peach

11 THURSDAY • *Tom Edison's Birthday* • *Our Lady of Lourdes*
Waning Moon   Moon Sign: Sagittarius
Moon Phase: Fourth Quarter Moon enters Capricorn 4:10 pm
Color: Turquoise   Incense: Laurel

12 FRIDAY • *Festival of Diana (Roman)* • *Abe Lincoln's Birthday*
Waning Moon
Moon Phase: Fourth Quarter   Moon Sign: Capricorn
Color: Pink   Incense: Floral

13 SATURDAY • *St. Matthias' Day*
Waning Moon
Moon Phase: Fourth Quarter   Moon Sign: Capricorn
Color: Blue   Incense: Thyme

14 SUNDAY • *St. Valentine's Day* • *Shrovetide* • *Carnival Begins*
Waning Moon   Moon Sign: Capricorn
Moon Phase: Fourth Quarter Moon enters Aquarius 12:57 am
Color: Orange   Incense: Ginger

FEBRUARY

15 MONDAY • *President's Day* • *Lupercalia*
Waning Moon
Moon Phase: Fourth Quarter   Moon Sign: Aquarius
Color: Lavender   Incense: Lavender

☽ TUESDAY • *Solar Eclipse* • *Mardi Gras* • *Chinese New Year*
New Moon 1:40 am   Moon Sign: Aquarius
Moon Phase: First Quarter   Moon enters Pisces 6:40 am
Color: White   Incense: Frankincense

17 WEDNESDAY • *Ash Wednesday* • *Lent Begins*
Waxing Moon
Moon Phase: First Quarter   Moon Sign: Pisces
Color: Brown   Incense: Cedar

18 THURSDAY • *Spenta Armaiti (Zoroastrian)*
Waxing Moon   Sun enters Pisces 9:47 pm
Moon Phase: First Quarter   Moon enters Aries 10:07 am
Color: White   Incense: Myrrh

19 FRIDAY • *Mahashivatri (The Great Night of Shiva)*
Waxing Moon
Moon Phase: First Quarter   Moon Sign: Aries
Color: Peach   Incense: Fruity

20 SATURDAY • *Day of Tacita (Roman)*
Waxing Moon   Moon Sign: Aries
Moon Phase: First Quarter   Moon enters Taurus 12:29 pm
Color: Gray   Incense: Sage

21 SUNDAY • *Feralia (Roman)*
Waxing Moon
Moon Phase: First Quarter   Moon Sign: Taurus
Color: Yellow   Incense: Sandalwood

PISCES

○ MONDAY • *St. Lucia's Day* • *George Washington's Birthday*
Waxing Moon   Moon Sign: Taurus
Moon Phase: Second Quarter 9:43 pm   Enters Gemini 2:54 pm
Color: Gray   Incense: Sage

23 TUESDAY • *Terminalia (Ancient Rome)*
Waxing Moon
Moon Phase: Second Quarter   Moon Sign: Gemini
Color: Black   Incense: Patchouli

24 WEDNESDAY
Waxing Moon   Moon Sign: Gemini
Moon Phase: Second Quarter   Moon enters Cancer 6:09 pm
Color: White   Incense: Vanilla

25 THURSDAY • *Day of Nut (Egyptian)*
Waxing Moon
Moon Phase: Second Quarter   Moon Sign: Cancer
Color: Violet   Incense: Lilac

26 FRIDAY • *Hygeia's Day (North African)*
Waxing Moon   Moon Sign: Cancer
Moon Phase: Second Quarter   Moon enters Leo 10:44 pm
Color: White   Incense: Almond

27 SATURDAY • *Feast of Esther (Hebrew)*
Waxing Moon
Moon Phase: Second Quarter   Moon Sign: Leo
Color: Brown   Incense: Woodsy

28 SUNDAY • *Buddha's Conception (Tibetan)*
Waxing Moon
Moon Phase: Second Quarter   Moon Sign: Leo
Color: Peach   Incense: Peach

MARCH

1 MONDAY • *Purim Begins* • *Matronalia (Roman)* • *Pulaski Day*
Waxing Moon   Moon Sign: Leo
Moon Phase: Second Quarter   Moon enters Virgo 5:05 am
Color: Silver   Incense: Temple

☺ **TUESDAY** • *Mother's March (Bulgarian)* • *Purim ends*
Full Moon 1:59 am
Moon Phase: Third Quarter   Moon Sign: Virgo
Color: Red   Incense: Cinnamon

3 WEDNESDAY • *Doll Festival (Japanese)*
Waning Moon   Moon Sign: Virgo
Moon Phase: Third Quarter   Moon enters Libra 1:34 pm
Color: Yellow   Incense: Sandalwood

4 THURSDAY • *Feast of Rhiannon (Welsh)*
Waning Moon
Moon Phase: Third Quarter   Moon Sign: Libra
Color: Green   Incense: Mint

5 FRIDAY • *Kite Festival (Japan)* • *Celebration of Isis (N. African)*
Waning Moon
Moon Phase: Third Quarter   Moon Sign: Libra
Color: Rose   Incense: Floral

6 SATURDAY • *Mars' Day (Roman)*
Waning Moon   Moon Sign: Libra
Moon Phase: Third Quarter   Moon enters Scorpio 12:23 am
Color: Indigo   Incense: Jasmine

7 SUNDAY • *Junonalia (Roman)*
Waning Moon
Moon Phase: Third Quarter   Moon Sign: Scorpio
Color: Orange   Incense: Orange

PISCES

8 MONDAY • *Working Women's Day* • *Birthday of Mother Earth*
Waning Moon   Moon Sign: Scorpio
Moon Phase: Third Quarter   Moon enters Sagittarius 12:47 pm
Color: Lavender   Incense: Lavender

9 TUESDAY • *Feast of the Forty Martyrs (Greek)*
Waning Moon
Moon Phase: Third Quarter   Moon Sign: Sagittarius
Color: White   Incense: Almond

☽ WEDNESDAY • *Siamese New Year* • *Holi (Indian)*
Waning Moon
Moon Phase: Fourth Quarter 3:41 am   Moon Sign: Sagittarius
Color: Peach   Incense: Peach

11 THURSDAY • *Hercules' Day (Greek)*
Waning Moon   Moon Sign: Sagittarius
Moon Phase: Fourth Quarter Moon enters Capricorn 12:54 am
Color: Turquoise   Incense: Laurel

12 FRIDAY • *Feast of Marduk (Mesopotamian)*
Waning Moon
Moon Phase: Fourth Quarter   Moon Sign: Capricorn
Color: Pink   Incense: Floral

13 SATURDAY • *Purification Feast (Balinese)*
Waning Moon   Moon Sign: Capricorn
Moon Phase: Fourth Quarter   Moon enters Aquarius 10:32 am
Color: Blue   Incense: Thyme

14 SUNDAY • *Veturius Mamurius (Roman)*
Waning Moon
Moon Phase: Fourth Quarter   Moon Sign: Aquarius
Color: Yellow   Incense: Sandalwood

MARCH

15 MONDAY • *Offerings to Ra, Asar, Horus (Egyptian)*
Waning Moon   Moon Sign: Aquarius
Moon Phase: Fourth Quarter   Moon enters Pisces 4:31 pm
Color: White   Incense: Frankincense

16 TUESDAY • *Feast of Heru-sa-Aset • Festival of Dionysus*
Waning Moon
Moon Phase: Fourth Quarter   Moon Sign: Pisces
Color: Gray   Incense: Sage

☽ WEDNESDAY • *St. Patrick's Day*
New Moon 1:48 pm   Moon Sign: Pisces
Moon Phase: First Quarter   Moon enters Aries 7:13 pm
Color: Brown   Incense: Cedar

18 THURSDAY • *Sheelah's Day (Icelandic)*
Waxing Moon
Moon Phase: First Quarter   Moon Sign: Aries
Color: White   Incense: Myrrh

19 FRIDAY • *Quintania (Greek) • Day of Aganyu (Santerian)*
Waxing Moon   Moon Sign: Aries
Moon Phase: First Quarter   Moon enters Taurus 8:09 pm
Color: Peach   Incense: Peach

20 SATURDAY • *Ostara/Spring Equinox • Feast of Ba-neb-dedet*
Waxing Moon   Sun enters Aries 8:46 pm
Moon Phase: First Quarter   Moon Sign: Taurus
Color: Gray   Incense: Sage

21 SUNDAY • *Tea and Tephi Day (Irish)*
Waxing Moon   Moon Sign: Taurus
Moon Phase: First Quarter   Moon enters Gemini 9:05 pm
Color: Gold   Incense: Sandalwood

ARIES

22 MONDAY • *Mesopotamian New Year Festival*
Waxing Moon
Moon Phase: First Quarter   Moon Sign: Gemini
Color: Gray   Incense: Sage

23 TUESDAY • *Summer Finding (Norse)*
Waxing Moon   Moon Sign: Gemini
Moon Phase: First Quarter   Moon enters Cancer 11:33 pm
Color: Black   Incense: Patchouli

☽ WEDNESDAY • *Day of Britannia* • *Day of Archangel Gabriel*
Waxing Moon
Moon Phase: Second Quarter 5:18 am   Moon Sign: Cancer
Color: Brown   Incense: Woodsy

25 THURSDAY • *Feast of the Annunciation*
Waxing Moon   Moon Sign: Cancer
Moon Phase: Second Quarter   Moon enters Leo 4:22 am
Color: Violet   Incense: Lilac

26 FRIDAY • *Arbor Day* • *Plowing Day (Slavic)*
Waxing Moon
Moon Phase: Second Quarter   Moon Sign: Leo
Color: White   Incense: Vanilla

27 SATURDAY • *Smell the Breeze Day (Egyptian)*
Waxing Moon
Moon Phase: Second Quarter   Moon Sign: Leo
Color: Brown   Incense: Cedar

28 SUNDAY • *Palm Sunday* • *Eid Al-Adha (Islamic)*
Waxing Moon   Moon Sign: Leo
Moon Phase: Second Quarter   Moon enters Virgo 11:35 am
Color: Peach   Incense: Peach

MARCH

29 MONDAY • *Festival of Ishtar (Babylonian)*
Waxing Moon
Moon Phase: Second Quarter   Moon Sign: Virgo
Color: Silver   Incense: Temple

30 TUESDAY • *Festival of Janus and Concordia*
Waxing Moon   Moon Sign: Virgo
Moon Phase: Second Quarter   Moon enters Libra 8:50 pm
Color: Red   Incense: Cinnamon

☺ **WEDNESDAY** • *Passover Begins*
Full Moon 5:50 pm
Moon Phase: Third Quarter   Moon Sign: Libra
Color: Yellow   Incense: Sandalwood

CUTTING REMARKS

If you cut your nails on a **Monday,** it will bring you news.

Cut your nails on a **Tuesday** for new clothes.

Cut your nails on **Wednesday,** and you'll have good health.

Cut your nails on **Thursday,** and you will have wealth.

Cut your nails on **Friday,** and you will have knowledge.

Cut your nails on **Saturday,** and you will travel.

ARIES

1 THURSDAY • *April Fool's Day*
Waning Moon
Moon Phase: Third Quarter   Moon Sign: Libra
Color: Green   Incense: Mint

2 FRIDAY • *Good Friday* • *Battle of Flowers (French)*
Waning Moon   Moon Sign: Libra
Moon Phase: Third Quarter   Moon enters Scorpio 7:49 am
Color: Rose   Incense: Floral

3 SATURDAY
Waning Moon
Moon Phase: Third Quarter   Moon Sign: Scorpio
Color: Indigo   Incense: Jasmine

4 SUNDAY • *Easter* • *Daylight Saving Time Begins at 2 am*
Waning Moon   Moon Sign: Scorpio
Moon Phase: Third Quarter   Moon enters Sagittarius 8:08 pm
Color: Gold   Incense: Sandalwood

5 MONDAY • *Tomb-Sweeping Day (Chinese)*
Waning Moon
Moon Phase: Third Quarter   Moon Sign: Sagittarius
Color: Silver   Incense: Temple

6 TUESDAY • *Ching Ming (Chinese)*
Waning Moon
Moon Phase: Third Quarter   Moon Sign: Sagittarius
Color: Red   Incense: Cinnamon

7 WEDNESDAY • *Blagini's Feast (Romanian)*
Waning Moon   Moon Sign: Sagittarius
Moon Phase: Third Quarter   Moon enters Capricorn 8:39 am
Color: Peach   Incense: Peach

APRIL

◖ THURSDAY • *Passover Ends* • *Flower Festival (Buddhist)*
Waning Moon
Moon Phase: Fourth Quarter 9:51 pm   Moon Sign: Capricorn
Color: Turquoise   Incense: Laurel

9 FRIDAY • *Orthodox Holy Friday*
Waning Moon   Moon Sign: Capricorn
Moon Phase: Fourth Quarter   Moon enters Aquarius 7:24 pm
Color: Pink   Incense: Floral

10 SATURDAY
Waning Moon
Moon Phase: Fourth Quarter   Moon Sign: Aquarius
Color: Blue   Incense: Thyme

11 SUNDAY • *Orthodox Easter* • *Feast of San Leo (Mexican)*
Waning Moon
Moon Phase: Fourth Quarter   Moon Sign: Aquarius
Color: Orange   Incense: Ginger

12 MONDAY • *Holiday*
Waning Moon   Moon Sign: Aquarius
Moon Phase: Fourth Quarter   Moon enters Pisces 2:35 am
Color: White   Incense: Vanilla

13 TUESDAY • *Holocaust Remembrance Day* • *Jefferson's Birthday*
Waning Moon
Moon Phase: Fourth Quarter   Moon Sign: Pisces
Color: Gray   Incense: Sage

14 WEDNESDAY • *Pan American Day* • *Sommarsblot (Norse)*
Waning Moon   Moon Sign: Pisces
Moon Phase: Fourth Quarter   Moon enters Aries 5:46 am
Color: White   Incense: Almond

TAURUS

☽ THURSDAY • *Tax Day* • *Feast of Tellus Mater (Roman)*
New Moon 11:22 pm
Moon Phase: First Quarter   Moon Sign: Aries
Color: Violet   Incense: Lilac

16 FRIDAY • *St. Padarm's Day (Celtic)*
Waxing Moon   Moon Sign: Aries
Moon Phase: First Quarter   Moon enters Taurus 6:07 am
Color: Peach   Incense: Peach

17 SATURDAY • *Islamic New Year* • *Eid-El Adha (Moslem)*
Waxing Moon
Moon Phase: First Quarter   Moon Sign: Taurus
Color: Brown   Incense: Woodsy

18 SUNDAY • *Rava Navami (Hindu)*
Waxing Moon   Moon Sign: Taurus
Moon Phase: First Quarter   Moon enters Gemini 5:39 am
Color: Yellow   Incense: Sandalwood

19 MONDAY • *Women's Celebration (Balinese)*
Waxing Moon
Moon Phase: First Quarter   Moon Sign: Gemini
Color: Gray   Incense: Sage

20 TUESDAY • *Yaqui Pageant (Native American)*
Waxing Moon   Sun enters Taurus 7:46 am
Moon Phase: First Quarter   Moon enters Cancer 6:28 am
Color: Black   Incense: Patchouli

21 WEDNESDAY
Waxing Moon
Moon Phase: First Quarter   Moon Sign: Cancer
Color: Brown   Incense: Woodsy

APRIL

◗ THURSDAY • *Earth Day* • *Take Your Daughters to Work Day*
Waxing Moon   Moon Sign: Cancer
Moon Phase: Second Quarter 2:02 pm   Enters Leo 10:06 am
Color: White   Incense: Frankincense

23 FRIDAY • *St. George's Day (British)*
Waxing Moon
Moon Phase: Second Quarter   Moon Sign: Leo
Color: Peach   Incense: Peach

24 SATURDAY • *Children's Day (Icelandic)*
Waxing Moon   Moon Sign: Leo
Moon Phase: Second Quarter   Moon enters Virgo 5:05 pm
Color: Gray   Incense: Sage

25 SUNDAY • *Feast of San Jorge (Mexican)*
Waxing Moon
Moon Phase: Second Quarter   Moon Sign: Virgo
Color: Peach   Incense: Peach

26 MONDAY • *Flower Parades (Dutch)*
Waxing Moon
Moon Phase: Second Quarter   Moon Sign: Virgo
Color: Lavender   Incense: Lavender

27 TUESDAY
Waxing Moon   Moon Sign: Virgo
Moon Phase: Second Quarter   Moon enters Libra 2:47 am
Color: Gray   Incense: Sage

28 WEDNESDAY • *Floralia Begins (Roman)*
Waxing Moon
Moon Phase: Second Quarter   Moon Sign: Libra
Color: Yellow   Incense: Sandalwood

TAURUS

29 THURSDAY

Waxing Moon
Moon Phase: Second Quarter
Color: Green

Moon Sign: Libra
Moon enters Scorpio 2:13 pm
Incense: Evergreen

 **FRIDAY** • *Walpurgis Night* • *Walpurgisnacht (German)*
Full Moon 9:55 am
Moon Phase: Third Quarter
Color: Rose

Moon Sign: Scorpio
Incense: Floral

SCOTT CUNNINGHAM'S MAGICAL PRINCIPLES

• *Magic is natural* • *Harm none, not even yourself, through its use* •
• *Magic requires effort. You will receive what you put into it* •
• *Magic is not usually instantaneous. Spells require time to be effective* • *Magic should not be performed for pay* •
• *Magic should never be used in jest or to inflate your ego* •
• *Magic can be worked for your own gain, but only if it harms none* •
• *Magic is a divine act* • *Magic can be used for defense but should never be used for attack* • *Magic is knowledge—not only of its way and laws, but also of its effectiveness. Do not believe that magic works—know it!* • *Magic is love. All magic should be performed out of love. The moment anger or hatred tinges your magic you have crossed the border into a dangerous world, one that will ultimately consume you* •

MAY

1 SATURDAY • *Beltane* • *May Day*
Waning Moon
Moon Phase: Third Quarter
Color: Brown

Moon Sign: Scorpio
Incense: Woodsy

2 SUNDAY • *Fire Festival of Bona Dea (Roman)*
Waning Moon
Moon Phase: Third Quarter
Color: Peach

Moon Sign: Scorpio
Moon enters Sagittarius 2:36 am
Incense: Peach

3 MONDAY • *Cruces (Mexican)*
Waning Moon
Moon Phase: Third Quarter
Color: Silver

Moon Sign: Sagittarius
Incense: Temple

4 TUESDAY • *St. Monica's Day (Irish)* • *Lag B'Omer (Jewish)*
Waning Moon
Moon Phase: Third Quarter
Color: Black

Moon Sign: Sagittarius
Moon enters Capricorn 3:12 pm
Incense: Patchouli

5 WEDNESDAY • *Feast of Banners (Japanese)* • *Cinco de Mayo*
Waning Moon
Moon Phase: Third Quarter
Color: Brown

Moon Sign: Capricorn
Incense: Woodsy

6 THURSDAY • *Eyvind Kelve (Norse)*
Waning Moon
Moon Phase: Third Quarter
Color: White

Moon Sign: Capricorn
Incense: Frankincense

7 FRIDAY • *Helston Furry Dance (Cornwall)*
Waning Moon
Moon Phase: Third Quarter
Color: Pink

Moon Sign: Capricorn
Moon enters Aquarius 2:40 am
Incense: Floral

TAURUS

◗ SATURDAY • *Stork Day (Danish)* • *Truman's Birthday*
Waning Moon
Moon Phase: Fourth Quarter 12:28 pm   Moon Sign: Aquarius
Color: Gray   Incense: Sage

9 SUNDAY • *Mother's Day* • *Lemuria (Roman)*
Waning Moon   Moon Sign: Aquarius
Moon Phase: Fourth Quarter   Moon enters Pisces 11:16 am
Color: Yellow   Incense: Sandalwood

10 MONDAY • *Tin Han's Day (Chinese)*
Waning Moon
Moon Phase: Fourth Quarter   Moon Sign: Pisces
Color: White   Incense: Myrrh

11 TUESDAY • *Ceremony for Rain (Guatamalan)* • *Teacher's Day*
Waning Moon   Moon Sign: Pisces
Moon Phase: Fourth Quarter   Moon enters Aries 3:54 pm
Color: Gray   Incense: Myrrh

12 WEDNESDAY • *Festival of Sashti (Indian)*
Waning Moon
Moon Phase: Fourth Quarter   Moon Sign: Aries
Color: Peach   Incense: Peach

13 THURSDAY • *Ascension Day* • *Our Lady of Fatima*
Waning Moon   Moon Sign: Aries
Moon Phase: Fourth Quarter   Moon enters Taurus 4:57 pm
Color: Violet   Incense: Lilac

14 FRIDAY • *Isis' Day (Egyptian)*
Waning Moon
Moon Phase: Fourth Quarter   Moon Sign: Taurus
Color: White   Incense: Vanilla

MAY

 SATURDAY • *Feast of Isidro (Filipino)* • *Armed Forces Day*
New Moon 7:06 am   Moon Sign: Taurus
Moon Phase: First Quarter   Moon enters Gemini 4:08 pm
Color: Blue   Incense: Thyme

16 SUNDAY • *Savitu-Vrata (Indian)*
Waxing Moon
Moon Phase: First Quarter   Moon Sign: Gemini
Color: Orange   Incense: Ginger

17 MONDAY • *Mut-L-Ard (Moroccan)* • *Victoria Day*
Waxing Moon   Moon Sign: Gemini
Moon Phase: First Quarter   Moon enters Cancer 3:40 pm
Color: Lavender   Incense: Lavender

18 TUESDAY • *Feast of Pan (Greek)*
Waxing Moon
Moon Phase: First Quarter   Moon Sign: Cancer
Color: Red   Incense: Cinnamon

19 WEDNESDAY • *Feast of Pudenciana (Mexican)*
Waxing Moon   Moon Sign: Cancer
Moon Phase: First Quarter   Moon enters Leo 5:38 pm
Color: Yellow   Incense: Sandalwood

20 THURSDAY • *Mjollnir (German)*
Waxing Moon
Moon Phase: First Quarter   Moon Sign: Leo
Color: Green   Incense: Mint

21 FRIDAY • *Shavuot* • *Day of Tefnut (Egyptian)*
Waxing Moon   Sun enters Gemini 6:52 am
Moon Phase: First Quarter   Moon enters Virgo 11:16 pm
Color: Peach   Incense: Peach

GEMINI

◯ SATURDAY • *Ragnar Lodbrok's Day (Odinist)*
Waxing Moon
Moon Phase: Second Quarter 12:35 am   Moon Sign: Virgo
Color: Indigo   Incense: Jasmine

23 SUNDAY • *Semik (Russian)*
Waxing Moon
Moon Phase: Second Quarter   Moon Sign: Virgo
Color: Gold   Incense: Sandalwood

24 MONDAY • *The Three Maries (French)*
Waxing Moon   Moon Sign: Virgo
Moon Phase: Second Quarter   Moon enters Libra 8:29 am
Color: Gray   Incense: Sage

25 TUESDAY • *Celebration of the Tao (Japanese)*
Waxing Moon
Moon Phase: Second Quarter   Moon Sign: Libra
Color: White   Incense: Vanilla

26 WEDNESDAY
Waxing Moon   Moon Sign: Libra
Moon Phase: Second Quarter   Moon enters Scorpio 8:05 pm
Color: Brown   Incense: Cedar

27 THURSDAY
Waxing Moon
Moon Phase: Second Quarter   Moon Sign: Scorpio
Color: Turquoise   Incense: Laurel

28 FRIDAY
Waxing Moon
Moon Phase: Second Quarter   Moon Sign: Scorpio
Color: Brown   Incense: Woodsy

MAY

29 SATURDAY • *Oak Apple Day (English)*
Waxing Moon   Moon Sign: Scorpio
Moon Phase: Second Quarter   Moon enters Sagittarius 8:37 am
Color: Blue   Incense: Thyme

 SUNDAY • *Frigg's Day (Odinist)* • *Enlightenment of Buddha*
Full Moon 1:40 am
Moon Phase: Third Quarter   Moon Sign: Sagittarius
Color: Peach   Incense: Peach

31 MONDAY • *Memorial Day* • *Day of Oggum (Cuban)*
Waning Moon   Moon Sign: Sagittarius
Moon Phase: Third Quarter   Moon enters Capricorn 9:06 pm
Color: Silver   Incense: Temple

SETTING THE DATE

Traditionally, it was considered unlucky to marry during the month of May—probably because it's a planting month, and workers were needed in the fields. June was the preferred month for marriage.

Flowers at the wedding represent wishes for the couple's happiness. Rice was thrown so that the couple would never go hungry. The bride wears something old for good memories, new to celebrate new friends and new life, borrowed to encourage frugality, and blue for serenity.

Rosemary is sometimes placed on the bride's bed for luck, or in her bouquet as an herb of remembrance.

GEMINI

1 TUESDAY • *Festival of Carna (Roman)*
Waning Moon
Moon Phase: Third Quarter   Moon Sign: Capricorn
Color: White   Incense: Vanilla

2 WEDNESDAY • *St. Elmo's Day*
Waning Moon
Moon Phase: Third Quarter   Moon Sign: Capricorn
Color: Yellow   Incense: Sandalwood

3 THURSDAY • *Chimborazo Day (Ecuadorian)*
Waning Moon   Moon Sign: Capricorn
Moon Phase: Third Quarter   Moon enters Aquarius 8:37 am
Color: Green   Incense: Evergreen

4 FRIDAY • *Socrates' Birthday*
Waning Moon
Moon Phase: Third Quarter   Moon Sign: Aquarius
Color: Rose   Incense: Floral

5 SATURDAY • *Sheela-Na-Gig (Irish)* • *World Environment Day*
Waning Moon   Moon Sign: Aquarius
Moon Phase: Third Quarter   Moon enters Pisces 6:01 pm
Color: Indigo   Incense: Jasmine

☾ SUNDAY • *D-Day*
Fourth Quarter 11:21 pm
Moon Phase: Fourth Quarter   Moon Sign: Pisces
Color: Gold   Incense: Sandalwood

7 MONDAY • *Vesta Aperit (Roman)*
Waning Moon
Moon Phase: Fourth Quarter   Moon Sign: Pisces
Color: Silver   Incense: Temple

JUNE

8 TUESDAY • *Lindisfarne Day (Odinist)*
Waning Moon   Moon Sign: Pisces
Moon Phase: Fourth Quarter   Moon enters Aries 12:09 am
Color: Red   Incense: Cinnamon

9 WEDNESDAY • *Vestalia (Roman)*
Waning Moon
Moon Phase: Fourth Quarter   Moon Sign: Aries
Color: Peach   Incense: Peach

10 THURSDAY • *Day of Anahita (Persian)*
Waning Moon   Moon Sign: Aries
Moon Phase: Fourth Quarter   Moon enters Taurus 2:44 am
Color: Turquoise   Incense: Laurel

11 FRIDAY • *King Kamehameha I Day (Hawaiian)*
Waning Moon
Moon Phase: Fourth Quarter   Moon Sign: Taurus
Color: Pink   Incense: Floral

12 SATURDAY
Waning Moon   Moon Sign: Taurus
Moon Phase: Fourth Quarter   Moon enters Gemini 2:49 am
Color: Blue   Incense: Thyme

☽ SUNDAY • *Tibetan All Souls' Day* • *Children's Day*
New Moon 2:03 pm
Moon Phase: First Quarter   Moon Sign: Gemini
Color: Orange   Incense: Orange

14 MONDAY • *Flag Day*
Waxing Moon   Moon Sign: Gemini
Moon Phase: First Quarter   Moon enters Cancer 2:14 am
Color: White   Incense: Almond

CANCER

15 TUESDAY • *St. Vitus' Day*
Waxing Moon
Moon Phase: First Quarter   Moon Sign: Cancer
Color: Black   Incense: Patchouli

16 WEDNESDAY • *Night of the Drop (Egyptian)*
Waxing Moon   Moon Sign: Cancer
Moon Phase: First Quarter   Moon enters Leo 3:07 am
Color: White   Incense: Frankincense

17 THURSDAY • *Ludi Piscatari (Roman)*
Waxing Moon
Moon Phase: First Quarter   Moon Sign: Leo
Color: Violet   Incense: Lilac

18 FRIDAY
Waxing Moon   Moon Sign: Leo
Moon Phase: First Quarter   Moon enters Virgo 7:12 am
Color: Peach   Incense: Peach

19 SATURDAY • *Waa-Laa Begins (Native American)* • *Juneteenth*
Waxing Moon
Moon Phase: First Quarter   Moon Sign: Virgo
Color: Gray   Incense: Sage

◯ SUNDAY • *Day of Ix Chel (Mayan)* • *Father's Day*
Waxing Moon   Moon Sign: Virgo
Moon Phase: Second Quarter 1:13 pm   Enters Libra 3:10 pm
Color: Yellow   Incense: Sandalwood

21 MONDAY • *Litha/Summer Solstice*
Waxing Moon   Sun enters Cancer 2:49 pm
Moon Phase: Second Quarter   Moon Sign: Libra
Color: Lavender   Incense: Lavender

JUNE

22 TUESDAY • *Feast of San Aloisio (Mexican)*
Waxing Moon
Moon Phase: Second Quarter   Moon Sign: Libra
Color: Gray   Incense: Sage

23 WEDNESDAY • *St. John's Eve*
Waxing Moon   Moon Sign: Libra
Moon Phase: Second Quarter   Moon enters Scorpio 2:18 am
Color: Brown   Incense: Cedar

24 THURSDAY • *Aztec Feast of the Sun* • *St. John the Baptist Day*
Waxing Moon
Moon Phase: Second Quarter   Moon Sign: Scorpio
Color: White   Incense: Myrrh

25 FRIDAY • *Well-Dressing Festival (British)*
Waxing Moon   Moon Sign: Scorpio
Moon Phase: Second Quarter   Moon enters Sagittarius 2:51 pm
Color: Rose   Incense: Floral

26 SATURDAY • *Green Corn Festival (Iroquois)* • *Mawlud*
Waxing Moon
Moon Phase: Second Quarter   Moon Sign: Sagittarius
Color: Brown   Incense: Woodsy

27 SUNDAY • *Day of Seven Sleepers (Muslim)*
Waxing Moon
Moon Phase: Second Quarter   Moon Sign: Sagittarius
Color: Peach   Incense: Peach

☺ **MONDAY** • *Festival of the Tarasque (French)*
Full Moon 4:38 pm   Moon Sign: Sagittarius
Moon Phase: Third Quarter   Moon enters Capricorn 3:12 am
Color: Gray   Incense: Sage

CANCER

29 TUESDAY · *Feast of Ogun (Santerian)•Carnation Day (Italian)*
Waning Moon
Moon Phase: Third Quarter   Moon Sign: Capricorn
Color: White   Incense: Vanilla

30 WEDNESDAY
Waning Moon   Moon Sign: Capricorn
Moon Phase: Third Quarter   Moon enters Aquarius 2:20 pm
Color: Yellow   Incense: Sandalwood

HIGH TIDES

The Norse, a sea-faring race, were especially attuned to the time of day when the tide came in, and they attrributed great significance to its arrival.

- Morning tides represented awakenings, fertility, and life.
- Day tides brought gentility, growth, and finances.
- A tide during midday represented sustenance, willpower, and perseverance.
- A tide before dusk offered change, perceptiveness, and parenting.
- An evening tide represented joy, spirituality, pregnancy, and children.
- A night tide meant creativity, deeper knowledge, and enlightenment.
- A tide at midnight meant recuperation.

JULY

1 THURSDAY • *Canada Day*
Waning Moon
Moon Phase: Third Quarter   Moon Sign: Aquarius
Color: Green   Incense: Bayberry

2 FRIDAY • *Feast of Expectant Mothers (European)*
Waning Moon   Moon Sign: Aqarius
Moon Phase: Third Quarter   Moon enters Pisces 11:35 pm
Color: Rose   Incense: Floral

3 SATURDAY • *Sothis (Egyptian)*
Waning Moon
Moon Phase: Third Quarter   Moon Sign: Pisces
Color: Indigo   Incense: Jasmine

4 SUNDAY • *Independence Day*
Waning Moon
Moon Phase: Third Quarter   Moon Sign: Pisces
Color: Gold   Incense: Sandalwood

5 MONDAY • *Old Midsummer's Day*
Waning Moon   Moon Sign: Pisces
Moon Phase: Third Quarter   Moon enters Aries 6:22 am
Color: Silver   Incense: Temple

◐ **TUESDAY** • *Feast of Julian the Blessed*
Waning Moon
Moon Phase: Fourth Quarter 6:57 am   Moon Sign: Aries
Color: Red   Incense: Cinnamon

7 WEDNESDAY • *Tanabata (Japanese)*
Waning Moon   Moon Sign: Aries
Moon Phase: Fourth Quarter   Moon enters Taurus 10:22 am
Color: Peach   Incense: Peach

CANCER

8 THURSDAY • *St. Sunniva's Day*
Waning Moon
Moon Phase: Fourth Quarter Moon Sign: Taurus
Color: Turquoise Incense: Laurel

9 FRIDAY • *Martyrdom of the Bab (Bahai)*
Waning Moon Moon Sign: Taurus
Moon Phase: Fourth Quarter Moon enters Gemini 11:59 am
Color: Pink Incense: Floral

10 SATURDAY • *Lady Godiva Day (English)*
Waning Moon
Moon Phase: Fourth Quarter Moon Sign: Gemini
Color: Blue Incense: Thyme

11 SUNDAY • *Naadam Festival (Mongolian)*
Waning Moon Moon Sign: Gemini
Moon Phase: Fourth Quarter Moon enters Cancer 12:27 pm
Color: Orange Incense: Orange

☽ MONDAY
New Moon 9:24 pm
Moon Phase: First Quarter Moon Sign: Cancer
Color: White Incense: Almond

13 TUESDAY • *Reed Dance Day (African)* • *Obon (Japanese)*
Waxing Moon Moon Sign: Cancer
Moon Phase: First Quarter Moon enters Leo 1:25 pm
Color: Black Incense: Patchouli

14 WEDNESDAY • *Bastille Day (French)*
Waxing Moon
Moon Phase: First Quarter Moon Sign: Leo
Color: White Incense: Frankincense

JULY

15 THURSDAY • *Day of Rauni (Finnish)*
Waxing Moon
Moon Phase: First Quarter
Color: Violet

Moon Sign: Leo
Moon enters Virgo 4:39 pm
Incense: Lilac

16 FRIDAY • *Rosa Mundi (Palestinian)*
Waxing Moon
Moon Phase: First Quarter
Color: Peach

Moon Sign: Virgo
Incense: Peach

17 SATURDAY • *Festival of Ama-terasu-O-Mi-Kami (Japanese)*
Waxing Moon
Moon Phase: First Quarter
Color: Gray

Moon Sign: Virgo
Moon enters Libra 11:19 pm
Incense: Sage

18 SUNDAY • *Birthday of Nephthys (Egyptian)*
Waxing Moon
Moon Phase: First Quarter
Color: Yellow

Moon Sign: Libra
Incense: Sandalwood

19 MONDAY • *Wedding of Adonis and Aphrodite (Greek)*
Waxing Moon
Moon Phase: First Quarter
Color: Lavender

Moon Sign: Libra
Incense: Lavender

○ **TUESDAY** • *Binding of Wreaths (Lithuanian)*
Waxing Moon
Moon Phase: Second Quarter 4:01 am
Color: Gray

Moon Sign: Libra
Enters Scorpio 9:30 am
Incense: Sage

21 WEDNESDAY • *Damo's Day (Greek)*
Waxing Moon
Moon Phase: Second Quarter
Color: Brown

Moon Sign: Scorpio
Incense: Cedar

LEO

22 THURSDAY • *St. Mary Magdalene's Birthday*
Waxing Moon   Moon Sign: Scorpio
Moon Phase: Second Quarter   Moon enters Sagittarius 9:49 pm
Color: Brown   Incense: Woodsy

23 FRIDAY • *Neptunalia*
Waxing Moon   Sun enters Leo 1:44 am
Moon Phase: Second Quarter   Moon Sign: Sagittarius
Color: Rose   Incense: Floral

24 SATURDAY
Waxing Moon
Moon Phase: Second Quarter   Moon Sign: Sagittarius
Color: Brown   Incense: Cedar

25 SUNDAY • *Feast of Salacia (Roman)*
Waxing Moon   Moon Sign: Sagittarius
Moon Phase: Second Quarter   Moon enters Capricorn 10:09 am
Color: Peach   Incense: Peach

26 MONDAY • *Sleipnir (Odinist)*
Waxing Moon
Moon Phase: Second Quarter   Moon Sign: Capricorn
Color: Gray   Incense: Sage

27 TUESDAY • *Hatshepsut's Day (Egyptian)*
Waxing Moon   Moon Sign: Capricorn
Moon Phase: Second Quarter   Moon enters Aquarius 8:55 pm
Color: White   Incense: Frankincense

☺ WEDNESDAY • *Lunar Eclipse* • *Pythias' Day (Greek)*
Full Moon 6:25 am
Moon Phase: Third Quarter   Moon Sign: Aquarius
Color: Yellow   Incense: Sandalwood

JULY

29 THURSDAY • *Feast of Santa Marta (Mexican)*
Waning Moon
Moon Phase: Third Quarter
Color: Green

Moon Sign: Aquarius
Incense: Mint

30 FRIDAY
Waning Moon
Moon Phase: Third Quarter
Color: Green

Moon Sign: Aquarius
Moon enters Pisces 5:27 am
Incense: Bayberry

31 SATURDAY • *Day of Loki and Sigyn (Odinist)*
Waning Moon
Moon Phase: Third Quarter
Color: Indigo

Moon Sign: Pisces
Incense: Jasmine

BIRTHSTONE   FLOWERS

January	Garnet	Carnations, Snowdrops
February	Amethyst	Violets, Primroses
March	Bloodstone	Daffodils, Jonquils
April	Diamond	Daisies, Sweet Peas
May	Emerald	Lilies of the Valley, Hawthorn
June	Pearl	Roses, Honeysuckle
July	Ruby	Water Lilies, Larkspur
August	Topaz	Gladiolus, Poppies
September	Beryl	Morning Glories, Asters
October	Opal	Calendula, Cosmos
November	Topaz	Chrysanthemums, Dahlias
December	Bloodstone	Narcissus, Holly

LEO

1 SUNDAY • *Lammas* • *Friendship Day*
Waning Moon
Moon Phase: Third Quarter
Color: Peach

Moon Sign: Pisces
Moon enters Aries 11:47 am
Incense: Peach

2 MONDAY • *Feast of Our Lady of Angels (Central American)*
Waning Moon
Moon Phase: Third Quarter
Color: Gray

Moon Sign: Aries
Incense: Sage

3 TUESDAY
Waning Moon
Moon Phase: Third Quarter
Color: Red

Moon Sign: Aries
Moon enters Taurus 4:08 pm
Incense: Cinnamon

☽ WEDNESDAY • *Feast of the Blessed Virgin Mary*
Waning Moon
Moon Phase: Fourth Quarter 12:26 pm
Color: Yellow

Moon Sign: Taurus
Incense: Sandalwood

5 THURSDAY · ST. OSWALD'S DAY
Waning Moon
Moon Phase: Fourth Quarter
Color: Turquoise

Moon Sign: Taurus
Moon enters Gemini 6:57 pm
Incense: Laurel

6 FRIDAY • *Tan Hill Festival (Celtic)*
Waning Moon
Moon Phase: Fourth Quarter
Color: Peach

Moon Sign: Gemini
Incense: Peach

7 SATURDAY • *Breaking of the Nile (Egyptian)*
Waning Moon
Moon Phase: Fourth Quarter
Color: Indigo

Moon Sign: Gemini
Moon enters Cancer 8:52 pm
Incense: Jasmine

AUGUST

8 SUNDAY • *Tij Day (Nepalese)*
Waning Moon
Moon Phase: Fourth Quarter   Moon Sign: Cancer
Color: Yellow   Incense: Sandalwood

9 MONDAY • *Milky Way Festival (Chinese)*
Waning Moon   Moon Sign: Cancer
Moon Phase: Fourth Quarter   Moon enters Leo 10:55 pm
Color: Lavender   Incense: Lavender

10 TUESDAY • *St. Lawrence's Day*
Waning Moon
Moon Phase: Fourth Quarter   Moon Sign: Leo
Color: White   Incense: Myrrh

☽ WEDNESDAY • *Solar Eclipse* • *Puck Fair (Irish)*
New Moon 6:09 am
Moon Phase: First Quarter   Moon Sign: Leo
Color: Peach   Incense: Peach

12 THURSDAY • *Lights of Isis (Egyptian)*
Waxing Moon   Moon Sign: Leo
Moon Phase: First Quarter   Moon enters Virgo 2:22 am
Color: White   Incense: Vanilla

13 FRIDAY • *Hecate's Day (Greek)*
Waxing Moon
Moon Phase: First Quarter   Moon Sign: Virgo
Color: Rose   Incense: Floral

14 SATURDAY • *Fieschi's Cake Day (Italian)* • *V-J Day*
Waxing Moon   Moon Sign: Virgo
Moon Phase: First Quarter   Moon enters Libra 8:25 am
Color: Blue   Incense: Thyme

LEO

15 SUNDAY • *Festival for Chang-O (Chinese)* • *Assumption Day*
Waxing Moon
Moon Phase: First Quarter   Moon Sign: Libra
Color: Orange   Incense: Orange

16 MONDAY • *Festival of Minstrels (European)*
Waxing Moon   Moon Sign: Libra
Moon Phase: First Quarter   Moon enters Scorpio 5:41 pm
Color: White   Incense: Almond

17 TUESDAY • *Amenartus (Egyptian)*
Waxing Moon
Moon Phase: First Quarter   Moon Sign: Scorpio
Color: Gray   Incense: Sage

☽ **WEDNESDAY** • *Blessing of the Grapes (Armenian)*
Waxing Moon
Moon Phase: Second Quarter 8:48 pm   Moon Sign: Scorpio
Color: White   Incense: Frankincense

19 THURSDAY • *Rustic Vinalia (Roman)* • *Ntl. Aviation Day*
Waxing Moon   Moon Sign: Scorpio
Moon Phase: Second Quarter   Moon enters Sagittarius 5:32 am
Color: Violet   Incense: Lilac

20 FRIDAY • *Day of Inanna (Mesopotamian)*
Waxing Moon
Moon Phase: Second Quarter   Moon Sign: Sagittarius
Color: Pink   Incense: Floral

21 SATURDAY • *Odin's Ordeal*
Waxing Moon   Moon Sign: Sagittarius
Moon Phase: Second Quarter   Moon enters Capricorn 5:59 pm
Color: Brown   Incense: Woodsy

AUGUST

22 SUNDAY • *Aedesia's Day (Greek)*
Waxing Moon
Moon Phase: Second Quarter   Moon Sign: Capricorn
Color: Gold   Incense: Sandalwood

23 MONDAY • *Moira's Day (Greek)*
Waxing Moon   Sun enters Virgo 8:51 am
Moon Phase: Second Quarter   Moon enters Aquarius 4:49 am
Color: Silver   Incense: Temple

24 TUESDAY • *St. Bartholomew's Day*
Waxing Moon
Moon Phase: Second Quarter   Moon Sign: Aquarius
Color: Gray   Incense: Sage

25 WEDNESDAY • *Paryushana Parva (Hindu)*
Waxing Moon
Moon Phase: Second Quarter   Moon Sign: Aquarius
Color: White   Incense: Almond

☉ **THURSDAY** • *Ilmatar's Day (Finnish)*
Full Moon 6:48 pm   Moon Sign: Aquarius
Moon Phase: Third Quarter   Moon enters Pisces 12:49 pm
Color: Violet   Incense: Lilac

27 FRIDAY • *Worship of Mother Goddess Devaki (East Indian)*
Waning Moon
Moon Phase: Third Quarter   Moon Sign: Pisces
Color: White   Incense: Vanilla

28 SATURDAY • *Nativity of Nephthys (Egyptian)*
Waning Moon   Moon Sign: Pisces
Moon Phase: Third Quarter   Moon enters Aries 6:09 pm
Color: Indigo   Incense: Jasmine

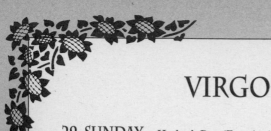

VIRGO

29 SUNDAY • *Hathor's Day (Egyptian)*
Waning Moon
Moon Phase: Third Quarter   Moon Sign: Aries
Color: Peach   Incense: Peach

30 MONDAY • *St. Rose of Lima Day (Peruvian)*
Waning Moon   Moon Sign: Aries
Moon Phase: Third Quarter   Moon enters Taurus 9:40 pm
Color: Lavender   Incense: Lavender

31 TUESDAY
Waning Moon
Moon Phase: Third Quarter   Moon Sign: Taurus
Color: Red   Incense: Cinnamon

THE 14 CONSTELLATIONS OF THE ZODIAC

Believe it or not, the Sun actually crosses through fourteen constellations— not twelve —in its annual trek past the stars.

Starting on the first day of spring, the Sun passes Pisces and Cetus, goes back through Pisces, and then crosses through Aries, Taurus, Gemini, Cancer, Leo, Virgo, Libra, Scorpius, Ophiuchus, Sagittarius, Capricornus, and Aquarius.

SEPTEMBER

1 WEDNESDAY • *Day of Radha (Indian)*
Waning Moon
Moon Phase: Third Quarter
Color: Peach
Moon Sign: Taurus
Incense: Peach

 **THURSDAY** • *Celtic Tree Month of Muin Commences*
Waning Moon
Moon Phase: Fourth Quarter 5:18 pm
Color: Violet
Moon Sign: Taurus
Enters Gemini 12:25 am
Incense: Lilac

3 FRIDAY • *La Kon (Native American)*
Waning Moon
Moon Phase: Fourth Quarter
Incense: Floral
Moon Sign: Gemini
Color: Rose

4 SATURDAY
Waning Moon
Moon Phase: Fourth Quarter
Color: Brown
Moon Sign: Gemini
Moon enters Cancer 3:10 am
Incense: Cedar

5 SUNDAY • *Day of Nanda Devi (East Indian)*
Waning Moon
Moon Phase: Fourth Quarter
Color: Gold
Moon Sign: Cancer
Incense: Sandalwood

6 MONDAY • *Labor Day*
Waning Moon
Moon Phase: Fourth Quarter
Color: Lavender
Moon Sign: Cancer
Moon enters Leo 6:29 am
Incense: Lavender

7 TUESDAY • *Festival of Durga (Bengalese)*
Waning Moon
Moon Phase: Fourth Quarter
Color: White
Moon Sign: Leo
Incense: Almond

VIRGO

8 WEDNESDAY • *Pinnhut Festival (Native American)*
Waning Moon
Moon Phase: Fourth Quarter
Color: Yellow

Moon Sign: Leo
Moon enters Virgo 10:57 am
Incense: Sandalwood

9 THURSDAY • *Horned Dance at Abbots Bromley (English)*
New Moon 5:03 pm
Moon Phase: First Quarter
Color: White

Moon Sign: Virgo
Incense: Vanilla

10 FRIDAY • *Rosh Hashanah Begins*
Waxing Moon
Moon Phase: First Quarter
Color: Pink

Moon Sign: Virgo
Moon enters Libra 5:16 pm
Incense: Floral

11 SATURDAY • *Egyptian Day of Queens*
Waxing Moon
Moon Phase: First Quarter
Color: Blue

Moon Sign: Libra
Incense: Thyme

12 SUNDAY • *Rosh Hashanah Ends* • *Astraea's Day (Greek)*
Waxing Moon
Moon Phase: First Quarter
Color: Orange

Moon Sign: Libra
Incense: Ginger

13 MONDAY • *Lectisternia (Roman)*
Waxing Moon
Moon Phase: First Quarter
Color: Gray

Moon Sign: Libra
Moon enters Scorpio 2:09 am
Incense: Sage

14 TUESDAY • *Feast of Lights (Egyptian)*
Waxing Moon
Moon Phase: First Quarter
Color: Red

Moon Sign: Scorpio
Incense: Cinnamon

SEPTEMBER

15 WEDNESDAY • *Birthday of the Moon (Chinese)*
Waxing Moon   Moon Sign: Scorpio
Moon Phase: First Quarter   Moon enters Sagittarius 1:35 pm
Color: White   Incense: Frankincense

16 THURSDAY • *St. Ninian's Day* • *Mexican Independence Day*
Waxing Moon
Moon Phase: First Quarter   Moon Sign: Sagittarius
Color: Green   Incense: Mint

◑ **FRIDAY** • *Hildegard of Bingen's Day (German)*
Waxing Moon
Moon Phase: Second Quarter 3:06 pm   Moon Sign: Sagittarius
Color: White   Incense: Myrrh

18 SATURDAY
Waxing Moon   Moon Sign: Sagittarius
Moon Phase: Second Quarter   Moon enters Capricorn 2:13 am
Color: Gray   Incense: Sage

19 SUNDAY • *Yom Kippur Begins* • *Octoberfest Begins*
Waxing Moon
Moon Phase: Second Quarter   Moon Sign: Capricorn
Color: Yellow   Incense: Sandalwood

20 MONDAY • *Yom Kippur Ends* • *Birth of Quetzalcoatl (Aztec)*
Waxing Moon   Moon Sign: Capricorn
Moon Phase: Second Quarter   Moon enters Aquarius 1:38 pm
Color: White   Incense: Vanilla

21 TUESDAY • *Raud the Strong's Martyrdom (Norwegian)*
Waxing Moon
Moon Phase: Second Quarter   Moon Sign: Aquarius
Color: Gray   Incense: Sage

LIBRA

22 WEDNESDAY • *Festival of the Sea Goddess (Alaska)*
Waxing Moon
Moon Phase: Second Quarter
Color: Brown

Moon Sign: Aquarius
Moon enters Pisces 9:51 pm
Incense: Woodsy

23 THURSDAY • *Mabon/Fall Equinox*
Waxing Moon
Moon Phase: Second Quarter
Color: Turquoise

Sun enters Libra 6:31 am
Moon Sign: Pisces
Incense: Laurel

24 FRIDAY • *Sukkot Begins* • *Feast of Obatala (Santeria)*
Waxing Moon
Moon Phase: Second Quarter
Color: Peach

Native American Day
Moon Sign: Pisces
Incense: Peach

☺ **SATURDAY**
Full Moon 5:51 am
Moon Phase: Quarter
Color: Indigo

Moon Sign: Pisces
Moon enters Aries 2:34 am
Incense: Jasmine

26 SUNDAY • *Sukkot Ends* • *Feast of Santa Justina (Mexican)*
Waning Moon
Moon Phase: Third Quarter
Color: Peach

Divali (Indian)
Moon Sign: Aries
Incense: Peach

27 MONDAY • *Day of Willows (Mesopotamian)*
Waning Moon
Moon Phase: Third Quarter
Color: Silver

Moon Sign: Aries
Moon enters Taurus 4:51 am
Incense: Temple

28 TUESDAY • *Confucius' Birthday*
Waning Moon
Moon Phase: Third Quarter
Color: Black

Moon Sign: Taurus
Incense: Patchouli

SEPTEMBER

29 WEDNESDAY • *Michaelmas*

Waning Moon
Moon Phase: Third Quarter
Color: Yellow

Moon Sign: Taurus
Mon enters Gemini 6:21 am
Incense: Sandalwood

30 THURSDAY • *Medetrinalia (Roman)*

Waning Moon
Moon Phase: Third Quarter
Color: Violet

Moon Sign: Gemini
Incense: Lilac

RITUAL DAYS

French occultist Eliphas Levi wrote that specific days of the week are best for certain ritual work. His suggestions:

Sunday	A day best suited for "light" work, especially work that combines the effects of gold and chrisolite.
Monday	Especially suited to divination and study of the greater mysteries. Wear yellow and pearls.
Tuesday	A day for spellwork based on justified wrath, while wearing red and using iron or amethyst.
Wednesday	A day for science and magic pertaining to the mind, while wearing green and using silver or agate.
Thursday	A day for religious and political rituals. Dress in purple and use tin or emeralds.
Friday	Cast love spells on Fridays. Wear blue robes and use turquoise.
Saturday	A day for mourning and for bidding farewell to old ways. Wear brownish colors and use lead or onyx.

LIBRA

☾ **FRIDAY** • *Octoberfest Ends*
Waning Moon
Moon Phase: Fourth Quarter 11:03 pm
Color: Peach

Moon Sign: Gemini
Enters Cancer 8:32 am
Incense: Peach

2 SATURDAY • *Sukkot Ends* • *Simchat Torah Begins*
Waning Moon
Moon Phase: Fourth Quarter
Color: Brown

Moon Sign: Cancer
Incense: Woodsy

3 SUNDAY • *Simchat Torah Ends* • *Moroccan New Year's Day*
Waning Moon
Moon Phase: Fourth Quarter
Color: Peach

Moon Sign: Cancer
Moon enters Leo 12:14 pm
Incense: Peach

4 MONDAY • *Elk Festival (Native American)*
Waning Moon
Moon Phase: Fourth Quarter
Color: Gray

Moon Sign: Leo
Incense: Sage

5 TUESDAY • *Romanian Wine Festival*
Waning Moon
Moon Phase: Fourth Quarter
Color: Red

Moon Sign: Leo
Moon enters Virgo 5:40 pm
Incense: Cinnamon

6 WEDNESDAY • *Water Festival*
Waning Moon
Moon Phase: Fourth Quarter
Color: Yellow

Moon Sign: Virgo
Incense: Sandalwood

7 THURSDAY • *Pallas Athena's Day (Roman)*
Waning Moon
Moon Phase: Fourth Quarter
Color: Turquoise

Moon Sign: Virgo
Incense: Laurel

OCTOBER

8 FRIDAY • *Chicago Fire Anniversary (1871)*
Waning Moon   Moon Sign: Virgo
Moon Phase: Fourth Quarter   Moon enters Libra 12:52 am
Color: White   Incense: Vanilla

☽ SATURDAY • *St. Denis' Day*
New Moon 6:34 am
Moon Phase: First Quarter   Moon Sign: Libra
Color: Gray   Incense: Sage

10 SUNDAY • *National Children's Day*
Waxing Moon   Moon Sign: Libra
Moon Phase: First Quarter   Moon enters Scorpio 10:01 am
Color: Yellow   Incense: Sandalwood

11 MONDAY • *Columbus Day* • *Canadian Thanksgiving*
Waxing Moon
Moon Phase: First Quarter   Moon Sign: Scorpio
Color: Lavender   Incense: Lavender

12 TUESDAY • *Farmer's Day* • *Fourth Gahambar (Zoroastrian)*
Waxing Moon   Moon Sign: Scorpio
Moon Phase: First Quarter   Moon enters Sagittarius 9:18 pm
Color: White   Incense: Almond

13 WEDNESDAY • *Floating of the Lamps (Siamese)*
Waxing Moon
Moon Phase: First Quarter   Moon Sign: Sagittarius
Color: Peach   Incense: Peach

14 THURSDAY • *Winter's Day (Northern European)*
Waxing Moon
Moon Phase: First Quarter   Moon Sign: Sagittarius
Color: White   Incense: Frankincense

SCORPIO

15 FRIDAY • *Ides of October (Roman)*
Waxing Moon
Moon Phase: First Quarter
Color: Pink

Moon Sign: Sagittarius
Moon enters Capricorn 10:02 am
Incense: Floral

16 SATURDAY • *Sweetest Day* • *Festival of Pandrosus (Greek)*
Waxing Moon
Moon Phase: First Quarter
Color: Indigo

Moon Sign: Capricorn
Incense: Jasmine

☽ SUNDAY • *St. Audrey's Day*
Waxing Moon
Moon Phase: Second Quarter 9:59 am
Color: Orange

Moon Sign: Capricorn
Enters Aquarius 10:17 pm
Incense: Ginger

18 MONDAY • *Alaska Day* • *Festival of Herne (Celtic)*
Waxing Moon
Moon Phase: Second Quarter
Color: White

Moon Sign: Aquarius
Incense: Myrrh

19 TUESDAY
Waxing Moon
Moon Phase: Second Quarter
Color: Gray

Moon Sign: Aquarius
Incense: Sage

20 WEDNESDAY • *Festival of Ancestors (Chinese)*
Waxing Moon
Moon Phase: Second Quarter
Color: Brown

Moon Sign: Aquarius
Moon enters Pisces 7:33 am
Incense: Cedar

21 THURSDAY • *Festival of Ishhara (Mesopotamian)*
Waxing Moon
Moon Phase: Second Quarter
Color: Violet

Moon Sign: Pisces
Incense: Lilac

OCTOBER

22 FRIDAY
Waxing Moon   Moon Sign: Pisces
Moon Phase: Second Quarter   Moon enters Aries 12:42 pm
Color: Rose   Incense: Floral

23 SATURDAY • *Mother-In-Law's Day*
Waxing Moon   Sun enters Scorpio 3:52 pm
Moon Phase: Second Quarter   Moon Sign: Aries
Color: Blue   Incense: Thyme

☺ SUNDAY • *United Nations Day*
Full Moon 4:03 pm   Moon Sign: Aries
Moon Phase: Third Quarter   Moon entersTaurus 2:26 pm
Color: Gold   Incense: Sandalwood

25 MONDAY • *St. Crispin's Day*
Waning Moon
Moon Phase: Third Quarter   Moon Sign: Taurus
Color: Silver   Incense: Temple

26 TUESDAY • *Aban Jashan (Japanese)*
Waning Moon   Moon Sign: Taurus
Moon Phase: Third Quarter   Moon enters Gemini 2:34 pm
Color: Black   Incense: Patchouli

27 WEDNESDAY • *Owagit (Native American)*
Waning Moon
Moon Phase: Third Quarter   Moon Sign: Gemini
Color: White   Incense: Vanilla

28 THURSDAY • *Fyribod (Celtic)*
Waning Moon   Moon Sign: Gemini
Moon Phase: Third Quarter   Moon enters Cancer 3:09 pm
Color: Turquoise   Incense: Laurel

SCORPIO

29 FRIDAY • *Iroquois Feast of the Dead (Native American)*
Waning Moon
Moon Phase: Third Quarter
Color: Peach

Moon Sign: Cancer
Incense: Peach

30 SATURDAY • *Los Angelitos (Mexican)*
Waning Moon
Moon Phase: Third Quarter
Color: Brown

Moon Sign: Cancer
Moon enters Leo 5:47 pm
Incense: Woodsy

☽ SUNDAY • *Samhain/Halloween* • *Day. Saving Time ends 2 am*
Waning Moon
Moon Phase: Fourth Quarter
Color: Peach

Moon Sign: Leo
Incense: Peach

BUTTONHOLING THE FUTURE

The first person you meet on Halloween can give you a glimpse of the year to come. Just count the number of buttons they're wearing.

One	Luck
Two	Happiness
Three	A new vehicle
Four	Another form of transportation
Five	New clothes
Six	Accessories
Seven	A new dog
Eight	A new cat
Nine	An unexpected letter
Ten	Pleasure
Eleven	Extreme joy
Twelve	A treasure soon to be discovered

NOVEMBER

1 MONDAY • *All Saints' Day*
Waning Moon
Moon Phase: Fourth Quarter
Color: Gray

Moon Sign: Leo
Moon enters Virgo 11:07 pm
Incense: Sage

2 TUESDAY • *Election Day* • *All Souls' Day* • *Animas (Mexican)*
Waning Moon
Moon Phase: Fourth Quarter
Color: Red

Moon Sign: Virgo
Incense: Cinnamon

3 WEDNESDAY • *Festival for the New Year (Gaelic)*
Waning Moon
Moon Phase: Fourth Quarter
Color: Yellow

Moon Sign: Virgo
Incense: Sandalwood

4 THURSDAY • *Will Rogers' Birthday*
Waning Moon
Moon Phase: Fourth Quarter
Color: Turquoise

Moon Sign: Virgo
Moon enters Libra 6:56 am
Incense: Laurel

5 FRIDAY • *Guy Fawkes' Day*
Waning Moon
Moon Phase: Fourth Quarter
Color: White

Moon Sign: Libra
Incense: Frankincense

6 SATURDAY • *Birthday of Tiamut (Babylonian)*
Waning Moon
Moon Phase: Fourth Quarter
Color: Brown

Moon Sign: Libra
Moon enters Scorpio 4:45 pm
Incense: Cedar

☽ SUNDAY • *Makahiki Festival (Hawaiian)*
New Moon 10:53 pm
Moon Phase: First Quarter
Color: Peach

Moon Sign: Scorpio
Incense: Peach

SCORPIO

8 MONDAY • *Festival of Kami of the Hearth (Japanese)*
Waxing Moon
Moon Phase: First Quarter   Moon Sign: Scorpio
Color: Lavender   Incense: Lavender

9 TUESDAY • *Feast of the Four Crowned Martyrs*
Waxing Moon   Moon Sign: Scorpio
Moon Phase: First Quarter   Moon enters Sagittarius 4:15 am
Color: White   Incense: Vanilla

10 WEDNESDAY • *Festival of the Goddess of Reason (French)*
Waxing Moon
Moon Phase: First Quarter   Moon Sign: Sagittarius
Color: Peach   Incense: Peach

11 THURSDAY • *Veterans' Day* • *Feast of Dionysus (Greek)*
Waxing Moon   Moon Sign: Sagittarius
Moon Phase: First Quarter   Moon enters Capricorn 5:00 pm
Color: White   Incense: Frankincense

12 FRIDAY • *Birthday of Baha'u'llah (Baha'i)*
Waxing Moon
Moon Phase: First Quarter   Moon Sign: Capricorn
Color: Pink   Incense: Floral

13 SATURDAY • *Festival of Jupiter (Roman)*
Waxing Moon
Moon Phase: First Quarter   Moon Sign: Capricorn
Color: Gray   Incense: Sage

14 SUNDAY • *Moccas' Day (Celtic)*
Waxing Moon   Moon Sign: Capricorn
Moon Phase: First Quarter   Moon enters Aquarius 5:46 am
Color: Orange   Incense: Orange

NOVEMBER

15 MONDAY • *Seven-Five-Three Festival (Japanese)*
Waxing Moon
Moon Phase: First Quarter
Color: White

Moon Sign: Aquarius
Incense: Myrrh

☽ TUESDAY • *Night of Hecate (Greek)*
Waxing Moon
Moon Phase: Second Quarter 4:04 am
Color: Gray

Moon Sign: Aquarius
Enters Pisces 4:21 pm
Incense: Sage

17 WEDNESDAY
Waxing Moon
Moon Phase: Second Quarter
Color: Brown

Moon Sign: Pisces
Incense: Cedar

18 THURSDAY • *Day of Ardvi Sura (Persian)*
Waxing Moon
Moon Phase: Second Quarter
Color: Violet

Moon Sign: Pisces
Moon enters Aries 10:58 pm
Incense: Lilac

19 FRIDAY • *Feast of Santa Isabel (Mexican)*
Waxing Moon
Moon Phase: Second Quarter
Color: Rose

Moon Sign: Aries
Incense: Floral

20 SATURDAY • *St. Edmund's Day*
Waxing Moon
Moon Phase: Second Quarter
Color: Indigo

Moon Sign: Aries
Incense: Jasmine

21 SUNDAY • *Feast of Hathor (Egyptian)•Day of Cailleach (Celtic)*
Waxing Moon
Moon Phase: Second Quarter
Color: Gold

Moon Sign: Aries
Moon enters Taurus 1:26 am
Incense: Sandalwood

SAGITTARIUS

22 MONDAY • *Ydalir (Norse)*
Waxing Moon   Sun enters Sagittarius 1:25 pm
Moon Phase: Second Quarter   Moon Sign: Taurus
Color: Silver   Incense: Temple

☺ TUESDAY • *Shinjosai (Japanese)*
Full Moon 2:04 am   Moon Sign: Taurus
Moon Phase: Third Quarter   Moon enters Gemini 1:14 am
Color: Black   Incense: Patchouli

24 WEDNESDAY • *Stir-Up Sunday (British)*
Waning Moon
Moon Phase: Third Quarter   Moon Sign: Gemini
Color: White   Incense: Vanilla

25 THURSDAY • *Thanksgiving Day*
Waning Moon   Moon Sign: Gemini
Moon Phase: Third Quarter   Moon enters Cancer 12:29 am
Color: Turquoise   Incense: Laurel

26 FRIDAY • *Festival of Lights (Tibetan)*
Waning Moon
Moon Phase: Third Quarter   Moon Sign: Cancer
Color: Peach   Incense: Peach

27 SATURDAY
Waning Moon   Moon Sign: Cancer
Moon Phase: Third Quarter   Moon enters Leo 1:18 am
Color: Blue   Incense: Thyme

28 SUNDAY • *First Day of Advent* • *Day of Sophia (Greek)*
Waning Moon
Moon Phase: Third Quarter   Moon Sign: Leo
Color: Peach   Incense: Peach

EXPLORE NEW WORLDS
OF MIND & SPIRIT

Just drop this card in the mail to get your FREE copy of *New Worlds*: it's 80 full-color pages packed with books and other resources to help you develop your spiritual and magical potential to the fullest.

New Worlds is your key for opening new doors to personal transformation. Get fresh new insight into the tarot, astrology, alternative spirituality and health, magick, the paranormal, and many other subjects, with:

- Articles and "how-tos" by Llewellyn's expert authors
- Tasty previews of Llewellyn's new books and features on classic Llewellyn titles
- Upbeat monthly horoscopes by Gloria Star
- Plus special offers available only to *New Worlds* readers

❑ **Please rush me my free issue of *New Worlds of Mind & Spirit*!**

Name _____

Address _____

City _____

State _____ Zip/Postal Code _____

MA99

LLEWELLYN PUBLICATIONS
P.O. BOX 64383
ST. PAUL, MN 55164-0383

NOVEMBER

☾ MONDAY • *Sons of Saturn Festival (Roman)*
Waning Moon   Moon Sign: Leo
Moon Phase: Fourth Quarter 6:19 pm   Enters Virgo 5:11 am
Color: Gray   Incense: Sage

30 TUESDAY • *St. Andrew's Day*
Waning Moon
Moon Phase: Fourth Quarter   Moon Sign: Virgo
Color: Red   Incense: Cinnamon

STONE DAYS

Some stones are especially powerful on certain days of the week.
Here's a guide to stones that can work for protection, and stones that
can be used in amulets. (The budget-conscious magician can
substitute other stones, candles, or cloths for more expensive gems.)

Sunday	Wear topaz, sunstone, or diamond. Use pearl in crafting talismans.
Monday	Wear pearl, moonstone, or crystal. Use an emerald for amulets.
Tuesday	Wear a ruby, star sapphire, or emerald. Use topaz for amulets.
Wednesday	Wear amethyst, star ruby, or lodestone. Use turquoise in amulets.
Thursday	Wear sapphire, cat's eye, or carnelian. Use sapphire in rituals.
Friday	Wear emerald or cat's eye. Use ruby.
Saturday	Wear turquoise, labradorite, or diamond. Use amethyst.

SAGITTARIUS

1 WEDNESDAY • *Festival of Poseidon (Greek)*
Waning Moon   Moon Sign: Virgo
Moon Phase: Fourth Quarter   Moon enters Libra 12:29 pm
Color: Brown   Incense: Woodsy

2 THURSDAY • *Feast of Shiva (Hindu)*
Waning Moon
Moon Phase: Fourth Quarter   Moon Sign: Libra
Color: Turquoise   Incense: Laurel

3 FRIDAY
Waning Moon   Moon Sign: Libra
Moon Phase: Fourth Quarter   Moon enters Scorpio 10:36 pm
Color: Peach   Incense: Peach

4 SATURDAY • *Chanukkah Begins* • *St. Barbara's Day*
Waning Moon
Moon Phase: Fourth Quarter   Moon Sign: Scorpio
Color: Brown   Incense: Cedar

5 SUNDAY • *Eve of St. Nicholas' Day*
Waning Moon
Moon Phase: Fourth Quarter   Moon Sign: Scorpio
Color: Yellow   Incense: Sandalwood

6 MONDAY • *St. Nicholas' Day*
Waning Moon   Moon Sign: Scorpio
Moon Phase: Fourth Quarter Moon enters Sagittarius 10:28 am
Color: Gray   Incense: Sage

☽ TUESDAY • *Burning the Devil (Guatemalan)*
New Moon 5:32 pm
Moon Phase: First Quarter   Moon Sign: Sagittarius
Color: Red   Incense: Cinnamon

DECEMBER

8 WEDNESDAY • *Day of Astraea (Greek)*
Waxing Moon   Moon Sign: Sagittarius
Moon Phase: First Quarter   Moon enters Capricorn 11:14 pm
Color: White   Incense: Frankincense

9 THURSDAY • *First Day of Ramadan*
Waxing Moon
Moon Phase: First Quarter   Moon Sign: Capricorn
Color: Violet   Incense: Lilac

10 FRIDAY • *Human Rights Day•Goddess of Liberty Day (French)*
Waxing Moon
Moon Phase: First Quarter   Moon Sign: Capricorn
Color: White   Incense: Myrrh

11 SATURDAY • *Day of Bruma (Roman)* • *Chanukkuh ends*
Waxing Moon   Moon Sign: Capricorn
Moon Phase: First Quarter   Moon enters Aquarius 11:59 am
Color: Blue   Incense: Thyme

12 SUNDAY • *Fiesta of Our Lady of Guadalupe*
Waxing Moon
Moon Phase: First Quarter   Moon Sign: Aquarius
Color: Gold   Incense: Sandalwood

13 MONDAY • *St. Lucy's Day (Swedish)*
Waxing Moon   Moon Sign: Aquarius
Moon Phase: First Quarter   Moon enters Pisces 11:18 pm
Color: White   Incense: Vanilla

14 TUESDAY • *Nostradamus' Birthday* • *Hopi Winter Ceremony*
Waxing Moon
Moon Phase: First Quarter   Moon Sign: Pisces
Color: Black   Incense: Patchouli

CAPRICORN

○ WEDNESDAY • *Festival of Alcyone (Greek)*
Waxing Moon
Moon Phase: Second Quarter 7:50 pm   Moon Sign: Pisces
Color: Peach   Incense: Peach

16 THURSDAY • *Festival of Sophia*
Waxing Moon   Moon Sign: Pisces
Moon Phase: Second Quarter   Moon enters Aries 7:30 am
Color: Green   Incense: Evergreen

17 FRIDAY • *Feast of Babaluaiye (Santerian)*
Waxing Moon
Moon Phase: Second Quarter   Moon Sign: Aries
Color: Pink   Incense: Floral

18 SATURDAY • *Saturnalia Begins (Roman)*
Waxing Moon   Moon Sign: Aries
Moon Phase: Second Quarter   Moon enters Taurus 11:45 am
Color: Gray   Incense: Sage

19 SUNDAY
Waxing Moon
Moon Phase: Second Quarter   Moon Sign: Taurus
Color: Orange   Incense: Ginger

20 MONDAY • *Mother Night (Odinist)*
Waxing Moon   Moon Sign: Taurus
Moon Phase: Second Quarter   Moon enters Gemini 12:39 pm
Color: Silver   Incense: Temple

21 TUESDAY • *Forefathers' Day*
Waxing Moon
Moon Phase: Second Quarter   Moon Sign: Gemini
Color: Gray   Incense: Sage

DECEMBER

🌝 **WEDNESDAY** • *Winter Solstice/Yule* • *Pryderi's Birthday*
Full Moon 12:31 pm   Sun enters Capricorn 2:44 am
Moon Phase: Third Quarter   Moon enters Cancer 11:52 am
Color: Yellow   Incense: Sandalwood

23 THURSDAY • *Secret of the Unhewn Stone (Celtic)*
Waning Moon
Moon Phase: Third Quarter   Moon Sign: Cancer
Color: White   Incense: Almond

24 FRIDAY • *Christmas Eve* • *Saturnalia Ends (Roman)*
Waning Moon   Moon Sign: Cancer
Moon Phase: Third Quarter   Moon enters Leo 11:32 am
Color: Rose   Incense: Floral

25 SATURDAY • *Christmas Day*
Waning Moon
Moon Phase: Third Quarter   Moon Sign: Leo
Color: Indigo   Incense: Jasmine

26 SUNDAY • *Kwanzaa Begins* • *Boxing Day*
Waning Moon   Moon Sign: Leo
Moon Phase: Third Quarter   Moon enters Virgo 1:34 pm
Color: Yellow   Incense: Sandalwood

27 MONDAY • *Feast of St. John the Evangelist*
Waning Moon
Moon Phase: Third Quarter   Moon Sign: Virgo
Color: Lavender   Incense: Lilac

28 TUESDAY • *Bairns' Day (Scottish)*
Waning Moon   Moon Sign: Virgo
Moon Phase: Third Quarter   Moon enters Libra 7:15 pm
Color: White   Incense: Myrrh

CAPRICORN

○ WEDNESDAY • *Birthday of Ra (Egyptian)*
Waning Moon
Moon Phase: Fourth Quarter 9:05 am | Moon Sign: Libra
Color: Brown | Incense: Woodsy

30 THURSDAY • *Birthday of Isis (Egyptian)*
Waning Moon | Moon Sign: Libra
Moon Phase: Fourth Quarter | Moon enters Scorpio 4:37 am
Color: Turquoise | Incense: Laurel

31 FRIDAY • *New Year's Eve*
Waning Moon
Moon Phase: Fourth Quarter | Moon Sign: Scorpio
Color: Peach | Incense: Peach

SEASON TO TASTE

Why don't seasons start on a regular schedule — December 21, March 21, June 21, and September 21 of each year? Why do the equinoxes skip around between the 20th and the 22nd?

Because the Earth takes more than 365 days to orbit the Sun. A year is actually 365¼ days long. As a result, the first day of each season starts six hours later than it did the year before.

To keep the seasons in their place, we add a leap day every four years. Otherwise, we'd wind up with some springs starting in September, and some autumns falling in March.

Jason and the Fairy Ring
By D. J. Conway

There aren't such things as fairies." Jason looked down at the face of his little sister. Jason was ten years old and didn't want Julie's talk about fairies to embarrass him in front of his friends. "Only little kids believe in fairies."

"There are too fairies," Julie answered, stamping her foot.

"Prove it," Jason said.

"Mom and Dad say there are fairies. There's even a fairy ring in our back yard where they come and dance." Julie started to cry because she was so upset with her brother. "I'll tell the fairies to take away your model airplane. That will teach you, Jason!" She turned and ran back to the house.

"Little sisters," Jason said to himself as he walked away to find his friends and play baseball. By the time he came home for supper, he had forgotten all about his argument with Julie and her threat about the fairies. But when he went into his room to go to bed, his model airplane was gone.

"I haven't seen your plane," his mother said when he asked, "and Julie hasn't been in your room."

Jason was very upset when he went to bed. He lay there a long time, wondering who had taken his plane. If Julie didn't take the plane, who did? He had a strange feeling that he should look outside at the back yard. The Moon was Full and bright, and its light made it possible for Jason to see as clear as day. He pressed his face close to the window and looked at the fairy ring. There in the center of the dark green circle of grass sat his model airplane.

Jason's bare feet made no noise as he quietly opened the back door and went out into the bright moonlight. He hurried across the lawn and stepped inside the dark ring of grass to pick up his airplane. But when he turned to go back, the house was gone. Little lights like fireflies darted all around him.

"What's happening?" Jason said, and he was afraid.

"You are between the worlds in the land of fairies," said a voice.

Jason turned and saw a man standing beside him. The man looked different somehow, but Jason couldn't decide why. "Who are you?" he finally asked.

"My name is Fire Glow, and I am a fairy," the man answered. "Hurry now. We must not be late for the Summer Solstice celebration, or the Fairy Queen will be upset."

"There aren't any fairies." Jason looked around for his house, but he still couldn't see it. "Fairies are make-believe."

"Is that so?" Fire Glow said. He reached out and gave a little pull on Jason's hair.

"Ouch! That hurt." Jason frowned, but Fire Glow grinned at him.

"How can that hurt?" the man asked. "After all, I don't exist. I'm only make-believe."

"Prove you are a fairy," Jason demanded. "Take me to this Fairy Queen of yours if you can."

"The magic words," Fire Glow said with a grin as he put three leaves into the pocket of Jason's pajamas.

"What are these?" Jason asked as he felt the leaves.

"Leaves of oak, ash, and hawthorn. They will help you travel to the court of the Fairy Queen, and they will help you return home when your visit is over."

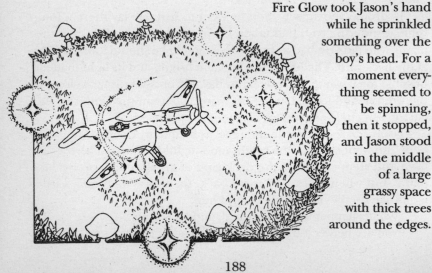

Fire Glow took Jason's hand while he sprinkled something over the boy's head. For a moment everything seemed to be spinning, then it stopped, and Jason stood in the middle of a large grassy space with thick trees around the edges.

"We are just in time," Fire Glow said. "Here comes the court and the Queen now."

Out of the trees came a parade of strange beings, some tall, some small, and others very tiny. They were laughing and singing as they came. Some walked, some rode horses, and, when Jason looked very carefully, he saw that the tiny ones rode on mice.

At the head of this parade rode a beautiful woman on a dappled gray horse. She wore a brightly-colored dress and had flowers in her long hair. The saddle and bridle of her horse were decorated with silver and gold. Beside her rode a man with dark hair and a sword by his side.

"I'm dreaming, that's all," Jason said, then jumped as Fire Glow laughed and tugged at his hair again. "It sure seems like it," Jason grumbled as he smoothed down his hair.

The parade of fairy beings poured into the clearing until they filled the space. The little darting lights he had seen when first he stepped into the fairy ring once more flew around his head. This time he saw that they were really tiny people with fluttering wings.

The Queen and King dismounted and sat on flower-covered chairs as their attendants led away their horses. All around the clearing tables were set up with food and drink. Some of the people began to play on pipes and harps, filling the moonlit night with music.

"Bring the boy Jason to us," called out the Queen. "I would talk with this human child who says we do not exist."

Fire Glow took Jason's arm and pulled him forward to stand before the Queen.

"Why do you say we are not real?" the King asked as he leaned forward to look at Jason with dark eyes. "You can see and hear and feel us. Does that not make us real?"

"Well, other kids don't see you," Jason answered. "And I never saw you before."

"Did anyone else see the deer you saw last fall along the road?" Jason shook his head. "So the deer does not exist then?"

"Yes, they exist. Everyone sees deer." Jason was beginning to feel he just might be wrong.

"Everyone?" The King raised his eyebrows in question.

"Well, no, I suppose everyone doesn't see deer," Jason answered. "You have to stand very still and be patient to see a deer."

"Have you ever seen a dinosaur or a dodo bird?" The Queen tapped her wand on her knee.

Jason shook his head. "They're all dead now."

"Then they never existed, if you haven't seen one." The King took a goblet offered to him. "They are make-believe."

"I've read books that tell all about them," Jason protested. He stopped and thought, I've read books about fairies too. And now I'm seeing them. Maybe I was wrong when I said there are no fairies.

"Yes, perhaps you were wrong in thinking that," the Queen said with a smile as she read his thoughts. "Like the deer, we do not show ourselves to just anyone. But fairies and other such creatures do like to meet with humans who believe in us. We sometimes help these believers and teach them ancient knowledge that is not written in books."

"Let us eat and drink and be merry while the night lasts," the King said.

Jason and Fire Glow sat on the grass by the Queen and King while the musicians played and food was passed around.

"Why did you bring me here?" Jason finally asked the Fairy Queen. "I was being rude when I said you didn't exist."

"You have a special task ahead of you when you grow up. You and many other humans will have the job of making your world a better place. Although we seldom live within your world, we are still part of it. If your world is destroyed, then so is ours. We are part of each other and must work together."

"At one time, in the distant past," the Queen said softly, "humans and the fairy folk were closer than we are now. We want to make the ties between us stronger, not weaker. Will you help?"

"If I can," Jason answered. "Will I remember you when I go home?"

"I will give you something to help you remember us." The King pointed at Jason's pajama pocket. "Take out the leaves and think of your home," he said.

Jason held the three leaves in his hands as he thought of the fairy ring in the grass in his back yard. Suddenly he stood in the center of the fairy ring outside his back door. He held his airplane in one hand. The leaves in his other hand crumbled into dust in the moonlight. The Fairy King was going to give me something, but he forgot, Jason thought, and he was sad.

Just then, something fell onto the grass and glittered in the light of the Moon. Jason picked it up and found that he held a silver ring in his hand. He smiled as he heard the laughter of the Fairy King.

The back door of the house opened, and Jason's mother stood there in her nightgown. "What are you doing?" she asked.

Jason ran to her and told her of his wonderful journey. He showed her the ring.

"I had forgotten," his mother said softly. "Feasting with the fairies is so wonderful." She touched a tiny ring she wore on her little finger, then patted Jason's shoulder. "Go back to bed now."

Jason peeked out the window before he went back to his room and saw his mother, her bare feet white in the moonlight, standing in the center of the fairy ring with her arms raised toward the Moon.

"I guess you don't have to be a kid to believe in the fairies," he said to himself.

MIDSUMMER NIGHT'S EVE

By Carly Wall, C. A.

It's the longest day of the year, called the Summer Solstice, and it has traditionally been a time of great feasting and merriment. These festivites arose from a fear that the waning light would disappear altogether, so ancient peoples built huge bonfires to warm the heavens and help keep the Sun going. As the years passed, magical rituals replaced the original rites and included many spells for romance and marriage.

Some girls set sedum plants in their bedroom windows on this night. The direction the plants pointed in the morning would tell the girl from which way her future husband would arrive.

Ferns have been said to bloom only at midnight on Midsummer's Eve, and can be used in a wide variety of ways. By gathering three grains of fernseed, it is believed that the gatherer can magically summon any living creature who walked, swam, or was able to fly. Worn in the shoe, these seeds can make one invisible. If carried in the hand, they can help one to find hidden treasures, especially gold. Gathering this seed is a risky proposition and must be done with the utmost of skill. Midsummer Night's Eve is the only time you can gather the seeds, between the hours of eleven and midnight. In silence, you must approach the fern and lay a white cloth under it. It is very dangerous to touch the fern with your bare hands, and the seeds must be allowed to fall of their own accord, although it has been deemed permissible to use a forked hazel rod to bend the plant so that the seeds may fall onto the cloth. The danger lies with the spirits who will try to prevent your collection of the fernseed. Many stories have been reported of past gatherers and their run-ins with mischievous spirits or demons who fly all about, bumping into one to cause one to touch the fern or drop the seeds (I couldn't find out what exactly can happen to you if you do touch the plant, but it seems ominous). They can also frighten the gatherer to illness or death if not properly prepared or protected, and

in some cases, the seeds have been stolen before the gatherer got home. If you can avoid the spirits and are prepared to follow collection methods to the letter, fernseed collecting would make a wonderful magical activity to top off the night for those who dare. Invite your closest friends and plan a party celebration to outshine all others. Of course, you will have your own ways to celebrate and feast, but I offer some suggestions here to get ideas flowing:

It's best to make it an intimate night with only a few close friends. A larger gathering can be expensive and hard to control. Send invitations with a sprig of thyme. Thyme has always been said to enable one to see the fairies dancing!

Bonfires are traditional and common to all the countries of Western Europe. In Sweden, Midsummer is still celebrated but it coincides with their midnight Sun and their celebrations consist of feasting, dancing, and tales of the supernatural. Their belief was that on this night, the Witches flew to see the Great Witch of the mountains. If a bonfire isn't practical, you can still have a small fire or use your barbecue pit to stand in for the symbolic fires. Have bundles of herbs for guests to throw on the dying embers while they chant:

May ill luck depart, as this is so burned.

Herbs good for this are thyme (helps one see into the other dimension), sage (cleansing and protecting), rosemary (for good luck and preventing others' negativity from affecting you), or lavender (for purification, enabling one to see ghosts, and is traditionally thrown on midsummer fires as a sacrifice to ancient gods).

Use lots of beeswax candles for atmosphere (especially on your table). Torches also help light up the area, because you want to hold your party from dusk until the wee hours.

Hold the party in your garden. Pretty it up with planters, streamers, and plenty of white lace on tables, chairs, etc. Be sure to get some music going for dancers too: soft melodies of flute and Celtic harp or invite someone who knows classical guitar.

The food can be as simple or complicated as you wish. Just make sure you have delectable eats so guests can enjoy themselves properly. Here are a few favorites I've enjoyed over the years. Now celebrate!

Nutmeg-Thyme Bread

2   cups flour
1   cup sugar
1   tablespoon baking soda
1   teaspoon salt
1   teaspoon nutmeg
1   cup minced thyme sprigs, plus extra for garnish
1   egg, beaten
1   cup applesauce
1   cup vegetable oil
1   cup walnuts

Preheat oven to 350°F. Mix together the dry ingredients except thyme and walnuts. Combine the thyme, egg, applesauce, and oil. Add to the dry mixture. Mix in walnuts. Pour the batter into two greased loaf pans. Sprinkle top with dried thyme. Bake forty-five minutes. Cool, remove from pans. Make a sweet sauce to pour over slices when served (make an herb tea, add honey, thicken with cornstarch). It freezes well, as the flavor is enhanced as it ages. Makes 2 loaves.

Chilled Lemony Cucumber Soup

1   cup lemon juice
2   cucumbers peeled, seeded and diced
1   yellow bell pepper, seeded and chopped
1   (10-ounce) package tofu
1   cup white wine

1 cup chopped seedless white grapes

1 cup diced melon

1 teaspoon turmeric

1 teaspoon dry yellow mustard

Purée in a food processor or blender (you'll have to do it in two batches). Chill several hours. Garnish with a slice of cucumber and sprinkle with a dash of nutmeg and some chopped lemon basil. Serves 4.

LAVENDER CHOCOLATES

2 cups sugar

1 cup milk

1 cup butter

1 cup cocoa

1 cup lavender flower buds

3 cups quick oats

1 teaspoon vanilla

Dash of salt

Mix the sugar, milk, butter, cocoa, and lavender buds together in a saucepan. Bring to a boil and boil for three minutes. Add oats, vanilla, and salt. Mix well. Quickly drop by teaspoonfuls onto waxed paper. When cool, place in sealed containers. Makes 2 dozen.

BORAGE PUNCH

Borage is said to make the heart glad and passions roar!

1 gallon dry red wine

1 cup lemon juice

1 cup sugar

1 borage stalk

In a large non-metal container, pour the red wine, lemon juice and sugar. Add a stalk of borage, cover and refrigerate overnight. To serve, remove the borage, pour into a punch bowl and decorate with borage flowers and lemon slices, and set the punch bowl in ice. 30 servings (enough to last all evening).

Herbal Drinks
for Summer and Winter

By Carolyn Moss

Many lovely drinks can be made using fresh herbs from the garden or market. Although you will see many recipes, particularly for herb teas, that utilize dried herbs, I would suggest you always try to use fresh herbs where possible. The difference is immense and will convert many who say they don't like herbal drinks.

I have divided the recipes by summer and winter as I live in England. I apologize for any confusion or irrelevance should your climate and the availability of herbs be different.

Summer

A Mixed Summer Cup

Make a strongish lemon verbena (*Aloysia tryphylla*) or lemon balm (*Melissa*) tea to which some mint and bergamot (*Monarda didyma*) sprigs have been added in moderation as undertones.

Float borage (*Borago officinalis*) flowers on top. Serve chilled with ice cubes made of lemon tea into which borage flowers have been frozen. If serving to a large party, make a giant ice cube from lemon tea in a ring mold and float this in the punch bowl. This is spectacular as well as effective. Making ice cubes from lemon tea avoids a nasty wateriness when they melt. You can add ginger beer, lemonade, or a spiking of vodka to the herb tea, just as an experiment. Add honey or sugar to taste. You will need less sweetener if your drink includes lemonade. For added interest, lightly beat an egg white and dip your glass rims in it and then into white sugar. Let this dry well before using.

"PERFECT" MINT TEA

Possibly the most refreshing drink in the heat is mint tea. The North Africans, particularly Moroccans, make this very strong, hot tea, which is sweet for most Western tastes. However, they do use an especially good, clear-tasting variety of mint, and you might find a plant labeled Moroccan mint at a specialist herb nursery. If you can't, simply use spearmint (*Mentha spicata*) or peppermint (*M. piperita*). Do not use the fancy eau de cologne, ginger mint, or the like, though. Make your tea by pouring boiling water onto a handful of leaves to which you have added just a couple of sprigs of lemon balm. This almost indiscernible hint of lemon adds a touch of complexity to the mint and raises it well above just plain good.

Chill the tea and add honey or sugar to taste. Even those who do not normally take sugar in tea or coffee may find that herb teas benefit from of touch of sweetener.

This tea can also be mixed in equal parts with ordinary tea to good effect.

A glass of mint tea, warm or chilled, is extremely effective for upset tummies and general feelings of nausea, and will settle the digestion after a large meal.

MAY WINE

For an easy and delightful drink, traditionally drunk on the first day of May in Germany (where it is known as *mei wein*), simply open a bottle of sweetish white wine and poke in some wilted sweet woodruff (*Galium odorata*). Re-cork the wine and leave it for a few days. On opening, the whole bottle will have taken on the warm sweet woodruff odor, and this makes a lovely drink when chilled. Some choose to add a little lemonade to give sparkle, and you can treat it as a fruit cup and float flowers and slices of fresh strawberries on top if you wish.

WINTER

In winter we look forward to warming drinks (either by temperature or effect) by the fire after coming in from long walks or returning from work on dark, cold nights. I have suggested some recipes that would make particularly welcome holiday gifts and that I hope will add interest to your holiday entertaining.

MULLED DRINKS

"Mulling" simply means warming an alcoholic drink with spices. Various alcoholic beverages have been used, with ale and cider being the traditional brew in the United Kingdom, and red wine being the base of the German *gluwein*. In Britain a variation was to float fluffy baked apple pulp on top of the mull, and the drink was then known as sheep's wool. During the holidays a mulled ale formed the basis of the wassail bowl, which in some areas was taken out to the fields and orchards to bless the trees in the hope of good fortunes in the coming year. Ancient in origin, mulling has become particularly popular in recent years, and for good reason. Mulled beverages can be delicious, comforting, and easy for entertaining. A large bowl or pan of mull can be prepared and served to all guests. Have another pan with the same fruit and spice mixture but with a grape juice base for non-drinkers, minors, or those who will be driving.

The basic mixture works well with red wine or beer. Pour a standard-sized bottle of wine or the equivalent amout of beer into a saucepan. Add two cinnamon sticks, a blade of mace (the outer coating of the nutmeg), one small orange stuck with several cloves and thickly sliced, one slice of lemon, and sugar to taste.

If you are multiplying the quantities, the above amounts will flavor up to two bottles. Add more cinnamon and citrus fruit for three bottles. The effect should not be too overpowering. Do not use an aluminium pan and do not boil.

Rose Brandy Liqueur

This is just one of an endless selection of liqueurs that are largely made by the same method of infusing fruit or petals in a ready-made alcoholic base, normally brandy, gin, or vodka. Flavorings and sweeteners are added and the whole left for a few months and then strained.

- 2 ounces fresh rose hips (or 1 ounce dried)
- 1 cup fresh rose petals (or ½ ounce dried)
- ½ cup red grape juice
- 3–4 tablespoons honey
  A good grating of nutmeg
- 2 teaspoons lemon juice
- 2 cloves
- 1½ cups brandy

Sterilize and rinse a wine bottle or similar bottle. If you use dried rosehips, soak them for 24 hours before use. Pour grape juice into a pan. Chop each rose hip in half and add, with all ingredients except petals and brandy, to grape juice. Warm over a gentle heat. When the mixture is warm and honey dissolved, allow it to cool. Put the petals in a sterilized bottle, and add the brandy and grape juice mixture. Seal it and store in a warm place, such as an airing cupboard, for 10 days. Strain and rebottle. This will be cloudy but will clear after a few weeks, at which point you can strain it off, leaving the sediment in the original bottle if you wish. The liqueur is ready to enjoy after 6–8 months after the original straining.

If you make one of these infused liqueurs and find the finished result disappointing, do not despair. Simply adjust the flavor with more sweetening, more brandy, some apple or grape juice, or other addition to balance the error.

Edible Solar Balls

By Edain McCoy

For this year's midsummer festivities, why not try serving something with a little finesse? These edible solar balls are round and fiery yellow, and their coconut coating mimics the shining rays of the Sun as we gather to celebrate it at its zenith. Similar recipes have been found in the regional cooking of New England and the Canadian Maritime Provinces in conjunction with Christmas, the time when the Sun is at its weakest, suggesting that this recipe already shares an archetypal link to turning-of-year celebrations.

Ingredients

- 1 (8-ounce) package of chopped dates (or 8 ounces of whole ones that you can chop yourself)
- 1 (8-ounce) package of candied fruit (or make your own by using any compote recipe then drying the finished product)
- 1 cup sugar
- ½ cup butter, softened
- 1 large egg
  Yellow food coloring (or red or orange if you prefer)
- 1 (8-ounce) package of shredded coconut

Mix all ingredients except the food coloring and the coconut in a heavy saucepan on medium heat until the mixture has thickened. Allow to cool at least one hour before continuing. After mixture has cooled, roll small portions into round balls no bigger than one inch across. Pour the coconut out into a small non-metal mixing bowl. Add a few drops of the solar-colored food coloring to the coconut, mixing with your fingers to ensure that it becomes evenly coated. If you want to mix food colorings, do this ahead of time in another small bowl until you get the desired shade. Pouring separate shades onto the coconut will cause a spotted effect. Roll the balls in the colored coconut and place them on wax paper to dry. Your solar balls will keep for about six weeks in cookie tins.

MOON LADY

BY CHRISTIE M. WRIGHT

Moon Lady.

I see your circled orb high in the skies of night;
   a ghostly galleon floating upon the cloudy seas of darkness.
Your gossamer veil cloaks the night sky in silvery softness,
   caressing the land with tender moonlight promises.
Your breath is the gentle breeze floating across the slumbering Earth,
   sighing in contentment and tickling the dreams of Man.
The brightest stars in the heavens glow in your dark velvet eyes.
Your hair, blacker than the blackest raven's wing,
   is adorned with twinkling stars and blazing comets.
You spread your black cloak over the land,
   taking all creatures under your protective wing,
   sheltering them until the dawn breaks over the horizon.

Your throne.

Silver shells from the sea,
   bathed in the moonlight.
Black obsidian kissed by the night.
Pearls of the whitest sheen,
   washed in the lake of dreams.
Brother Raven's feathers adorn your Moon Scepter,
   dipped in purity.

You who are the protector and bringer of dreams:
   bring me a sweet dream of moonlit
   lakes and silver sands.
   bring me a sweet dream of the
   one whom I love,
   bathed in your protective light.
Send me visions of the future,
   soft and silver,
   flowing on the river of Time.

Keeper of Dreams.
Dark Mother.
Moon Lady.

A Moon Myth

By Chris Cooper

My young niece was asking me about the Moon, and so I explained the science of it to her—how it reflects sunlight, how its phases are the result of seeing its half-lit orb from different angles, how its period of rotation matches its period of revolution so that the same side of the Moon always faces the Earth, how its gravity produces tides—and while it was all true, I realized there was another aspect to the Moon, a metaphorical level that speaks less to the empirical reality and more to our internal lives, our search for our place in the universe. It's the Moon of poetry, the Moon of myth and legend. So I offered her this myth of my own making, in the hope that it might help her find added meaning in the moonlight.

The goddesses Maia and Luna, twin sisters who love each other deeply, had long shared that love with Cosmos, the Lord of the Stars. Soon Maia's womb bore the fruit of Cosmos' love, and she gave birth to the millions of lifeforms that populate the Earth. Cosmos was so pleased that he plucked out his flaming right eye and set it in the heavens to watch over the sisters and his children; and so was born the Sun, Sol, the Luminous Eye. Luna too was overjoyed for her sister, but that joy was tinged with sadness, for though she and Maia were twins, they weren't identical; while Maia was incredibly fertile, Luna had proven barren. So Luna adopted her sister's children as her own and resolved to nurture and help them.

One day, the children of Maia beseeched Luna for just such help. "The Eye of Cosmos watches over us," they cried, "but we fear the coming of Night, when Sol sleeps; for who will watch over us then?"

Luna did not understand their fear of Night, for in the darkness he keeps perfect watch, since no shadows are hidden from him. But she was moved by their pleas, so she turned her gaze forever away from the other worlds and stars and instead agreed to face evermore toward her sister's children, to watch over them whenever the Luminous Eye slept. But soon, Maia's children cried for her help once more.

"Lady," they wept, "we fear the coming of Night, for in the darkness we cannot see and cannot know what lurks in the shadows."

This perplexed Luna, for the mystery of Night was what beguiled her about him the most. But

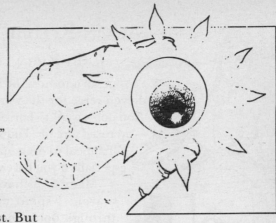

once more she was moved by their pleas, and so she gave up the dark that beguiled her so and took up a great lamp. Holding it aloft, she set sail in a boat and commanded the waters to rise up and lift her into the sky, so that the light could be seen far and wide. And to this day the waters rise and fall in tune to Luna's wishes, hurling her boat into the sky so that her lamp can light the darkness for Maia's children. And for a while, they were pleased...until they felt old age rumbling through their bones, and knew that Death was coming to take them to her father.

"Lady, help us!" they wailed. "We fear the coming of Night, for it means the end of all our days!"

And now Luna was truly baffled, for she knew that all things return to the Great Goddess only through Night's embrace, and this was bliss and nothing to be feared; besides, everyone ought to know that Night is always followed by a new day. But Luna also knew that as an immortal goddess, she could not comprehend what Maia's mortal children were facing. So Luna made her greatest sacrifice: she went to Chronos, shepherd of time, and asked him to lift her immortality—let time do with her what it would. Only that way could she understand the children's fears. And so each month, Luna goes from slender youth to radiant womanhood to the stark beauty of old age, then dies, and then is reborn; for that is the promise of Luna's example, the promise of new life from death. But before she dies each month, Luna lowers her veil over her face, so that what happens to her as she passes through Night's realm remains unseen by mortal eyes; there are some things that must remain forever a mystery. Upon her rebirth, she slowly lifts her veil again, to reveal her smiling face to Maia's children, who now slept in peace.

Moon Ritual Treats

By Kirin Lee

I t's your turn to host the Esbat ritual, but what do you serve for the wine and cakes portion? You don't want to borrow a recipe that's been overused already. Finding a good recipe that will appeal to everyone can be a challenge, especially if you have vegans in the group.

Many of us have been through this search. I spent a lot of time sifting through books looking for that special recipe that would delight my guests and prove I could be a great hostess. One day I was visiting my mother when she was baking cookies for Christmas. I watched as she formed cookie dough into little crescent Moons. It turned out that she made her "Moon cookies" every year, and those who received them as gifts always requested them. I had found my special recipe at last.

Moon Cookies

- 1 cup shortening or ½ cup shortening and ½ cup butter
- ⅓ cup sugar
- ⅔ cup ground blanched almonds
- 1⅔ cup flour
- ¼ teaspoon salt
- 1 cup confectioner's sugar
- 1 teaspoon cinnamon

Mix together shortening, sugar, and almonds. Sift together flour and salt, then stir into almond mixture. Chill dough for at least one hour. Break off pieces and roll pencil thin. Cut in 2½-inch lengths and form dough into crescent shapes with fingers. Bake on an ungreased cookie sheet until set, but not brown. Set oven on 325°F for about 14–16 minutes. Cool on pan, and while slightly warm, carefully dip each in a mixture of confectioner's sugar and cinnamon. Makes approximately 5 dozen crescent Moons. For vegan guests, use a natural sugar substitute in place of the refined sugar.

Making Mooncakes

By Breid Foxsong

Mooncakes are a part of nearly every ritual, a celebration of the connection between ourselves and the land. Bread of any kind is made of the four elements—earth, the grain; water, the liquid; air, any fresh bread has an unmistakeable scent; and the fire of the oven to bake it. There are several simple recipes for mooncakes, but this one is easy to make and can be adapted to any season by changing a few ingredients

- 2 cups sifted flour (not self-rising)
- 3 teaspoons baking powder
- 1 teaspoon salt
- 2 teaspoons sugar
- ¼ cup shortening
- ½ cup milk
- 1 slightly beaten egg

Sift together flour, baking powder, salt, and sugar. Cut in shortening until mixture is crumbly. Stir in milk and egg to form a soft dough. Round dough on a lightly floured cloth-covered board. Knead lightly (about 30 seconds). You can chant while doing this, but it only takes a couple of rounds. Roll or pat out until dough is evenly spread about ¼-inch thick. Cut into small crescents. With a sharp knife carve runes or symbols of your hopes for the next month into the tops of the crescents. Place cresents on an ungreased baking sheet. Bake at 450°F for 10–12 minutes or until golden brown. These are best if eaten while still warm, so make them just before you have your circle.

To adapt the recipe around the wheel of the year, you can sprinkle spices on top of the cakes. In the winter, I put a little sugar on top of each one, symbolizing the snow. For spring, add a candied violet to the top or grate the rind of an orange into the dry ingredients. For summer, add ¼ cup of minced parsley for flecks of green throughout. Autumn can be enhanced by dropping the sugar and adding a teaspoon each of sage, basil, oregano, and thyme, or by placing a sprig of the herb on top of the cakes.

DR.PRICE'S CREAM BAKING POWDER

NEW MOON RITE

BY JIM GARRISON

In a private place, in the deepest, darkest hour of the night of the New Moon, assemble a simple altar on a black cloth. At the center of the altar, place a small mirror wrapped in black cloth. If you are outside, place three lamps on the altar, one each for the Lady, Lord, and ancestors. If you are inside, three gray or black candles will suffice. It is best to do this rite without steel, without iron, and without clothes or robes.

When you are ready to begin, light the candles or lamps, pause, breathe deeply, and clear your mind. Relax, spread your arms wide, and listen to the night noises. Feel yourself extending downward into the earth like a tree. Feel your roots drawing energy up from the deepest places within the crust of the world. Slowly and deliberately bring your hands together. Rub your hands together and gather the energy you are drawing up from the depths.

Go to the north and extend your left hand, or a wand held in your left hand, into the darkness. Visualize the energies you are drawing up from the earth swirling around your hand and creating a barrier of living energy. Scribe a widdershins circle with your hand or the wand. Feel the deep energies of the Earth stream forth from your hand or the wand. Go around three times, then tap the wand or touch your hand to the ground.

Cleanse this place with consecrated salt water and the smoke of a resinous incense, such as dragons' blood. It is best that this part be done in silence. Return to the north and recite the following:

In the beginning was darkness, and from the womb of darkness came all else. In this place made sacred by my hand, I call upon the spirits of the land. Great and small, I welcome you all. Attend this rite and watch over me that I might work my spell and blessed be.

Walk to the west and recite the following:

Tears and kisses, joy and sorrow, I call upon the spirits of water, you who guard the gates of tomorrow. By river, lake, and stream, share this circle and share this dream.

Walk to the south and recite the following:

Fire and flame, I call you to this place, in passions' sweet name I seek your grace.

Walk to the east and recite the following:

By word and thought, alone in the night, I call upon the winds of inspiration and insight.

Return to the center of the space and sit down facing the quarter that pertains to the area of your life in which you most wish to experience change. Face north for material/monetary things, west for emotional issues, south for motivation and taking action, or east for learning and communication. Get comfortable. Close your eyes. Re-establish your connection with the deep energies of the earth. Visualize the attainment of your goals. See them as reality. Draw upon the energy of the earth and direct it into the images of your desire. Try to incorporate all of your senses as much as possible in visualizing your success. Focus as intensely as you can manage upon the image, the sensation, the taste, etc. of manifesting your desires. When it is as real to you as possible, release the image.

Pause. Stand up. Silently go to the north and dismiss each quarter in turn, moving widdershins. Upon returning to the north, reach up to the New Moon and stretch your hands upward to it. Feel the energy that is there for you. Pull this energy down from the New Moon. Let it course through your body, and mingle it with the energy from the earth. Feel it cleanse your aura and invigorate your body with its feathery touch. Touch the ground or floor and release the excess energy down into the earth.

This ends the rite. Clean up your space, and go for a walk or do something similar, especially something physically active. The key is to take your mind off of the visualization, and to let the subconscious take over. Let it go, let it happen, let it be.

HEALING BY THE MOON

BY RACHEL RAYMOND

Moon goddesses are also goddesses of magic and herbal healing. Isis, Artemis, Hecate, and Diana are just a few of the many lunar deities who were invoked in herbal healing rituals and spells.

The very first forms of magic were healing magic. Healers used the energies and properties of the world around them to bring their ailing patients back into a state of health. They observed that all living things responded to the waxing and waning of the Moon. During the Full Moon shellfish are plumper and more succulent, and mammals have more blood in their bodies and stronger heartbeats. Women tend to menstruate during the New Moon and ovulate during the Full Moon. The herbs used by ancient healers were said to be best when picked during a particular phase of the Moon.

As a modern herbalist, I have found the Moon to be a powerful healing ally. Unlike my healing predecessors, I am spoiled by a ready supply of prepared herbs. Therefore, I don't spend a lot of time picking my herbs during the optimal phase of the Moon. However, I have found using herbal therapies in harmony with the phases of the Moon to be a very powerful healing strategy.

WAXING MOON

The waxing phase of the Moon is the best time to build the body up. This is when I use nurturing herbs and tonics to strengthen the body's natural immunities. Raspberry leaf is an excellent tonic for female reproductive organs; hawthorn berries are good for the cardiovascular system; nettle is a great blood tonic; marshmallow root is a soothing tonic for the urinary tract; astragalas is a wonderful immune system tonic; burdock is a good liver tonic; red clover builds fertility; oat straw is good for the nervous system; and alfalfa is a fantastic all-around nutritive tonic.

These herbs are simple and gentle. They are best taken in a cup of tea, three to five times a day. During the waxing phase I also like to increase water intake to avoid water retention. The more water we ingest, the less water our bodies attempt to retain.

This is also a good time to apply medicinal salves and to take therapeutic baths. Most importantly, I work during the waxing Moon to ensure that the body has all the nutritional support it needs. This is the body's building time, and it needs a good supply of minerals, vitamins, carbohydrates, lipids, and amino acids to be healthy. I would also not attempt to fast or to lose weight during the waxing Moon.

Use energy healing techniques to strengthen and reconnect with the earth. Be careful to ground and center when healing so that you never use up your own life force energy. The universe is full of energy to use, and by tapping into it you will be able to help many more people than you could by using just your energy alone.

FULL MOON

The Full Moon lasts about three days. It is a very intense phase. Many women still ovulate with the Full Moon. This is the time when I apply the most powerful herbs. I like to use cayenne capsules to treat infections of any kind. Goldenseal is a well-known herbal antibiotic. Echinacae and lomatium are anti-viral. Dong quai is an excellent herb for female hormonal fluctuations.

Energy healing work during the Full Moon is very powerful. On the energetic level, it acts like a magnifying mirror. The strong lunar energy pulls everything out of hiding and reflects it back at us. This is often the time during an acute illness when people feel their worst. The Full Moon intensifies whatever else is going on. Often people aren't even aware that they're sick until the Full Moon hits.

This is also an excellent time for psychological therapy. Emotions seem closer to the surface than usual and social inhibitions melt away. Agendas that have been simmering under the surface tend to come out under the light of the Full Moon. This is a time to strengthen relationships and reaffirm bonds. Never underestimate the healing power of simply holding someone's hand and listening. This is not the time for isolation or introspection. The Full Moon draws all of life toward it. Even the solid ground rises several inches when the Full Moon passes overhead!

WANING MOON

The waning Moon is the best time to employ therapeutic fasts. I avoid drastic fasting. There is usually no need to starve the body to heal it. However, I found it helpful to limit my intake to juices and soups for a few days during the waning Moon, particularly when I was struggling with the flu. I like to use purifying herbs in moderation at this time. Sage, usnea, ginger, lemon, thyme, lavender, and peppermint are all cleansing and clearing herbs.

The waning Moon is also a good time to do sweats and diaphoretic (sweat producing) baths. In addition, if I was trying to kick a habit, I would do it during the waning phase. Full body massages help circulation and strengthen the eliminative systems. Use energy healing techniques to sever unhealthy bonds and strengthen boundaries.

NEW MOON

The New Moon is as powerful in its own way as the Full Moon. It is a time for taking stock. It is a phase of hibernation, retreat, and contemplation. Avoid crowds and gatherings and seek a little time for yourself. Unless an illness is at a critical phase, I frequently cease all therapies for a day or so and allow the body to seek its own level. Rest is crucial during the New Moon. Simple foods and quiet times are powerful healers.

Many women menstruate with the New Moon. It is natural to want to curl up in bed with a good book and nice cup of chamomile tea. Stronger nervines (relaxing herbs) are skullcap, hops, catnip, oatstraw, and valerian.

After the New Moon ends and that first crescent appears, then the healing lunar cycle begins all over again. Most acute diseases do not last a full lunar cycle.

The information in this article is only intended to be an educational tool, not a prescription. It is always wise to consult with your health care provider when experiencing any illness or discomfort.

Awareness of the rhythms of nature can assist you and your health care provider in determining the best course of treatment at any given time. Naturally, some conditions will require that you apply therapies that don't necessarily "fit" with the phase of the Moon. However, I have found that my own therapies are much more effective when I am not fighting the tides that flow around and through us.

May the lunar goddesses of healing—Artemis and Isis, Diana and Hecate—bless your healing efforts with Moon wisdom and Moon magic.

KITCHEN MEDICINE

BY ELLEN EVERT HOPMAN

WINTER REMEDIES

HEALING WITH HONEY

When you select honey for medicinal use, always buy a variety that is produced by an apiary local to your area. Ingesting local pollens found in honey can build resistance to allergies over time. The honey should be raw, not heated or processed.

HONEY FLU REMEDY

Take a six-inch ginger root and slice it. Put it in a non-aluminum pot with about 3 cups of fresh water. Cover the pot tightly and bring to a simmer. Allow the water to simmer (not boil) for about twenty minutes. Remove from the stove and add the juice of half a lemon, a pinch of cayenne pepper, and honey to taste. This is a great remedy for bronchitis and flu.

HONEY THROAT SYRUP

Take several cloves of fresh garlic. (Please don't use the genetically altered, odorless variety. It has lost its healing virtue.) Place the garlic in a blender with the juice of half a lemon. Blend until smooth. Add 1 cup raw honey and blend again. This mixture can be taken as it is in teaspoon doses for a sore throat, or strained through a cheesecloth and bottled for later use.

GARLIC AND HONEY WOUND DRESSING

If you have a cut or a wound, wash it carefully and then apply chopped or mashed raw garlic, which will kill any bacteria or viruses. Cover the garlic with a slather of honey and apply a clean bandage. The honey will keep the wound anaerobic (without oxygen) so bacteria will be unable to grow in it.

Roasted Garlic Sore Throat Remedy

Take unpeeled cloves of fresh, raw garlic and place them in a pan over medium heat (do not use oil). Gently roast the cloves until they are soft to the touch. Remove them from the pan and allow them to cool. Peel and eat.

Ginger Ale

This is a good remedy for stomach flu and also makes a tasty beverage. Chop a large ginger root. Place the slices in a non-aluminum pot and cover with several cups of fresh, cold water. Bring to a simmer

Jewelweed

and then simmer for twenty minutes. Remove the pot from the burner and, while the liquid is still hot, strain out ginger, and add honey or maple syrup to taste. Allow the mixture to cool. To make the ginger ale fill a glass half full of the cooled mixture and add sparkling water until the glass is full. Voilà!

Summer Remedies

Poison Ivy Wash

Gather sweet fern (*Comptonia peregrina*), a woody-stemmed herb that grows in wild places at the edges of fields and forests. Place the leaves in a clean glass jar until the jar is two-thirds full. Add plantain leaves and jewelweed (impatiens) until the jar is packed full. Pour vodka over the herbs to the level of the top of the jar. Cover with a lid and allow the tincture to sit for three days. When the herbs begin to wilt and the liquid is brown, strain out the herbs and reserve the liquid. Apply locally to poison ivy with a cotton ball four

Plantain

times a day. You will also want to take burdock root capsules (two capsules, three times a day for a 150-pound adult) for about a week to clear the ivy out of your system.

Scrape, Sunburn, and Burn Salve

Take equal parts of three or more of the following: plantain leaves, pine needles, comfrey leaves,

Sarsaparilla

elecampaign roots, baby oak leaves (not old ones), wild sarsaparilla roots, bee balm leaves, chopped horse chestnuts (the meat of the nut and the shiny brown covering), and/or fresh, chopped green walnut hulls. Add calendula blossoms and lavender flowers, fresh or dried. Place the herbs in a non-aluminum pot and cover with good quality olive oil. Bring to a simmer and simmer with a tight-fitting lid for 20 minutes. In a separate pot bring fresh beeswax to a simmer. When both pots are of equal temperature, add three tablespoons of the hot beeswax for every cup of olive oil to the pot with the herbs. Stir, strain, and seal in a clean jar. This salve is great for diaper rash, and if you add the horse chestnuts it makes a wonderful remedy for piles.

Calendula

Queen of Hungary Rosemary Cologne

Use this cologne as a facial spray in the heat of summer or as a gentleman's aftershave any time. Fill a glass jar with fresh rosemary greens. Add a small amount of fresh lavender blossoms, lemon balm leaves, a fragrant rose or two, and a little lemon zest if desired. Cover the herbs with gin (gin is flavored with juniper berries), place a lid on the jar and let the mixture sit in the hot Sun for two days. Strain and bottle.

Lemon Zest

Food From the Garden

Flower Tea

This magical and delicious tea is also a love potion. Share it with your beloved on a Full Moon night. Take equal parts lemon balm leaf, rose buds, and chamomile flowers, fresh or dried. Add ¼ part lavender blossoms. Place the mixture in a pot of freshly boiled water that you have removed from the stove. Cover tightly and allow to steep. (Do not let the herbs steep more than ten minutes or the delicate flowery aroma will be lost.) Serve with a touch of honey.

Rose

NASTURTIUM FLOWER SANDWICHES

Take slices of crusty whole wheat bread and slather on thick coats of natural cream cheese. Place peppery nasturtium flowers on top of the cream cheese. Serve the sandwiches open faced.

CLOVER BLOSSOM TEA SANDWICHES

Cut the crusts off of delicate white bread slices. Spread with real butter and then place fresh *Nasturtium* red clover blossoms on each slice. Cover with watercress leaves and top with another slice of buttered bread. Serve this with organic black tea in the garden.

FLOWER SALAD

To a salad of fresh mixed lettuces add fresh rose petals, johnny jump up blossoms, violet flowers and leaves, red clover blossoms, baby dandelion leaves and flowers, and daisies. Sprinkle with grated carrot and thinly sliced spring onion. Use a delicate lemon juice and olive oil dressing. Top with a pinch of sea salt.

Violet

VIOLET OR DANDELION JELLY

Fill a glass jar with either dandelion flowers (remove the stems) or blue violets. Pour boiling hot water over the flowers until the jar is filled. Allow the jar to sit overnight. Strain out the flowers and reserve the liquid. To 2 cups of liquid add the juice of 1 lemon and a package of powdered pectin. Place the liquid in a non-aluminum pot and bring to a boil. Add a tiny piece of butter (to prevent froth) and 4 cups of sugar and bring to a boil again. Boil for 1 minute, pour into sterilized jars, and seal.

RASPBERRY HONEY

Dandelion

Take raspberries, blackberries, or strawberries and place them in a non-aluminum pot. Cover with fresh, raw honey and gently bring to a simmer. Cook for 2 minutes and allow to cool. Pour into jars and store in the refrigerator. Great on waffles and pancakes.

Blackberries

FLOWER CAKE

Make a delicate yellow layer cake batter and put five fresh rose geranium leaves in the bottom of each cake pan before you pour the batter into it. Cover the cooled cake with a thick white frosting. Into the frosting press rose petals or entire roses, fresh day lily blossoms, daisies, johnny jump ups, or violet flowers. Place fresh mint leaves around the base of the cake. Eat the whole thing.

Day Lilly

ST. JOHN'S WORT LIQUEUR

Gather fresh St. John's wort blossoms at the Summer Solstice. Place 2 cups of chopped organic oranges (keep the peel on) in a non-aluminum pot with 2 cups of fresh, cold water and 2 cups of sugar. Cook until the sugar dissolves. Pour the mixture into a large glass bottle and add 2 cups of vodka and 2 teaspoons of vegetable glycerin. Add 2 cups of the flowers and stir or shake. Keep the mixture in a cool, dark place for 6 months, shaking occasionally. Strain and bottle. The beauty of this process is that the flowers are picked at the height of summer *St. John's wort* and the liqueur is ready in the dark of winter, on the Winter Solstice. St. John's Wort is a solar herb, the perfect herb for a Winter Solstice ritual celebration.

ZUCCHINI PANCAKES

Sauté half of a small onion (chopped) and set aside. Grate a medium zucchini and place it in a bowl with the onion. Add a pinch each of fresh chopped basil and marjoram. Grate in ½ cup cheese. Add 1 cup whole wheat flour, 1 teaspoon of salt, 1 teaspoon of baking powder, 1 beaten egg, and a dash of cayenne. Pour in enough milk to make a batter. Cook like pancakes and top with a mixture of yogurt *Basil* and sour cream. Garnish with fresh chopped parsley.

Lavender: The All-American (and British) Herb

By Therese Francis

If I could only have one herb in my house, lavender would be my choice because it can be used for so many things, including culinary, cosmetic, medicinal, and aromatherapy purposes.

Although there are many subspecies of lavender, the two most commonly used are *Lavandula angustifolia* (in the U. S.) and *Lavandula officinalis* (in Britain and Europe). The flower is gathered just before it opens, between June and September. The fresh flowers contain 0.5 percent of volatile oil that contains linalyl acetate, linalol, geraniol, cineole, limonene, and sesquiterpenes.

Some recipes call for fresh flowers, while others use dried ones. To dry, tie a bundle of flowers together and hang upside down until dry to the touch, or spread the flowers out on a cookie sheet or drying rack at room temperature. Once dry, lavender stores readily in bags or glass jars. Do not store fresh flowers in airtight containers, or they may mold.

Culinary Uses

Lavender water is used in cooking, just like rose water. Use a commercial lavender water or make your own. Soak a handful of lavender (fresh is best) in a quart of warm water for at least five hours but not longer than overnight. Strain out the lavender.

My favorite use of lavender water is in icing on cakes and cookies. Add lavender water to icing, starting with a few drops and adding more to taste. As with all extracts, a little goes a long way.

Aromatherapy Uses

Lavender is best known as an aromatherapy oil. (Never take the essential oil internally.) The distilling process is rather intense, so buying a commercial essential oil is the easiest. Be careful that you get a distilled oil and not a chemically extracted oil (the distilled oils are more expensive but do not contain foreign chemicals).

Lavender oil is used to relax. The oil is gentle enough that it can be applied directly on the skin or added to a massage oil or aloe vera gel. Since the aromatherapy property of the oil is to promote relaxation, lavender can be good for headaches and muscle fatigue due to stress.

Another aromatherapy use of lavender is to place dried flowers in a pillow or stuffed animal to use as a sleep pillow. The soothing scent promotes deep, dream-filled sleep.

COSMETIC USES

Lavender water can be used as a tonic or added to a moisturizer to help promote strong skin cells. Use lavender water as a daytime perfume or cologne substitute. Most people who are scent-sensitive will be okay around lavender.

Lavender water can also be used as a hair tonic after shampooing. Add the lavender water to vinegar, rinse your hair with the mixutre, and let dry.

Lavender essential oil can be applied directly to the skin as a moisturizer and to promote strong skin cell development.

MEDICINAL USES

In *The Holistic Herbal,* David Hoffman recommends lavender tea for mild depression (alone or in combination with rosemary, kola, or skullcap). Pour 1 cup boiling water onto 1 teaspoon dried herb and steep for 10 minutes. Take up to three times daily. Lavender is safe for children. Hoffman also recommends using the essential oil as a rubbing oil to help ease the pain of rheumatism.

In *Aromatherapy for Women,* Maggie Tisserand recommends using lavender in combination with rose and bergamot as a douche against vaginal candida infections, and in combination with rosemary, eucalyptus, and geranium to kill lice and promote healing following a lice infection.

My favorite use of lavender oil is on mild burns and sunburns. I add a few drops of the essential oil to a handful of aloe vera gel and apply liberally every few hours until the skin returns to normal color. Lavender oil can also be applied to cuts, scratches, and scrapes to promote healing. I have successfully used lavender oil on scars to get them to fade.

BACH FLOWER REMEDY

The Flower Essence Repertory recommends using lavender flower remedy for "nervousness and overstimulation of spiritual forces that deplete the physical body." You can find flower remedies at most health food stores. Generally, flower essences are used by taking one dropperfull four times a day for seven to fourteen days at the onset of the indicated symptoms.

Lavender is a truly versatile herb and one that needs to be in everyone's home.

REFERENCES

Hoffman, David. *The Holistic Herbal.* Dorset, England: Element Books, Ltd., 1983.

Kaminshi, Patricia, and Richard Katz. *Flower Essence Repertory.* Nevada City, CA: Earth-Spirit Inc., 1986.

Tisserand, Maggie. *Aromatherapy for Women.* Rochester, VT: Healing Arts Press, 1985.

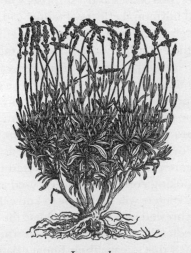

Lavender

THE MAGIC OF FENNEL

BY NUALA DRAGO

The lore and magic of fennel transcends the ages. The Greek physician Hippocrates wrote of the virtues of this sweetly aromatic herb more than 2,300 years ago. For the last two millennia it has been used to flavor foods and beverages, cleanse the skin and banish wrinkles, cure illnesses, lose weight, neutralize curses, and much more.

Ancient gladiators ingested fennel on a daily basis to make themselves more ferocious in battle. They wore it on their bodies as a protective talisman and used it in the treatment of their battle wounds. Ancient practitioners administered it as a stimulant and prescribed it for menstrual cramps, indigestion, flatulence, and colic. Moreover, it was used as an eyewash and treatment for cataracts and blindness. Because of its natural estrogen-like effect, it was given to menopausal and lactating women. Milk production was increased in cows, sheep, and goats by adding fennel to their diets.

Today, modern science has proven many of the beliefs of our ancestors to be based in fact. For those of us who believe in the magic of nature, this comes as no surprise. The antispasmodic, antibacterial, and hormonal effects of fennel can give us a more natural and kinder alternative to harsher medicines in many instances. With the exception of the essential oil, which should not be ingested, we can take a lesson from generations past in using fennel as a natural remedy, and there is more good news.

Fennel is probably one of the best beauty secrets of the centuries. It can be used in facial saunas, perfumed soaps, bath oils, and face creams. The flowers and stalks of the plant make a wonderful sachet or potpourri, while the seeds and stalks can be chewed to sweeten the breath. It is reputed to promote a clear and younger-looking complexion when used as a beverage or applied topically. Dieters will be happy to know that when the seeds are chewed or brewed as a tea, fennel has the ability to curb the appetite. In medieval times, when food was scarce, peasants would take advantage of this to ease their hunger pangs.

Indeed, in medieval times and well before, the magical properties of fennel were as well recognized as the practical ones. In ages past it was believed that fennel could repel evil spirits and ward off curses. This is yet another reason that it was used to season the food of humans and beasts alike. In fact, large swags of fennel would be placed over doorways, used in protective sachets and amulets, and burned as an incense to protect the home. If you would like to add a little fennel magic to your life, here are some suggestions:

* Add fennel seed to a dream pillow.

* Make a natural cough syrup by boiling 1 tablespoon of fennel seeds with a pint of water. Cool, strain, sweeten with honey, and use as needed.

* To soothe tired eyes and reduce puffiness, use strained and cooled fennel tea to soak a cloth. Lie down, close your eyes, and apply the cloth to your eyes for ten to fifteen minutes.

* Burn fennel stalks with your firewood for a pleasing fragrance and magical atmosphere.

* Drink fennel tea to improve your vision before consulting your tarot cards or scrying.

* Make a sachet out of the stalks and seeds and add it to your bath water before performing a ritual.

* Burn fennel as an incense on a charcoal tablet during rituals or ceremonies or to cleanse the atmosphere after something unpleasant has happened.

FENNEL CAKES

One of my favorite ways to use fennel is to make fennel cakes. These small tea cakes, or cookies, can be eaten for pleasure or protection, used as altar cakes, or given as gifts. Some say they even have an aphrodisiac-like effect. If you are among those who believe in the Good People or Faery Folk, I have been told that these are among their favorite foods!

FENNEL CAKES

2½ cups flour

2½ teaspoons baking powder

¼ cup butter

⅔ cup sugar

3 large eggs

1 teaspoon lemon extract

½ teaspoon vanilla

1 tablespoon fennel seed

ICING

¼ cup plus 1 teaspoon water

3 cups confectioners' sugar

1 teaspoon lemon extract

Combine flour with baking powder and set aside. Preheat the oven to 375°F. In a large bowl cream butter, and gradually add sugar. One at a time, beat in eggs. Beat for one minute after each one is added. Next, stir in lemon extract, vanilla, and fennel seed. Add the flour mixture and stir with a spoon until the dough is smooth. Using a level tablespoon of dough for each, roll into small balls and place on a parchment-lined baking sheet. Bake on the center rack of the oven for about 15 minutes. Move to the top rack for another 5–7 minutes or until they are a very pale brown. Remove them from the baking sheet immediately and place on racks to cool.

After they are completely cooled, prepare the icing on the stovetop. It will not set properly if made in the microwave. Be careful when dipping the cakes because this icing is very hot.

Bring water for icing to a full boil in a large saucepan. Immediately stir in confectioners' sugar and lemon extract. Turn the heat to low, and as soon as the icing is smooth, remove it from the heat. Working quickly, dip the tops of the cakes into the hot icing and place them on racks over waxed paper to catch the drips. Allow the icing to harden completely before storing. These taste even better the next day.

WEDDING HERBS

By Carolyn Moss

A wedding is the perfect time to indulge a passion for herbs, be it a formal affair with all the neighborhood dignitaries, or an intimate one with a few close friends and family. Herbs can provide romantic, muted colors and fragrances coupled with unique symbolism. An especially appealing aspect of planning herbs into a wedding celebration is that they can be carried right through from invitations to church and reception arrangements, bouquets, food and drink, and even confetti. Any herbs and flowers used can be dried and incorporated into keepsake pictures or potpourri. Needless to say, herbs are suitable for use in ceremonies for all religions and denominations or in non-religious commitment festivals.

Here are some ideas on how to use herbs at a wedding. I assure you that once you start you will get carried away and will only be bound by time and imagination.

TUSSIE MUSSIES

Tussie mussies are herb posies made by gathering herbs and flowers around a central feature, e.g., a perfect rosebud or a wired fir cone for a winter bunch. Bind the stalks, stripped of any excess leaves or twigs, in green florist tape, and cover with wide ribbon or lace. The whole is finally surrounded by a doily

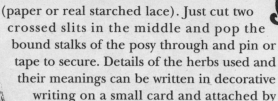

(paper or real starched lace). Just cut two crossed slits in the middle and pop the bound stalks of the posy through and pin or tape to secure. Details of the herbs used and their meanings can be written in decorative writing on a small card and attached by ribbon. Further ribbons may be added, from which dangle a lucky horseshoe charm, a miniature lavender bag, and a card with the bride's and groom's names and the date.

Large tussies would be suitable for a bride or attendants at a more informal wedding. They also make lovely mementos for the bride's and groom's mothers and godmothers. For a small party (or if you are ambitious!) a small tussie mussie could be made for each female guest.

Choose sturdy herbs that will dry well, such as roses, rosemary, marjoram, lambs ears, and gypsophila.

POTPOURRI

It would be lovely to make a batch of potpourri with some of the wedding flowers, either from bouquets or table and church arrangements. A helpful mother or bridesmaid will need to be at the ready to salvage the flowers as soon as possible after the event, as trying to make potpourri with wilted flowers will end in disappointment. The simplest thing is to air dry leaves and petals on kitchen paper. To add further fragrance, combine a few drops of essential oil of your choice with a fixative such as powdered orris root (available in natural or synthetic form from craft suppliers), and mix in with the petals, using half a teaspoonful of fixative per two cups of petals.

Another charming use for potpourri is as natural confetti for a change from rice or paper. Make up a quantity of a flowery fragrance. Three parts pink rose petals to one part lavender is lovely. Either bag it up and use it as normal or have a young bridesmaid circulate round the guests with a basket of the flowers and a supply of small card cones so all can take a small scoop with which to shower the bride.

Cones can easily be fashioned from circles of pastel colored card, six inches in diameter. Cut a slit to center and overlap the paper until the desired shape is reached. Fasten the cones with glue, staples, or tape. Decorate with paper or cotton lace as desired.

Some of this potpourri could be bagged up to send to absent friends along with a piece of the cake.

BOUQUET

If tussie mussies are unsuitable for your wedding plans, herb leaves and flowers can add beauty and fragrance to formal or free-form bouquets for the bride and attendants. A glance at the list below will show the scope of herbs available. Herbs are often very economical compared to other flowers available and many may be available in your own or friends' gardens.

Herbs can be fashioned into corsages to pin onto dresses. The corsages are ideal for attendants or for the bride at a more informal function. Other brides like to have a perfect flower or tiny posy, maybe of roses, pinned onto a wide heavy ribbon and carried in a prayer book, or maybe a book of meaningful poetry for a secular ceremony. Bridesmaids of all ages can enjoy hair bands, circlets, or decorated hair combs with an herbal theme. Again, choose robust varieties that won't wilt, such as rosemary or myrtle rather than fennel and the like.

OTHER FLORAL DECORATIONS

Make up large arrangements for the room where the ceremony will be held. If you have access to the countryside, an informal rural effect and great savings can be made by gathering wild flowers such as cow parsley, which can be accented with just a few expensive blooms.

Tie small posies to each pew or end chair of each row. If there is to be a formal sit-down meal, attach an herbal posy with ribbon on to each lady's chair.

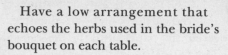

Have a low arrangement that echoes the herbs used in the bride's bouquet on each table.

KEEPSAKES FOR THE BRIDE

DRESS BOX

Cover a large, lidded box with a thin layer of wadding topped with material (glazed cotton works well) between which you have sandwiched lavender or potpourri sachets. Cut a piece of card the size of the box lid. Cover with wadding and material and place in after material has been fitted to the lid to cover the raw edges. Do the same on the base and cover the insides of the base with card stock cut to reach just below upper edge for a neat finish. This makes a beautiful gift for a bride to keep her wedding dress in. Include some acid-free tissue paper and a shoe bag.

WREATH

Make up an herbal wreath as a gift for the bride, her mother, and mother-in-law. Use herbs that will dry well, such as sage or lavender (soft herbs such as dill and mint just wilt and shrivel). The following message was given to me by Madeleine Siegler and can be altered according to what flowers have been included. Write it on a card and attach to wreath with ribbon.

Your herbal wedding wreath contains lavender for devotion, rosemary for remembrance, marjoram for joy, sage for wisdom, rosebuds for undying love, and chamomile for patience in adversity. The circle, symbol of unending life, is wound with artemisia, which was named for the goddess of fertility.

HERB GARDEN

Whether the newlyweds are to live in a sky scraper or a ranch, an herb garden would be sure to be a welcome gift. It can be a container planted up with a few well-chosen plants. Try a dwarf marjoram, lemon thyme, chives, and parsley. Alternatively, you could present an herb garden design together with the plants or a gift voucher for the local herb supplier. Along with the design, add recipes, remedies, folklore, and a yearly maintenance schedule for the suggested herbs if the wedding couple are novice gardeners. Gear the design of the gift to the couple's interests. For example, use predominantly culinary herbs for cooks, dye herbs for spinners or crafts people, medicinal herbs for those interested in natural remedies, or Native American herbs for those interested in United States history and Native American folklore and medicines. Any library should be able to provide books about herbs.

HERBS AND FLOWERS FOR A ROMANTIC DAY

ROSEMARY: In *Hamlet,* Shakespeare wrote, "There's rosemary, that's for remembrance; pray you love remember."

THYME: for strength and courage

SAGE: for long life and domestic virtue

ROSES. for love

IVY: for fidelity—the female plant to the holly's male

CARAWAY SEEDS: should be placed by the bride in the groom's pocket to ensure fidelity, although in the interests of equality perhaps the groom could put some in the bride's pocket too!

WHITE LILAC: for youthful innocence

HONEYSUCKLE: for devotion

LILY OF THE VALLEY: sweet innocence

MYRTLE: for love (the sprigs found in all British royal wedding bouquets are taken from a bush at Osbourne on the Isle of Wight, which is a direct descendant of one that Queen Victoria planted)

LAVENDER: for devotion

MARJORAM: for joy

BERGAMOT: for compassion

CLOVE PINKS: for the bonds of affection

GYPSOPHILA: for gentleness

This list is by no means exhaustive—the joy of herbs is that there is no need for formality or correctness. Just use what you have and what you enjoy, and have a lovely herbal wedding day.

HELPFUL SCENTS FOR MEDITATION

BY CARLY WALL, C. A.

S cent has been used by humankind since the beginning of time for a variety of reasons. Because scent alters our perceptions (sometimes in radical ways), it has had an air of mystery and magic surrounding it. Indeed, the plants themselves have a vibration all their own, and the scented liquids we distill from them, called essential oils, also have particular vibrations. These vibrations can alter our moods and feelings. In addition, since scent is a doorway into the depths of our minds, it is also helpful in altering our perceptions and gaining access to other realms. The ancients had knowledge of this, and were careful to use particular scents for their incenses used during religious ceremonies and other rituals.

Today, we can use particular scents to help deepen our meditation experiences, to help expand our psychic awareness, and to encourage astral dreams. Use the scents in the following ways.

Light a candle and place two to three drops in the melted wax (careful, don't touch the burning wick—essential oils are flammable). Put one to three drops on a cotton ball—inhale one minute at a time or place the cotton ball in your pillowcase.

You can also place drops in a lamp ring diffuser or room diffuser so the scented air can fill the bedroom. Here are a list of essential oils and what they can help you accomplish.

MEDITATION

FRANKINCENSE: Frankincense has a long religious history because of its ability to help one access the spiritual realms. It awakens higher consciousness and is good for meditation. It has a spicy, woody scent.

MYRRH: To help deepen the meditation experience, inhale this rich, slightly bitter scent. It helps you to become aware that this reality isn't the only one.

SANDALWOOD: Slow, yet powerful, Sandalwood has been said to be in charge of opening the highest and lowest chakras, so is helpful for unleashing the kundalini energies while keeping one grounded. It helps guide one toward enlightenment.

ENHANCING PSYCHIC AWARENESS

BAY: Bay purifies negativity, releasing you to your psychic self. It is also the scent used by the Delphic Oracle in Greece.

CINNAMON: Cinnamon arouses the physical senses beyond the normal limits. It helps increase psychic abilities and increases vibratory qualities.

LEMONGRASS: Lemongrass awakens the psychic mind, and is very opening. It helps concentration and purifies.

YARROW: Yarrow opens to cosmic energies, is balancing, and also good for strengthening intuitive abilities.

EXPLORING THE ASTRAL THROUGH DREAMS

CLARY SAGE: This scent is centering for the soul. It is very relaxing and can be narcotic. Clary sage helps one access the creative element within, and is famous for inducing exciting and very interesting dreams. Inhale for a short period before sleep, while using affirmations to induce lucid dreams.

HOPS: Hops is a tranquilizer that has been used often as an ingredient in sleep pillows. It is very relaxing. It can also free the soul during sleep.

JASMINE: Calming and relaxing, Jasmine also lifts the spirits. Psychic dreams result from inhalation, although the essential oil is expensive.

Kitchen Witchery 101

By Denise Dumars

Many practitioners new to the magical arts believe that before casting a spell or performing a ritual, one must drive across town to the occult supply store and spend money getting just the right ingredients. In reality, the ingredients to many successful spells, rituals, and other magical practices may be right there already—in your own kitchen! Here are some suggestions as to how to transform common items in your kitchen cabinets and refrigerators into the accoutrements of magical practice.

Herbs

Need some fast cash? All out of money-drawing incense? Look at your spice rack for some leafy green herbs such as mint, oregano, basil, or parsley. Write the amount of money you need right now on a piece of plain white paper. Place the paper beneath a candle and light the candle. Scatter the herbs on a piece of charcoal in your incense burner. You can also scatter herbs around the candle if you wish. Use dried herbs for this: fresh ones won't burn. Supplement the herbs with any abundance-type self-burning incense to help the herbs burn if you wish.

Forgetful? Try a "rosemary for remembrance" pillow. Simply tie some dried rosemary into a piece of cheesecloth and place it inside your pillowcase. Then you'll remember that you need to restock your money drawing incense! If you check your spellbooks, aromatherapy guidebooks, and natural medicine books, you'll find many more uses for common kitchen herbs.

Extracts

Remember when Granny Clampett on *The Beverly Hillbillies* had Ellie Mae put vanilla extract behind her ears before a prospective beau arrived? Turns out the old back country wise woman was right. Studies have shown that sweet aromas, such as vanilla, are alluring to men. Many perfumes on the market now contain vanilla. Make sure you include vanilla in the baked goods that you make for your favorite suitor (vanilla improves even the flavor of chocolate). Why not dab a bit on the pulse points if you're hoping for a night of passion?

Perhaps you're up late studying for a big test. Instead of taking one of those harmful caffeine tablets, try sharpening your tired mental faculties by taking a whiff of the peppermint extract in your cupboard. If that doesn't do the trick, try taking the top off a jar of peppercorns and alternately inhaling the peppermint and the peppercorn aromas. Now you're awake!

APPLE CIDER VINEGAR

Feel the need for a cleansing or purification ritual? Before you begin, take a purifying bath by putting a cupful of apple cider vinegar in the bath. If showering, warm a Pyrex cupful in the microwave for thirty seconds; pour over yourself in the shower. As you bathe, visualize a pure white light surrounding and protecting you. Chiropractors, massage therapists, and other body workers also recommend the apple cider vinegar bath after a treatment.

People in New England and in the South often recommend tonics to stimulate the system, especially in the spring. A simple tonic is made by adding one teaspoon each of apple cider vinegar and honey to a little water. Sip slowly and visualize your system being renewed and energized.

Learn the correspondences between common herbs and astrology, Witch workings and natural healing methods, and you'll find a wealth of simple abundance right there in your cupboards!

MULLED WINE

BY BREID FOXSONG

Rather than simply pouring a ritual wine from the bottle to the chalice, it is sometimes a nice touch to "mull" it, or warm it gently with a few carefully chosen herbs or spices. This not only invests the wine with the qualities of the chosen herbs or spices, it adds a special touch toward individualizing each ritual. "Wine" is used loosely here. You can mull anything! I personally feel that grape juice takes a mull better than any other juice, but experiment on your own.

Select the herbs used on a basis of compatibility, taste, properties, mood, and season of the Sabbat/Moon involved, and to aid any magical undertakings planned for the evening. You can also add herbs that are sacred to your particular deity(s) if you wish, being sure, of course, that all the herbs used are edible.

While you are learning, I strongly suggest you start with a red wine; it tolerates a heavier hand with the herbs and spices. White wines are much more delicate. For a red wine you can use up to a teaspoon of each herb, but start with a quarter teaspoon or less per quart, especially with the stronger flavors. You can always add more; it is difficult to remove it once it's been added. With white wines, use only a small pinch per quart.

To mull wine, warm it gently on low heat with the herbs wrapped in cheesecloth and suspended in the liquid for several minutes until you can taste the herbs in the wine. Serve warm or re-chill, depending on taste and the season. Just because it's mulled does not mean it has to be hot. In fact, some taste better cold.

As far as adding the herbs, some people prefer to add each herb separately, focusing on the herb's properties and concentrating on allowing the herb's virtues to mingle with the wine as it is stirred. Others add them all at once, concentrating on the combined effects. Both methods are effective, depending only on how you like to work. Remember that some spices are stronger than others and should not be allowed to cook for long. The following are a few suggested herbs and spices listed according to correspondences (and my personal preferences). Compile your own lists as you experiment with combinations.

FULL MOON

Rose hips (psychic awareness); pomegranate seeds (creativity and fertility); orange peel (purification); cinnamon (psychic awareness, love); nutmeg (psychic awareness); and cloves (protection).

NEW MOON

Cloves (protection); red clover blossoms (growth and prosperity); chamomile (renewal); and thyme (purification).

THE SABBATS

MABON

Sage (longevity); basil (protection); apple (health); and cloves (protection). This can be done with cider, too, if you omit the apple and add a pinch of cinnamon or nutmeg.

SAMHAIN

Apple peel (health); sage (longevity); rosemary (protection and mental stimulation); one bay leaf (manifesting reality and increasing protection); one acorn meat (harvest and potential); a half-pinch of cayenne (purification); and one cinnamon stick (psychic awareness/love). Note: Don't try this combination with a white wine or cider it tastes awful! A strong red or burgundy is good.

YULE

Chamomile (renewal); wintergreen (renewal); cardamom (love); nutmeg (psychic awareness); and a pinch of pine needles (renewal).

IMBOLC

Small dash of cayenne (purification); peels of orange (purification) and lemon (happiness); cinnamon (psychic awareness and love); basil (protection); and one bay leaf (manifesting reality and increasing protection).

OSTARA

Cloves (protection); jasmine or rose (love and renewal); and a pinch of basil (protection).

BELTANE

Fruit sections: orange (purification), lemon, apple (health); strawberries (two per quart); pomegranate seeds (creativity and fertility); one cinnamon stick (psychic awareness and love); orange peel (purification); rose hips (psychic awareness); cloves (protection); and rose petals (love). This is a good combination in champagne also (see note below).

MIDSUMMER

Fennel seed (strength); mugwort (psychic awareness); sage (longevity), bay leaf (manifesting reality and increasing protection); and cinnamon (psychic awareness and love).

LUGHNASAAD

Rosemary (protection/mental stimulation); basil (protection); cinnamon (psychic awareness and love); blackberry leaves and/or fruit (money and harvest); and a few corn or wheat kernels (protection, spirituality, and transformation).

ETHNIC BLENDS

For a more traditional spicing, or if you are honoring your forebears, you can try these "ethnic" mulls.

AMERICAN INDIAN

Sage (longevity); sweetgrass (purification) or pine needles (renewal); and clover (growth). A more traditional blend would include tobacco (spirituality), but this will turn very bitter if soaked for more than about forty-five seconds, so I don't recommend it. Instead of mulling the tobacco, consider combining it with the above ingredients after mulling and burning it as an aromatic.

CELTIC

Clover (growth); an acorn meat (harvest and potential); apple peel (health); and a teaspoon of orange marmalade (purification).

GREEK/ROMAN

Bay leaf (manifesting reality and increasing protection); apple peels (health); pomegranate seeds (creativity and fertility); and one olive (spirituality and health). A grape leaf (dream fulfillment) can add flavor also, but add it to the warm wine and remove it in less than two minutes or it will make the wine bitter. In the winter, a dash of oregano (peace) is also good.

HINDU/EAST INDIAN

A combination of basil (protection) and lotus (peace), or a combination of cumin (peace and happiness); peppercorns (protection and health); tamarind fruits (protection); and coriander (protection and love).

NORSE

Cloudberries or lingenberries (prosperity); and acorn meats (harvest/potential). Don't let the acorns soak for more than a few minutes or the wine will become bitter.

EGYPTIAN

Horehound (prosperity); peppercorns (protection and health); and catnip (purification).

HELPFUL HINTS

Champagne should never be mulled. If you should use champagne, a few drops of herbal extract can be added to get a similar benefit to that of mulling. Another way to attain the mulling effect is to use sliced peeled fruit or fruit juices to get the desired flavoring.

Besides the listed flavors, you may wish to add herbs for healing, growth, insight, love, and other qualities. Keep in mind that the whole mixture should be compatible in flavor. Experiment for yourself using small batches to test.

Inside a Kiva

Hopi Kivas of the Southwest

By Bernyce Barlow

The first homes of the Hopi ancestors were pit houses dug deep in the Earth and covered on top. Later, as the West populated, the People came together and built structures in cliffs and canyons above the ground, but they continued to keep their corn and crops below ground in pits. Later, when storage bins were developed above ground, the pits were used to bury the dead, linking life with death, as the Earth had also housed, protected, and fed the Hopi. Finally, large settlements made up of the Hopi clans evolved and the ground pits became *kivas*, or places of ritual and worship.

Kiva means "world below." Kivas are eigther round or rectangular, but the interior plans of both are basically the same. Some kivas are small and others are large enough to hold several clans. There are usually four pillars of stone or wood supporting the kiva walls, and the pillars often rest on four large stones. The pillars represent the four Hopi emergences. The last emergence was said to take place on reed rafts that came from the west. Therefore, crossed logs of cedar or reed mats are placed within the kiva's interior, mimicking the rafts. Around the walls are openings with ladders of cedar, each with five rungs. The rungs represent the five worlds of emergence (four have been completed and there is one more to come). In the larger kivas the ladderways open up into a chamber of twelve areas where the initiates or clan members sat. This chamber represented the heavens and the constellations. The floor of the kiva was reserved for the priests and ritual. A vault or pit was constructed into the lower kiva chamber to hold ceremonial objects. A fire altar was also built into the lower chamber for ritual purposes. The eastern half of a kiva was slightly raised above the western half.

Throughout the kiva there are small openings called *sipapuni,* representing the umbilical cord connecting earth and the human family as well as underworld emergences. The ground floor has one. Sipapuni has the combined meaning of "navel" and "path from." It usually remains covered unless an emergence act is required in ritual. There are many symbols of sipapuni in the kiva, each representing an emergence, such as a ladder leading to the outside of the kiva, which is called the *kivaove* (the above part). The kivaove represents the world we now are involved with—the fourth emergence.

So, let's take a basic look at the Hopi kiva. Most are multi-level, and the ladder leading into the kiva represents emergence. The opening in the roof that the ladder(s) peek through frames the constellations and stars that are used to begin and end ceremonies. It also serves as a kind of sipapuni. Eventually, the ladder(s) lead to the underworld/fire pit or the symbol of the first emergence where the Hopi believe all life began. The center ground floor altar represents the second world, the raised floor where the ladder sits is the third world, and the kivaove, the fourth. A vault in the kiva holds the masks of the kachinas and the pahos (prayer feathers) of the clans as well as certain stones and charms.

Obviously, there is much more to the ceremonial chambers of the Hopi than meets the eye. It is worth mentioning that Hopi kivas are different than other kivas around the southwest. Taos pueblo built their kivas in a sixfold system (for the six directions) and the pueblos near the Rio Grande used a double kiva system. Many public dances that help to tell the story of the Hopi people take place in the plazas of the Hopi, but the ceremonies within the kiva walls are the true enactments of their origin and magic. If you happen to find yourself in Arizona, try to visit the Hopi people, buy their crafts, and listen to their stories. You might come away with a new way of looking at this world, the fourth emergence. HO!

TAKE ME OUT
TO THE OLD BALL GAME

By Leanna K. Potts

One of the favorite pastimes of millions of Americans is watching a ball game. We tend to think of ball games and our fascination with them as a fairly recent fixation. However, ball games have been recorded as early as 1200 BC in the Americas. Throughout Mesoamerica, a game known by the Nahuatl (Aztec) word of *ulama* was played with great fervor. In these games, the losing players were not traded, nor were the coaches fired. In these games, people tended to lose their heads—literally.

Ulama was played by many of the people inhabiting the Mesoamerican region. The best known ballcourts were those of the Aztecs and Mayas. Ulama was a Mesoamerican combination of modern-day football, soccer, basketball, and baseball, all rolled into one game. By the time the Spanish Conquistadors arrived, the games had already reached their height and were on the decline. Shortly after the arrival of the Spaniards and their priests, the games began to disappear. They were banned by the church because of their sacrificial nature, and games were forbidden among the conquered peoples. Ulama almost died out in all but the back reaches of Mesoamerica. However, many of the Spanish scribes and scholars did record some information about the games before their disappearance. Today, anthropologists and archaeologists are discovering that a few villagers still know some of the skills used by their ancestors in playing the game. Combined with the knowledge that is being unearthed and deciphered on the glyphs and in the codices, they are beginning to piece together the true importance of this game by a society that believed they would cease to exist if it were not played.

Ulama was generally played on an I-shaped court surrounded by sloping walls of stone slabs. The rules of the game, the manner in which it was played, the protective clothing that was worn, and the design of the ball court depended on where and by whom the game was played.

The Maya played a game in which the object was to send a rubber ball through the center of a stone ring mounted on the sides of the court. The ball was nearly the same size as the hole. This immediately won the game as it was a nearly impossible feat, especially since the only means of aiming the careening ball was by bouncing it off the hip, shoulder, or knee. Protective gear ranged from a mere leather loin cloth to complete protection such as a *yugo;* a padded shoe for the left foot; arm, leg, loin, and hand wraps; cotton pads for the knees; and a leather pouch worn over the thigh. A yugo was a U-shaped stone belt that was worn over the left hip. It was sometimes elaborately carved with ball game symbols that included toads, jaguars, and death heads. This belt was used to deflect the hard rubber ball back into the opponent's court. Once the ball was brought into play by throwing, it could never again be touched by the hands. To do so resulted in a forfeiture of the game. The ball had to be kept in constant motion. Depending on whether the game was played by the Aztecs or the Mayas, the ball was either played to be kept in the air and aimed to go through one of two hoops on either side of the court, or kept moving low to the ground without ceasing movement or missing a return. The latter required a lot of footwork, necessitating the padded toe shoe which kept the players from breaking their toes. It also required the players to drop to the ground on stone paved flooring in order to propel the ball

with either a hit from the knee, shoulder, or hip. Despite the protective gear, many times players would have to stop to have ball-inflicted hematoma lanced before they could continue play. In some cases, if a ball hit an unprotected area, it could rupture the bladder or break a bone.

The ball itself was of hard rubber extracted from latex and formed into a ball using a wooden or stone-carved two-piece mold.

Teams consisted of one to seven players on each side. The losing team was sacrificed so that their shed blood might ensure the survival of the crops and the people, and in greater terms, the world. Occasionally the game was played to settle political, military, and boundary disputes, but for the most part it was the reenactment of the Sun's passage through the underworld and eventual return to the heavens.

According to the mythology of the Popul Vuh, the creation story of the Quiche Maya, the game originated when two brothers, Hunahpu and Xbalanque, descended into Clubalba, the Mayan underworld. Here they were engaged by the Lords of the Underworld in a ball game. After losing the game to the Lords of the Underworld, they sacrificed each other, returned to life, and rose into the heavens to become the Sun and Moon.

The Aztecs also had a similar belief. They believed the ball represented the Sun, which sank into the underworld where it was devoured by the Earth Monster. Only a blood sacrifice could bring it back.

This game was so culturally and religiously important to these groups that, according to Fray Diego Duran in the *Madrid Codex,* they gambled their homes, their fields, their granaries, and their maguey plants, and sold their children in order to bet. Some even staked themselves and became slaves.

This may be the ending of the twentieth century, but some things never seem to change.

Pai Pai Hut

Baja Mexico: The Pai Pai Tribe

By Bernyce Barlow

Baja is the peninsula of land that extends from Southern California into the lower regions of Mexico, bordered by the Pacific Ocean on one side and the Sea of Cortez on the other. During the era of early exploration and colonization by Spain, Baja was considered a wasteland with little to offer. Later, in 1847, when California secured its grip on Upper California, Baja was included in the deal, but was again rejected due to its inhospitable and desolate character.

The Indian population of Baja was one of the poorest groups in all of Mexico. Other indigenous tribal systems of Mexico rejected the Baja native population as a subgroup and treated them as a lower-caste ethnic bevy. In particular, the Pai Pai Indians (located in the Pacific/Ensenada district) seemed to suffer the most abuse. Their isolation was geographical as well as social. Although the desert was sparse, the Pai Pai lived near an abundant ocean in a region whose winters were mild and whose summers were long. They ingeniously combined both their environments to suit their needs.

Above the seaport town of Ensenada are a number of hot springs and caves. These springs are/were used by the Pai Pai for their healing properties, irrigation, and ceremonial rituals. Water was sacred to all desert cultures, and the Pai Pai were no exception. By the way, these healing springs are accessible to Baja tourists!

The caves scattered throughout the hills of Ensenada were not only used as shelter, but for ceremonies more common to the Southern California Chingichngich cult than the Mezoamerican religious system. This may account in part for the social isolation cast upon the Pai Pai by interior tribes. Within the caves are paintings that depict the visions and dreams of the Pai Pai shamans under the influence of a hallucinogenic tea called *tolche*. Out of respect for the Pai Pai shamans, the location of these caves should remain anonymous because they are still being used today by ancient way practitioners and healers.

The Pai Pai understood the ways of the stark land they inhabited and used local plants as hunting aids, food, and curatives. Most plants had a myriad of applications, such as turkey mullin, a roadside weed found abundantly in Southern California and Northern Baja. Turkey mullin was used as a tea to bring on sweats, soothe the lungs, cure acute diarrhea, and stabilize heart palpitations. The Pai Pai understood that turkey mullin was not a plant that could be used on a long-term basis because of its powerful constituents. They also knew how to use the leaves of this plant to stun and poison fish in order to bring them to the surface for collection.

The Pai Pai were master fishermen who harvested the sea regularly for fish, sea mammals, shellfish, and kelp. Medicines were made from certain ocean life such as sea slugs, and different types of kelp were used to restore and maintain what modern day medicine calls body trace elements. Shells were also collected and used as tools, in ceremony, or as ornaments. The abalone shell was especially used in a variety of practical ways.

When the mission system finally assimilated the Pai Pai, it changed their way of life forever, but their wisdom and spirit has not been lost despite the intrusion. I had the opportunity to spend a day horseback riding into the hills above Ensenada to a

Pai Pai encampment set along the trade route connecting Mission San Diego with Baja. My guides were enchanting, and we spent much of our time talking about coastal and mesa healing plants, as well as Pai Pai history. The Spanish influence was obvious, but the Pai Pai spirit was dominant. I was extremely impressed with their natural ability to ride. They rode their horses like an eagle rides the wind. As I watched them dart in and out of the bush, it reminded me why I love the spirit of the West.

When we arrived on top of the mesa where the huts were located, we were greeted with smiling faces and goodwill. My trail guides retired into one of the huts for lunch, but I ate mine on the edge of the mesa overlooking the Pacific among spring wildflowers. The tortillas and chorizos, fresh fruit, and lemonade were just what I needed after my ride up the mountain. The cheerful spirit of the Pai Pai was the only thing that competed with their cooking!

If I could sum up the spirit of the Pai Pai, I would say it was a spirit of survival. It comes to light in their eyes and smiles. There is a proud look among them, content in who they are and what they know. Is this not true identity? It has been said that the Pai Pai identity was taken away and no longer exists; it was crushed by disease, poverty, and assimilation. With all due respect, that is not what I experienced. I met a group of people who strengthened themselves through spirit, a quiet people whose ways were old and wise. The Pai Pai learned to adapt in order to survive, and just as they adapted to the conditions of the sparse northern Baja coast, they also adapted to the new cultures that eventually surrounded them. Like I said, you can see it in their eyes and in their smiles.

I visit Baja often because of its beauty, the charm of the people, and the colorful cultures that are found there. If I was told I could only visit one part of Baja, I would choose the north coast because it combines the spirit of the land and its people with the sea and the sky, the way of the Pai Pai.

THE DIFFERENCE BETWEEN HIGH AND LOW MAGIC

BY SILVER RAVENWOLF

What is "high" magic? How about "low" magic? Does it matter which one you practice? Is one method better than the other? Is it true that once Wiccans get tired of low magic they leave the faith and become ceremonial magicians so that they can advance their magical practice? (I'll jump the gun on this one: the answer is no.)

As with all buzzwords, interpretation lies within the mind of the author, and the discussion of high and low magic is no exception. Let's begin with the basics, and take it from there. In most magical circles, "high magic" refers to practices associated with ceremonial magicians and some Wiccans (Gardnerians and Alexandrians specifically, but not entirely). High magical practices can incorporate intricate scripts (where deviation is not permitted), specific tools, celestial energies (both positive and negative), or practices associated with other religious theologies such as the Tree of Life from the Kabala; the Lesser Banishing Ritual, LBR, recited in Hebrew, and the Middle Pillar Ritual, also recited in Hebrew; or the Rose Cross, recited in Greek. High magics usually incorporate detailed and intricate methods of achieving a desired end. It is said that the high magic influences we find in Wicca today can be directly attributed to the writings of Aleister Crowley and the influence of the Golden Dawn on Gerald Gardner, though there is still staunch debate in some Wiccan circles on this issue.

Low magic, on the other hand, relies more on the gut instinct of the practitioner, rather than a set methodology of performance, though there are basic techniques available. In low magic we find a more shamanic influence, such as totem animals, drums and rattles, short chants and charms, a heavy dose of folklore, and the use of practical tools for magical purposes, such as raw herbals and household items. Where high magical practices can take from thirty minutes to an hour or more (full ritual) to perform, low magic techniques can be done in less than five minutes. Practices such as drum trancing, however, can last thirty minutes or more, depending on the magical individual.

Wiccans normally employ both high and low magical methods, though usually a particular group or individual will lean more toward one type of practice than the other. Wiccans with high ceremonial flavor will normally produce more rigid rituals where change of basic elements is not an option, and Wiccans using low magical applications tend to be more spontaneous and allow deviation or extended use of creativity in their ritual format. If you visit a Wiccan circle where the group calls the Watchtowers, casts a triple circle (with sword, wand, and athame), uses an athame or sword to open the quarters, calls the quarters starting at the East, and creates magic with pomp and circumstance, you are dealing with ceremonial influences. If you attend a Wiccan circle that calls totem animals, casts a single circle with a visualization technique, opens the quarters by using their hands, begins calling the quarters at the North, and uses as few tools as possible when working magic, you are dealing with shamanic influences. Few Wiccan circles will be strictly ceremonial or absolutely shamanic, though by sticking to one method your circle energies will be purer.

Does one format produce better results than the other? I personally feel that a magical person's rate of success with either system depends on the energy manipulation, desire, confidence, and faith of the individual. For example, Luann may have great success with high magic, but low magical applications elude her. Thomas may be a whiz at any practical magical techniques, but fail miserably time after time with high magic methods. Is there anything wrong with either individual? Absolutely not. Along comes Marni who has been studying magic for over twenty years, and she has no difficulty with either system, but prefers low magic over high, as she has little time to devote to a long ritual working. I found also that one's religious background before he or she entered the Craft has a lot to do with the method (high or low) they will choose to support his or her Wiccan faith.

Is there a difference in energy vibrations between high and low magical applications? Yes, but again, this will rely on personal interpretation. To me, high magic vibrates at a higher, smoother rate, where low magic has a raw power that pulses. Anything using angelic energies, even if you are working a low magic technique, will result in high magical energy flow. Why? Because of the angelic energies. Anything using the energies of the dead, even if you are working high magic techniques, will have the underlying energy flavor of that type of spirit. If you employ drums, the voice of low magic, into a Wiccan ceremonial circle, you will change the flow of energy from smooth to pulsing. Bells, on the other side of the pentacle, bring a higher energy vibration into the circle.

Does any of this really matter? Again, this depends on who is working the magic, and who is talking about it. We can argue points of technique until heck freezes over, but the proof will always be in your successes or your failures. If a ceremonial Wiccan argues that her way is best and all other methods are for the lowly masses, yet she has a habit of extorting money from others, guess what I'm going to think? Likewise, if a shamanic Witch tells me that ceremonial Wicca is for the common-sense impaired, but he just had his car repossessed, his wife left him, and his best friend wants to beat the tar out of him, again, guess what will come to mind? Believe it or not, the mixture of both high and low magics in a circle can work. I've seen this done in hundreds of rituals as my husband and I toured the United States magical community. I can tell you that there is an energy drag when a ritual begins with ceremonial techniques, then switches in the middle to shamanic, then back to ceremonial to close. Is this bad? Not really, and if you are aware of this potential drag when writing a ritual, you can work around it by using bells and drums together, allowing one sound to overcome the other as you move into the energy change.

Most Wiccans will, over the course of time, work with both types of magic, blissfully unaware about the nuances of either technique, where others will feel it necessary to delineate at all times. When I began practicing Wicca, I threw everything into the cauldron not knowing or understanding there was a difference. These days (now that I supposedly know what I'm doing), I prefer low magical operations. They are quick, easy, fulfilling, and successful for me; however, I had to try both systems to give myself the benefit of choosing wisely. I hope you will do the same.

ELEMENTAL INCENSES

BY EDAIN MCCOY

Magical people quickly find themselves on intimate terms with the four elements: earth, water, fire, and air. As basic as the elements are, their associations are vitally important to all our magical and ritual workings because they make up the four-squared foundations on which our successes are constructed. Newcomers and elders alike need to seek out new ways to align with these energies and to keep their associations fresh and at the forefront of the magical consciousness.

One of the easiest ways to accomplish this is to work with incenses that embody the energies of each element, changing each formula when it grows too familiar. Incenses can be ignited in small, heat-resistant bowls and placed at the four cardinal points of our sacred circles, or at the four points of a personal altar when all four need to be present in balance. They can be used individually when a spell or other magical working requires us to attune with one particular element that is related to our goal.

To use homemade incenses you will need to purchase charcoal incense blocks that can be found in occult and metaphysical shops, religious supply stores, or can be ordered from many occult mail order houses. Avoid using the fast-lighting charcoal designed for use in outdoor barbecue grills. These brands contain substances that are not meant to be used in unventilated areas and they can be harmful if inhaled.

Incenses can be made from any dried, non-toxic plant. This includes stems, petals, blades, bark, and roots. Fresh plants can be tied in small bundles and hung up in an arid area of your home to dry. When the plants have dried, measure out a small amount and begin to grind them slowly into a powder, keeping in mind the whole time the precise purpose for which they are being created. This is the beginning of the magical process when you start yourself moving toward your goal by your will power and visualizations. Many powdered herbs are readily available in

culinary shops, and these can also be used, but you should first handle them extensively in order to imbue them with your personal energy.

Make sure the charcoal block is lit and burning evenly before applying any incense. Most of these "blocks" are round, and you can estimate the amount of incense it can easily take by matching it to its diameter. For example, a charcoal block with a ½-inch diameter can take about a level half teaspoon of powdered incense. Incense can be reapplied when at least three-quarters of what was already applied has burned off.

The following recipes can get you started working with elemental incenses. When you feel it's time for a change, take a look at the list of alternate herbs provided to begin experimenting with your own elemental blends. As you will see from this list, several herbs have more than one elemental attribute.

EARTH INCENSE

Earth is usually associated with the direction of north. This element is feminine in nature, and its attributes include stability, fertility, prosperity, grounding, money, planting, home life, the Mother Earth herself, and many types of healing. For the basic earth incense combine the following:

3   parts patchouli

2   parts pine

1   part bistort

1   part vervain

Other earth-related herbs and plants include barley, cedar, corn silk, juniper, magnolia, oak bark, soybeans, and wheat.

WATER INCENSE

Water is usually assigned to the direction of west. This is the element of the natural psychic, one related to pregnancy, birth, rebirth, death, regeneration, divination, purification, psychic endeavors, spirit contact, and past life exploration. Water is the other feminine element. To make the basic water incense try using the following:

3 parts lavender
1 part willow bark
1 part catnip
¼ part valerian

Other water-related herbs and plants include cypress bark, jasmine, kelp, lotus, moss, myrtle, myrrh, rue, sandalwood chips, seaweed, and vanilla.

FIRE INCENSE

Fire is a masculine element, one usually associated with the south in the Northern Hemisphere. Its energies govern the areas of protection, employment, sex magic, the law, exorcism, strength and courage, and profound transformations or change. A basic fire incense recipe contains:

4 parts frankincense
3 parts cinnamon
1 part dried orange peels
¼ part thyme

Other fire-related herbs and plants include allspice, basil, bay, black pepper, clove, cumin, dill, garlic, ginger, nutmeg, onions, and thistle.

AIR INCENSE

Air is the other masculine element and it is usually associated with the east. Areas governed by this element are education, communication, weather magic, general power raising, and music magic. The following combination makes a basic air incense:

4 parts rosemary
2 parts mugwort
1 part chicory
½ part coffee beans

Other air-related herbs and plants include benzoin, elm bark, lavender, parsley, sage, spearmint, and wormwood.

The Magical Diary

By Cerridwen Iris Shea

Grimoire. Book of Shadows. Book of Mirrors. Book of Lights and Shadows. Diary. Journal. Pillow Book. What's a Witch to use when she wants to keep records of what she does? Hopefully, these ideas will give you a beginning point. That way, you can experiment and see which type of record-keeping system works best for you without losing track of your magical workings.

Why Is Record-Keeping So Important?

As a Witch, you are a type of natural scientist. You are learning and re-learning the natural ways in which the Earth moves and the cycles change. You are also integrating that knowledge with modern technology, finding out what works, what doesn't, what the variables are, and why. When a spell works, you want to know the ingredients, as one does with any good recipe. When it doesn't work, you want to be able to retrace every step to find out why, see what you can change, make note of it, and make it work the next time. While memory is a wonderful thing and many people have excellent memories, we live in an age of information overload, and writing one's work down is the best way to ensure it is saved.

Diaries have been used in personal and spiritual record keeping from Japanese pillow books to Samuel Pepys to Virginia Woolf to Anais Nin, one of the most famous diarists of all time. The listing of hopes, fears, and the daily minutiae of life are a way to keep in touch with one's own past and the past of one's society. For inspiration, go to your local library and look up some diaries or diary anthologies. My personal favorite is called *A Book of One's Own,* edited by Thomas Mallon. It's a wonderful tome to dip into when feeling tired or out of sorts.

The biggest thing to remember is that there is no right or wrong way to keep a diary. The only "must" is that each entry must be dated. Diaries are a personal place where you can express yourself without fear. No one under any circumstances has the right to read your diary without your permission. If that means buying a locked box and wearing the key around your neck, do it, and then start rethinking your living situation.

Magical record-keeping differs from general diary keeping in the need to be as precise as possible. As mentioned earlier, there is no right or wrong way to keep a diary. You can write stream of consciousness, portraits, lists, or dialogues with parts of yourself (see *The New Diary* by Tristine Ranier for some wonderful ideas). With magical diary-keeping, however, precision is important. What day is it? What time is it? What phase of the Moon? What ingredients did you use, and how did you mix them in? Did you say the incantation before or after you lit the candle? How did it feel? Did you cast a full ritual circle, or do something simpler? What colors and astrological correspondences did you use? At the end of the "how to" section, leave room for reflection. Sometimes I reflect at the end of the ritual. Sometimes I wait a few hours or even a few days, just to make sure my thoughts and feelings are in order.

If you like extreme organization or follow Ira Progroff's theory in his *Intensive Journal Workshop,* you can do all of this in three-ring binders. You can decide on how to separate your sections, have an index, and cross-reference rituals under headings like love, money, rosemary, bay, water, and the waxing Moon.

I'm sure that if I did it that way, I'd be Organizational Witch of the Year, but I'm not, and that way feels too structured. So I have a couple of different organization setups that I will share with you.

THE DIARY

First and foremost is my diary. This is the depository of my daily life. It is a bound book that I often carry in my purse and scribble in whenever I get the chance. It is full of random thoughts, joy, and, of course, anything that is bugging me at the time. It is my mirror self, my balancing agent, and my best non-human friend apart from my cats. Magically, I also write in my morning and evening devotionals any daily tarot guidance or meditative work that I do. I write

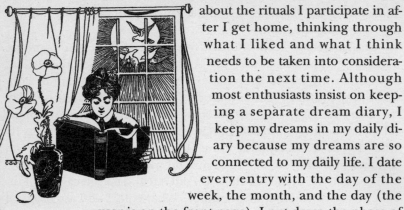

about the rituals I participate in after I get home, thinking through what I liked and what I think needs to be taken into consideration the next time. Although most enthusiasts insist on keeping a separate dream diary, I keep my dreams in my daily diary because my dreams are so connected to my daily life. I date every entry with the day of the week, the month, and the day (the year is on the front page). I put down the phase of the Moon, what astrological sign the Moon is in, and the weather. The weather is a new addition, suggested by Silver RavenWolf, and I found it makes an enormous difference when I go back to look things up. I go through about one blank book every month or two, and I write a book blessing on the front page of each one.

MIRROR BOOK

For several years I kept a Mirror Book where I wrote only about magic. I made passing references to my magical work in my daily diary, but took my Mirror Book to ritual (Circle of Muses, one of my covens, uses journal-writing often in ritual to center and get the creative juices flowing). As I integrated my life and my spirituality and each became indivisible in my daily life, I found that keeping a diary and Mirror Book made me feel fragmented. Since my life was now integrated, those journals needed to be integrated, too.

I tried to integrate my tarot readings, animal oracle and Celtic tree oracle readings into the daily diary as well, and I ran into trouble there. It was difficult to go back and check how things had played out. I like to go back over my reading several months later to see how it worked out. Did I misrepresent something? Was I warned about something and did I take the correct action to prevent pain or mistakes? How could I have interpreted the cards better? It's a good way to use twenty-twenty hindsight to help one's foresight. Keeping a separate book for divination helps me keep track of progress that way. I still often discuss the readings in my daily diary as well as in the reflection section of the readings, so there is overlap.

BOOK OF SHADOWS

As far as my circle work goes, I do keep a Book of Shadows for each group with which I work, and a Book of Shadows for rituals I pull from the online services. I have them in date order, with the most recent ritual at the front. Around every Samhain, I go back and re-read all the rituals in which I've participated for that year, and do an evaluation. I also jot down the various deities we've worked with so that I can thank them in my annual ritual of thanks. These are kept in three-ring binders and stored under my main working altar. At the end of various rituals, I also make sure I write down any extemporaneous changes or inspirations that happened during the course of the ritual. It's helpful in tracking patterns.

What about a grimoire? I keep one of those, too. My grimoire is entirely handwritten in a bound blank book. I put the spells that have been tested, re-tested and tested some more, having a high rate of success. Basically, my grimoire has my "kick ass" spells in it, whether for healing, protection, or hex-breaking. My grimoire contains the experiments that work.

Record-keeping is extremely important. Sometimes the last thing you want to do after an intense ritual is sit there and write about it, but it's important to your continuing progress to know what worked and didn't work so you can find out why. Try different kinds of record keeping. Use loose-leaf, your computer, a bound book, preprinted forms, or make lists. When you find what works for you, you will know it because it will feel right. You will feel more integrated. Remember, you can always change your mind and keep a different set of books. Merry writing!

SOURCES

Mallon, Thomas. *A Book of One's Own.*

Progoff, Ira. *At A Journal Workshop.* New York: Dialogue House Library, 1975.

Rainer, Tristine. *The New Diary.* New York: Jeremy P. Tarcher/Putnam, 1978.

RavenWolf, Silver. *To Stir a Magick Cauldron.* St. Paul: Llewellyn Publications.

MAKE AN INSTANT CIRCLE

BY ESTELLE DANIELS

Sometimes you need a circle but don't have the time, energy, or resources to put one up. With preparation beforehand you can make yourself an instant circle, ready for you at a moment's notice.

What is an instant circle? It is a permanent, yet portable, circle, ready for activation whenever you need it. It is easily carried and stored, yet already charged so all you have to do is set it up and put a minimal amount of energy into it to activate it.

These portable circles are great for traveling. You get to a motel room and want to keep out the noise and energies of other people so you can rest. Once you have locked yourself in for the night, activate your instant circle, and you are able to sleep in sacred space, with a good insulation between you and the rest of the world. Or if you are staying for some time, just leave your circle up, with the understanding people will be in and out, and reinforce it with a jolt of energy each night before you go to sleep. When you are camping it can be put up inside your tent or around your campsite, depending on how weatherproof your materials are.

One place it is NOT recommended is in your car while driving. Even though you might feel more protected, you need to be aware of the other drivers and what is going on around you outside the car. A circle might cut you off from the rest of the traffic, and that can be dangerous while driving. If you stop to take a nap at a rest stop, then a portable circle, put up before your nap and taken down afterwards, is helpful in getting good rest.

To make a portable circle, you start at home, in your own private circle or other sacred space. You select the materials beforehand and prepare them as you want. You can use rocks, or sticks, natural materials either as they are or painted with the appropriate

symbols. You can
use cords woven es-
pecially to contain
the energies of a
circle. You can use
purchased items that
symbolize the ener-
gies you want. Post-
card-sized pictures are
usable, though you
might want to encase
them in plastic.

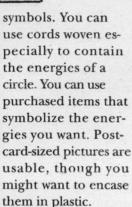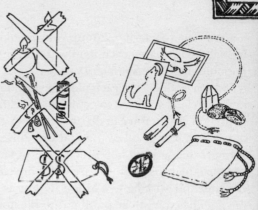

How you construct your circle will determine how many items
you have. My circles are three dimensional, the four directions/el-
ements (east, south, west, north), above, and below. Some people
only use the four elements. Some use the four elements and center (or ether, the fifth element). It's up to you.

I would recommend using items that are fairly common and
inexpensive in themselves, like rocks, sticks, or postcards. The
more elaborate and expensive you get, the more distressed you will
be if one item is misplaced or lost. This will be something you use
while traveling, and sometimes things get lost or misplaced, so stay
away from the expensive one-of-a-kind items. I do NOT recommend candles, incense, or anything that burns. This is for safety;
many motels do not allow open flame in their rooms (outside of
smoking). Items that are perfumed or fancy oils don't work well either. They may clash with the natural smells of the room you are in,
and oils can spill and are really difficult to clean up. Keep it simple
so that it reacts minimally with the environment.

Once you have your items chosen, clean and gather them at
your personal altar. Have a bag or other carrier so they are easy to

grab as you are packing. Put up your regular circle, and your working will be to charge each item with the energies you want in your portable circle. I recommend you have each item distinct enough to tell which is which. Let each piece be distinct for the part it will have in the circle. If you want to paint/inscribe the items, now is the time to do it in circle. You can do one item per circle and working time, or you can charge all of them at one time. It depends upon how strongly charged and how much time and energy you are willing to put into the project. If you are charging each item separately, you can time the working to a Moon sign or aspect that resonates with the energies you will be putting into the item.

Once you have charged your item, you will then put it into your holder, and let it stay there. Once all are done, you might want to try out your portable circle. Take each item and place it in the appropriate quarter, recalling the energies you have placed in each item. Once all are placed, sit quietly and link them with an energy cord, thereby activating the circle. You should have a good circle, not as strong or tangible as one you might do at home, but adequate for shielding and basic protection. It also has the advantage of being quick, quiet, and easily portable. If you use common items, most people will not even be aware there is a circle in place. When you are ready to go, sit quietly again, take up the energy cord linking the items and gather them up and put them back into their carrier. The circle is down.

If you take time and energy to plan ahead, and do a good job of charging each item, you will have a portable circle that will work time and again for years to come. If you did it right the first time, each time you activate your instant circle you are recharging each item. Blessed Be.

Choosing A Magical Name

By Silver RavenWolf

Many beginning Wiccans and Pagans choose a magical name when embarking upon the path of Wiccan mystery. There are several types of names within Craft Tradition. For example, some covens use a "spiritual name" that only the individual to whom the name is given and the High Priest and High Priestess know. Other covens have "circle names," where the name you choose is used only within the confines of the circle. Still other Witches use magical names much like an author uses a pen name—such as mine—where people all over the world, Craft or no, know me by that name.

How does one go about choosing a Craft name, and is it all that necessary? That really depends on you. When embarking on magical study, some Witches feel the need to choose a magical name to assist them in grooming their personality in a positive direction. Practicing the Craft changes you from the inside out, meaning it isn't necessary to wear particular garb, do your hair differently, or wear unusual make-up. The spiritual manifestation begins within. Choosing an appropriate magical name can assist you in your studies by giving you a trigger for positive reinforcement of the changes you wish to make within yourself.

What name, then, would be appropriate for you to choose? Again, this decision lies solely with you and your needs. Because magical people believe that words carry power, choosing a new name should be done with serious thought, as you will manifest through that name its history or properties. For example, I chose Silver (years ago when there were no other Silvers other than the Lone Ranger's horse) because the astral cord that connects our spirit to our bodies is said to be silver. To me, silver meant "that which binds the spirit to the human." I wanted to write spiritual books, so I thought this name would be appropriate.

You may come up with a name immediately, or you might wait months until an appropriate name makes itself known to you. Remember that you take on the history of any name, so choosing the name of a god or goddess may not be the wisest choice, given the personal attributes of these archetypes. The name you choose will pull particular energies toward you that you may not be ready to handle, or indeed, have no desire to deal with at all.

Try to be original in your choice, especially if you plan to do a lot of community service or write for magical publications. For years I was confused because there were at least five public Rhiannons and I never knew which Rhiannon was which. Argh! (I'm not picking on Rhiannons, that's just the name that came to mind.) Naturally, there will probably be some duplication somewhere, but please try to be as original as possible. Imagine my surprise, when at a festival several years ago, I discovered that Raymond Buckland had used the magical name RavenWolf years before! Astounded comes to mind. I thought the name was entirely my own. And yes, I did apologize to Mr. Buckland when I was lucky enough to meet him, as I have always felt that it is personally inappropriate to take another magical person's name as one's own.

Your magical name should "ring true" to you. You should be absolutely comfortable with what you have chosen. If you aren't, keep looking. The right name will come along.

What if you don't see the need for a magical name? Why, that's okay too. Our given names have great power, and if you feel comfortable with Janice, Alexander, or Hope, that's wonderful! What isn't okay is to make fun of another person because they did choose to take a magical name.

Once you've chosen a magical name, how do you incorporate that name into yourself? You might like to begin with a ceremony. You should write the ritual yourself so that the entire process will be tailored to your personal energies, rather than looking for such a ceremony in a book. You may wish to purchase a gift for yourself, such as a necklace, ritual robe, a ring, statue, wall hanging, plaque, or bracelet to signify this step forward in your spiritual training. Designing a personal sigil that incorporates your name is another way to manipulate the energies that you wish to manifest.

What happens if you grow out of your name? This does sometimes happen. In ceremony, lay the old name to rest with honor, and take on the new name. Perhaps you had a magical name, but now you wish to use your given name. There's nothing wrong in that. The only caution I will present is that of popping from one name to another, and then another, and so on, in a short span of time. Yes, we can grow out of our names, or even get tired of them, but choosing too many names actually minimizes the original spiritual significance. So too, if you have used a magical name for many years and are well known in the magical community, it may be difficult, if not impossible, for those who know you to let that name go because you have taken on its symbiotic identity.

Can you use your magical name as your legal name? Yes you can. Consult your nearest Pagan-friendly attorney to find out the expense and legal process required. It used to be that the IRS didn't really care what your name was on your income tax form as long as your social security number remained the same, and you paid your taxes. Now, with the new tax laws this is not so.

Finally, there is a practical reason for using a magical name, especially if you are one of the hundreds of thousands of magical people who are not ready (or willing) to come out of the proverbial closet, yet desire to network with others at festivals, magical shops, on the Internet, or through the mail system. Magical names will protect your identity to a point, but should not be used as a shield to insult or harm others.

I hope that your name gives you as much pleasure, power, and positive change as mine has.

Create points A and B

How to Draw
a Pentagram

By John Michael Greer

S ome of the symbols commonly used in magic are fairly easy to draw accurately. The pentagram, unfortunately, isn't one of them. Trying to draw a pentagram freehand and make it come out evenly can be a difficult proposition. The inner structure of the pentagram, though, makes it possible to approach it in a different way—geometry.

Several different geometrical ways of constructing a pentagram have been circulated in different parts of the magical community; some are very complex, and at least one of them doesn't do the job accurately. The following method is quick, easy to learn, and effective. It looks complicated written out, but with a little practice you'll find that you can do it in a couple of minutes. You'll need a pencil, a ruler, a geometer's compass (the kind you probably used in school, with a little yellow pencil clipped to one side, is fine) and a sheet of paper.

Step One

Draw a circle with the compass, making it as large across as you want the pentagram to be.

Step Two

Draw a horizontal line through the center point of the circle, dividing the circle in half. Mark the two ends of the line, where it touches the edge of the circle, A and B.

Step Three

Draw a line up from the center of the circle to the top. This line has to be at a right angle with the first line, and getting this exact is the tricky part of this method. You can use a drafting square if you have one, or set the compass points a little farther apart than you set them to draw the circle,

Create point C

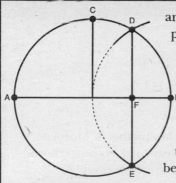

and then, putting the metal point first on point A and then on point B, draw a pair of short arcs that cross each other above the circle's center, as shown. If you draw a line from the center through the point where the two arcs intersect to the edge of the circle, you'll have your right angle. Mark the point where the new line touches the edge of the circle C; this will be the top point of your pentagram.

Create points D, E, and F

Step Four

Set the compass points to exactly the same setting you used to make the circle. Put the metal point on point B, and draw two more short arcs across the side of the circle at D and E, as shown in the diagram. Draw a line from D to E, and mark the point where that line crosses the line from A to B. This is point F.

Step Five

Put the metal point of the compass on point F and change the setting of the points until the pencil point is on point C, up at the top. Draw an arc down from C until it crosses the line from A to B, and mark the point where the arc and the line cross as point G.

Step Six

Put the metal point of the compass on point C at the top and change the setting so that the pencil point is on point G. Draw an arc all the way across the circle from side to side, touching the circle at H and I; these are the left and right points of your pentagram. If you leave the compass at the same setting and put the metal point first at H and then at I, you can mark the two lower points, J and K, by making two short arcs as shown. Finally, with your ruler, connect points C and J, J and I, I and H, H and K, and K and C, and you have your pentagram.

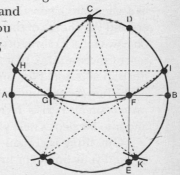

Create points G, H, I, J, and K

261

BLUE MAGIC

BY JIM WEAVER

In a remote village near the Atlas Mountains of Morocco, a simple adobe home stands on a dusty road. Its only colorful detail is the front door, which is painted a vivid royal blue.

In a small town in southern Spain, several cottages are accented with window shutters painted in such a heavenly blue that they rival the color of the Spanish sky.

To the casual observer the scenes described above are nothing more than charming sights you may encounter while traveling abroad. Those who are familiar with folk magic, however, will realize that the blue trim used on these dwellings isn't just there for decoration. Instead, they know that in certain parts of the world the use of blue on the exterior of a structure has a deep mystical significance.

Welcome to the world of blue magic. For centuries, many of the world's oldest cultures have used the color blue as a simple but powerful magical tool to protect homes and people against evil spirits and negative magic of all kinds.

As is the case with many magical beliefs, exactly when and where blue was first used for protection against evil may never be known for sure. My personal theory is that the belief in using blue as a safeguard against curses and hostile energy probably began around the shores of the eastern Mediterranean. In this region, blue was most likely associated with the aquamarine life-giving waters of the sea. Also, blue served as a reminder of the clear skies the region is noted for, and thus, its link to the heavens. Mysteriously, however, a similar belief in blue being used as a color of protection also exists in certain areas of the American Southwest and into Mexico as well, proving how widespread this belief is.

One thing is certain—using blue in all its soothing shades around your home, or in jewelry, is a time-honored method of protecting yourself against any negative energy that may come your way.

Naturally, for many of us it isn't practical to paint our doors or the trim around our windows blue. No problem! There are other easy ways to bring this peaceful hue into our lives with the same magical benefits. Here are a few ideas to get you started.

Wear blue turquoise. In Greece and Turkey, for example, wearing small charms or pendants set with a blue turquoise bead or stone is thought to repel bad luck, including the dreaded evil eye. Any turquoise jewelry will do, but it must be blue turquoise. According to personal taste, it may be set in either gold or silver. If you wish to make your own charm or necklace, you may even use blue beads made of glass or plastic. They will have the same magical effect. Remember, it's the brightness of the blue that matters.

The blue gazing globe, which has been used as a focal point in gardens for years, also lends itself beautifully to blue magic. It's interesting to note that the original purpose of a gazing globe was magical. Their reflective surfaces were thought to attract friendly garden spirits, while at the same time deflecting any negative energy directed at a home by passers-by. Recently, I've begun to see miniature blue gazing globes that are small enough to be used indoors, perhaps in front of a window if you wish.

Don't forget that blue flowers in the garden are highly prized by gardeners, and can help surround your home with a protective curtain during the warmer months.

Try blue flowers such as violas, delphinium, lobelia, and monkshood. You can continue your blue garden right up to hard frost with blue asters and morning glory vines.

I'm sure that you can think of other ways to bring blue magic into your life. Remember, sometimes having the blues isn't such a bad thing after all.

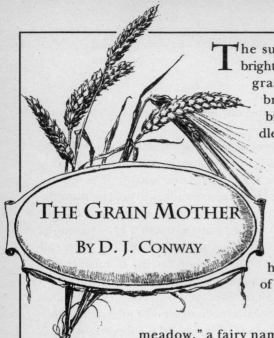

THE GRAIN MOTHER

BY D. J. CONWAY

The summer Sun was very bright and hot. It turned the grass in the meadow brown and dry. All the birds and animals huddled in the shade under the trees so they could be cool in the heat of late summer. Deep under the roots of the giant oak in the shady forest, a group of fairies sat in their home, drinking glasses of cool flower nectar.

"It will soon be time for us to go to the meadow," a fairy named Lilac said as she fanned herself with an oak leaf. "It seems as if we have been harvesting food forever."

"The squirrel says winter will soon come, and we will need the food to eat then." Little Meadow-Grass sighed and looked around at the baskets of grass seeds, dried mushrooms, acorns, and sweet-smelling flower petals that filled the shelves around all the rooms. "Surely this will be enough food for us."

"What is winter?" asked Rose, as she finished making a hat of leaves and moss to keep off the Sun. "We have never seen winter."

"The squirrel says winter is very, very cold." Daffodil piled the last of their empty baskets near the door. "He and the birds say the wind blows, it rains, and then it snows."

"I don't think I will like snow." Dandelion put an apron on over her white dress. "I asked the Great Oak today about snow, and it told me that snow is wetter and colder than anything we have ever seen."

"Then I don't think I will like snow, either." Elder Blossom finished weaving her big grass-stem basket and set it aside.

"The fairies who live under the big maple tree near the pond told me there will be a special celebration tonight when the harvest is finished," Lilac said. "They said the Grain Mother will be there."

All the fairies looked in surprise at Lilac, who shrugged and shook her head.

"When I asked them who the Grain Mother was, they laughed at me," she said. "I was embarrassed that I didn't know."

"We don't know either," the other fairies answered. "Will the others let us go to the celebration if we don't know who the Grain Mother is?"

Lilac shrugged again. "I don't know," she answered.

There was a knock on the door to their underground home.

"Open up, fairies," called a voice. "It's time to go harvesting."

Rose opened the door, and the little gnome Brown Knobby hurried inside. He took off his brown hat and smiled at the fairies. The sleeves of his brown shirt were rolled up above his elbows. Several grass-woven bags were thrown over his shoulder. One of the bags held his fiddle.

"Brown Knobby, who is the Grain Mother?" Daffodil asked, as she poured the gnome a glass of flower nectar.

"The Grain Mother is just another face of the Great Mother," the gnome answered, as he looked at the fairies with round dark eyes. "When the Mother appears as the Grain Mother, the humans sometimes called Her Demeter or Ceres. She blesses the grain and all the food that is harvested for the winter." His eyes twinkled. "Maybe I shouldn't let you go to the celebration if you don't know about the Grain Mother."

"Don't tease us, Brown Knobby!" Little Dandelion looked as if she were going to cry. "We're only new fairies. We are still learning, you know."

The gnome smiled and bowed to the fairies "You can come with me," he said, his dark eyes twinkling. "I will introduce you to the Grain Mother when She comes to the harvest festival." He smiled wider, and then said, "The Sun King will be there, too."

The fairies gathered up their baskets and bags and a picnic lunch. Then they all hurried out toward the meadow with Brown Knobby. Other fairies, gnomes, elves, and brownies were already filling their pouches and bags with the last of the grass seeds.

"Look! There is the Queen of the fairies, and the King!" Rose pointed across the meadow. A regal looking woman, with her long

hair braided back, was helping with the harvesting. Beside her worked a handsome man with dark hair, his sleeves rolled up like Brown Knobby's.

"Everyone helps at the harvest," the gnome said. "Everyone must gather food for winter."

The gnome and the fairies began to fill their baskets with grass seeds. They gathered the fallen acorns and the mushrooms that grew at the edges of the forest. Finally, the Sun went down, and a round Moon came sliding up the sky.

"It's cooler now," said Elder Blossom as they stacked all their filled baskets and bags together. "Look at the Moon. Isn't she beautiful tonight?"

The gnome and the fairies went to the edge of a stream and washed their hands and faces. Brown Knobby brought out the big picnic basket and a jug of apple cider. Rose and Dandelion spread a blanket on the grass near a tree, and they all sat down to eat.

"Listen!" said Brown Knobby. "She is coming! The Grain Mother is coming!"

The fairies listened. Everyone in the meadow was quiet. Lilac saw several deer silently step out of the trees and wait along the edge of the meadow. A white owl settled on a limb above their heads, and a pair of squirrels dashed down a tree trunk to sit beside the fairies.

"I don't hear anything," Lilac said, looking around.

"Listen to the breeze," answered the gnome. "You can hear the footsteps of the Grain Mother."

The fairies listened very carefully and heard the sound of someone walking through dry grass. Swish, swish, went the sound. They watched as the fairy King and Queen stood up and faced the far end of the meadow.

A tall woman stepped out of the forest and walked out into the meadow. She wore a gold and green dress. Her bright yellow hair was braided around Her head, and She was smiling.

"Is that the Grain Mother?" Elder Blossom's little mouth made an 'O' of delight, as she looked at the beautiful lady. "Oh, look! The Sun King is coming along behind Her, and His arms are full of ripe grapes and fruit."

"And there is the Maiden and the Old Wise One." Rose clasped her hands together in joy. "Oh, it's so wonderful, Brown Knobby! And listen. Even the trees and wind are singing to Her."

The fairies all looked up at the great trees of the forest and heard the wind whispering through the branches. The rustle of the leaves and movement of the tree limbs made a special song. The white owl hooted once, spread its mighty wings, and flew to meet the Grain Mother. The golden-haired Mother raised her arm, and the owl settled gently on it.

"Greetings, my children." The Grain Mother's voice carried like music on the little night breeze. "I am so glad you remembered to come and celebrate the harvest with me."

Everyone around the meadow bowed to the Lady as She walked along, blessing each of them. When She came to the little fairies, She stopped and touched each one of them on the head with Her hand.

"Welcome, little ones. I am so happy to see new children at My festivals. Are you all happy?"

"Yes, Lady," they all said together as they looked up into Her beautiful eyes.

The Grain Mother moved on to a fallen tree, where the Maiden spread a green cloak for Her to sit upon.

"Her eyes were blue as the hot summer sky," Lilac said.

"Yes, but they were also the blue of the secret, shady forest pond, where the turtles and fish live," Rose answered.

The little fairies watched in fascination as the Sun King squeezed the juice from the grapes and fruit into a big cauldron that the Old Wise One set near the Grain Mother.

"Now we will all have even more fun," said Brown Knobby as he took his fiddle out of one of his bags and began to tune it. "Tonight we will dance in honor of the Lady and the Sun King."

Other fiddles and bagpipes and flutes sounded all around the clearing, making beautiful music. Soon everyone there, even the new little fairies, were dancing and laughing to the music. The Sun King and the Grain Mother danced together, while the Old Wise One took a ladle and filled all the cups and glasses with the juice.

Once the Maiden came to Brown Knobby and made him put down his fiddle to dance with Her. Brown Knobby's cheeks turned pink with surprise and happiness. He bowed to the Maiden, and they whirled out onto the meadow in a spinning dance.

"Now I see," said Dandelion when she and her sisters stopped dancing for a while to rest. "Harvest isn't all work. It is also a celebration that we have food for the coming cold times. It is all very wonderful."

The fairies watched the dancers and the fireflies for a time, before they fell asleep on the blankets, tired and happy. When Brown Knobby woke them to take them home, he was humming a dance tune. And he hummed it all the way back to the great oak and the fairies' little home.

SUN LORD

BY CHRISTIE M. WRIGHT

Sun Lord.

I laugh from joy to see your shining orb ride the blue skies of day!
Your golden light illuminates all things;
    nothing can hide from the light of your truth.
You blaze! You shine!
Each new day, we are greeted by your golden smile.
In all your glory,
    you ride across the burning blue sky in your blazing chariot,
    never deviating from your course.
All who see you riding the oceans of sky are filled with bliss.
They see your laughing eyes,
    hear your infectious laughter and cannot help but smile.
Small children clap their hands in delight as they wake to see
    your chariot peaking over the windowsill.

Your throne.

Golden smiles of children.
Golden obsidians washed in sunbeams of purest joy.
Softest drapery,
    woven from the whitest clouds and purest rainbows.
Sister Eagle's feathers adorn your Sun Scepter,
    dipped in Warmth and Light.

You, who are protector of all that is free:
    light the road of my taking,
    and banish the black shadows from my path.
    Fill my life with light and love,
    and let your beams of
    truth shine through
    those who would seek to
    deceive me.

Protector of Freedom.
Golden Father.
Sun Lord.

Goddess Tales from Wailea, Maui

By Bernyce Barlow

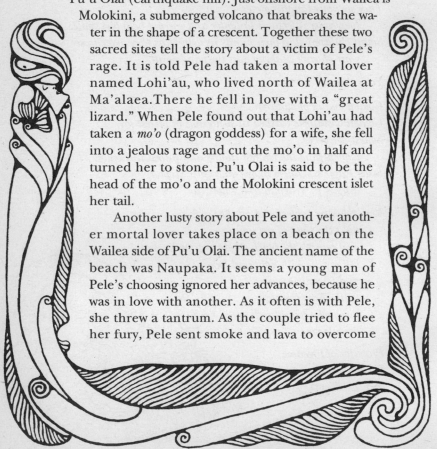

One of my favorite things to do when I visit Hawaii is to explore the legends and sacred sites of the goddesses of the islands. Each island has individual *meles* (chants) that tell of the times when the goddesses intermingled with mortals. Three tales come to mind from the island of Maui, an enchanting paradise full of color and lore. The fiery goddess of the volcanoes, Pele, used to call Maui her home when she lived in the House of the Sun, Haleakala. It is during this time our first story originated.

On the southern coast of Maui there is a town called Wailea. Near Wailea there is a cinder cone emerging from the beach called Pu'u Olai (earthquake hill). Just offshore from Wailea is Molokini, a submerged volcano that breaks the water in the shape of a crescent. Together these two sacred sites tell the story about a victim of Pele's rage. It is told Pele had taken a mortal lover named Lohi'au, who lived north of Wailea at Ma'alaea. There he fell in love with a "great lizard." When Pele found out that Lohi'au had taken a *mo'o* (dragon goddess) for a wife, she fell into a jealous rage and cut the mo'o in half and turned her to stone. Pu'u Olai is said to be the head of the mo'o and the Molokini crescent islet her tail.

Another lusty story about Pele and yet another mortal lover takes place on a beach on the Wailea side of Pu'u Olai. The ancient name of the beach was Naupaka. It seems a young man of Pele's choosing ignored her advances, because he was in love with another. As it often is with Pele, she threw a tantrum. As the couple tried to flee her fury, Pele sent smoke and lava to overcome them but, guided by a star, they made it safely to a canoe and escaped. When the lava merged with the sea it created a huge explosion that broke loose one point of the guiding star. When the point broke off it fell into the sea, then came to shore on a set of gentle waves. The star point merged with the island to become a bush with flowers shaped like small white stars with one point missing. The flower is also called naupaka. Occasionally, a naupaka is found with all its points intact. This is considered a very lucky omen by islanders.

Not all the goddesses of Maui were so temperamental. Lea, the goddess of canoes, was a gentle spirit who lovingly protected the canoe makers and their families. Meles sing that Lea could turn herself into a native bird called the elepiao. As an elepiao, Lea would choose logs worthy of a canoe. When she walked the length of a log without stopping, it meant the log was fine craft material, but if elepaio stopped to peck insects along the way, the log would be weak and rotten from within.

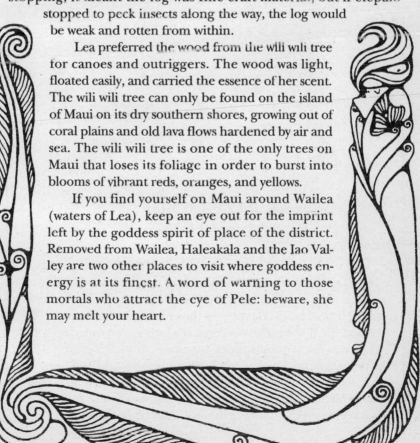

Lea preferred the wood from the wili wili tree for canoes and outriggers. The wood was light, floated easily, and carried the essence of her scent. The wili wili tree can only be found on the island of Maui on its dry southern shores, growing out of coral plains and old lava flows hardened by air and sea. The wili wili tree is one of the only trees on Maui that loses its foliage in order to burst into blooms of vibrant reds, oranges, and yellows.

If you find yourself on Maui around Wailea (waters of Lea), keep an eye out for the imprint left by the goddess spirit of place of the district. Removed from Wailea, Haleakala and the Iao Valley are two other places to visit where goddess energy is at its finest. A word of warning to those mortals who attract the eye of Pele: beware, she may melt your heart.

Crazy Horse:
The Mystic Warrior

By Marguerite Elsbeth

An Oglala/Brule Sioux Indian boy, named Curly because of his wavy hair, was born around 1842 in the Pa'ha Sap'a, or Black Hills, of South Dakota. As the child grew, his father could see that the boy was chosen for sacred things. So one day Curly went on a vision quest to seek his *wakan,* his spirit power. This he did at a time when the Lakota people were cold and hungry, their lodges old and torn; and it was too dangerous to hunt buffalo so far away from camp in the deep-snow winter. They needed a very great man to save them. Could he be the one?

As Curly sat in prayer to the Great Spirit, he saw his horse break free of its hobble. He watched as the animal ran in a zigzag pattern, floating through dazzling light, turning rainbow colors. Soon Curly saw that the horse bore a ghost rider on its back, a phantom warrior who wore a pebble behind one ear, a lightning bolt across his face, and a single hawk feather in his hair.

From this time forward, Curly became Tashunka Witco, or Crazy Horse, the great mystic warrior-chief of the Lakota Sioux. Fasting made him wiry and lean. He fasted so that the children would have more food, as well as to increase his *wakan*. Unlike other Indian war chiefs, Crazy Horse never sat for a photo. Some say he thought the camera would steal his wakan, because other chiefs had been photographed and lost their fighting spirit.

Crazy Horse always remained true to his vision. He wore a sacred medicine bag over his heart, and carried a pebble behind his ear to make him bulletproof. Only one hawk feather graced his hair instead of the elaborate, eagle-feathered war bonnet that was his due. Protective hailstone medicine paint, a design meant to confuse the evil spirits, covered his body. In time, his wakan became so strong that bullets melted in the air around him. Sometimes his wakan showed itself, shimmering about him like an aura as he rode fiercely into battle.

Crazy Horse never signed a treaty and never took a drink of alcohol. He led the Lakota people proudly through many battles, always guided by his spirit power. The Battle of Little Big Horn, where General Custer made his last stand, was Crazy Horse's most famous fight. The Battle of Wolf Mountain was his last. Throughout his days as a warrior-chief and mystic, Crazy Horse was immune to bullets as long as he followed his vision. He was in custody and on foot when he was killed on September 5, 1877, by an enemy soldier's bayonet.

Taoist Magic

By deTraci Regula

I n China there are rumors of odd beings inhabiting remote high mountains, far from the hustle and bustle of
modern Shanghai or Beijing, up where the air is pure and
herbs are abundant. The beings are said to be immortals,
living on little more than dew or the occasional mushroom
of longevity. Scarcely part of the earth, they can appear and
disappear at will, transform themselves into animal shapes
(cranes are a favorite) and generally content themselves
with the company of spirits rather than humans. Tai chi
and qi gong assist them in extending their lives through the
harnessing of chi, the power of life.

As in many world religions, there are two sides of Taoism: one, a high and pure spiritual philosophy filled with its
own brand of enchantment, and the more common, popular
Taoism, filled with paper charms, magical chants, clouds of
incense, and busy, well-paid clergy. Where one ends and the
other begins, and which is preferable, is very subjective.

Throughout Asia, the written word has been held to be particularly sacred, and even in the West we come across the occasional charm written in ink that is meant to be washed off and drunk by a patient, or carried on the body for one purpose or another. In Taoist magic, this reverence for the mystic powers of the word has evolved into alternate languages, where the usual rules of Chinese calligraphy are thrown aside in favor of flowing water or cloud-like scripts that can only be read by initiates. Sometimes these special characters are integrated into a painting of a Chinese landscape so cleverly that these words of power will not even be visible to the average viewer, but to the Taoist magician, these paintings may speak volumes. Even sculptures may take on the form of magic words, lost on most collectors. Oddly pierced objects deserve special attention. If, when you hold one of these objects up to the light, you can see small openings, try to figure out which constellation they may represent. The Big Dipper is a common one, believed to possess special power, but others may also be represented and are in fact talismans of the celestial powers.

With the popularity of feng shui, the art of placing dwellings and furniture to maximize good fortune, or to amend places that are not so favorably located, other Chinese mystical practices are spreading as well. Some shops catering to western feng shui practitioners will also carry the popular new year charms. The paper charms usually come in sets of five, all on different colored paper. These are derived from a five-based system, referring to the Chinese five directions and five elements. Western Pagans familiar with the five-pointed pentagram will have little trouble adapting to the Chinese point(s) of view on this subject.

A popular Taoist and feng shui charm is a small mirror surrounded by the eight trigrams, the arrangement of three broken and unbroken lines that are the building blocks of the Hexagrams of the I Ching. These mirrors are believed to reflect away misfortune and repel evil or negative spirits. Do you have trouble with your neighbors? Hang one of these in the direction of their houses.

One of the best known manifestations of popular Taoism is the reverence paid to the eight immortals. While the true number of immortals is limitless, these eight are practically patron saints in the popular imagination. They are believed to have once been humans who learned the secrets of immortality from other immortals or from the gods and goddesses themselves. A diverse group, these spirits came from a wide variety of backgrounds. Han Zhong I was a general; Cao Guo Jui was the nephew of an empress; Lan Cai He was an androgynous lover of nature and flowers; He Xian Gu was a mere shopkeeper's daughter; Lu Dong Bin Was a scholar; and Zhang Guo Lao a recluse. Han Xiang Zi, a musician, obtained his immortality directly from Xi Wang Mu, the goddess of the western region of paradise. The crippled Li Tie Guai was a compounder of medicines who mastered the art of astral projection. Unfortunately, his student thought he was dead during one journey, and cremated him. Li Tie Guai was forced to reanimate the body of a deceased beggar, and take on the new, but damaged, physical form.

Taoist healing treatments often border on the magical, at least to Western eyes. Chi gong is a method of circulating qi, the Chinese term for both air and spiritual energy, through the body using a series of exercises. Tui na, or pointing therapy, is a lesser-known healing art that consists of directing energy at specific points on the body, employing the same meridians used in acupuncture.

The highest magic of Taoism pays little attention to the manifestations of folk belief. Union with the infinite is the goal, to attain the state of *wu-wei,* "without effort," emerging naturally with the tides of the universe, at one with them. The Tao that can be spoken is not the Tao. Sometimes the vision clears and for a moment, the great flow that is Tao can be glimpsed in the skittering of clouds across the Moon or in the swirling of turbulent water, or in our own souls at a moment of peace and oneness with the universe.

THE MAGICAL JOB INTERVIEW

BY DENISE DUMARS

Preparing for a job interview is an exciting, scary, and mind-numbingly complex ordeal. Just about anyone could use a little help getting ready. Whether you get a serious case of pre-job interview jitters, or if you just want to have a bit of an edge on the competition when you get in there, read on. The following ritual can be performed the night before your job interview (for morning interviews) or the morning of your interview if it is in the afternoon.

The ritual begins before the interview is even set up. If you have a choice, schedule your interview for a Thursday. Thursday is ruled by Jupiter, the planet generally associated with success in business or any money-making opportunity.

Next, plan the outfit you will wear for your interview. One of the colors of Jupiter should be found within the clothing you wear. The jacket of my "interview suit" is royal purple with black piping and gold buttons. A ring with an amethyst (also my birthstone) set in gold completed the outfit. However, if you are interviewing for a conservative company or line of work (such as banking) it is best to avoid Jupiter's royal purple and instead count on the navy blue suit. Men can, of course, wear a tie that includes some of the other colors of Jupiter: royal blue, turquoise, and any shade of purple. Women can wear lapis lazuli (a Jupiter stone that looks wonderful with navy) or turquoise jewelry. Any metal worn (watch, rings, modest earrings, etc.) should be gold or goldtone.

Now you know you will look fabulous. What next?

Gather together your magical equipment. Any ritual gear you normally work with can be present. You should feel comfortable and adapt the ritual to the tradition that you follow. Even if you don't belong to an earth religion or follow a magical tradition you can customize this ritual to your belief system.

The basic ingredients for the ritual are: candles, incense, oils, and a mirror. You can also add an image of Kwan Yin, Juno, Jupiter, or, if you're working the ritual on a Thursday or if you have obtained a Thursday interview, Thor.

You will need two green, royal blue, or purple candles. If you need the job right now, use green. Green is not for long-term monetary gain, but for fast cash when needed. Otherwise use royal blue or purple. Incense can be lavender, sage, road opener (*abre camino*), or a combination. Oils can be botanical, such as lavender and carnation, or magical, such as success and John the Conqueror. The mirror should sit on your altar or table where you can gaze into it, preferably situated between the two candles.

Now you are ready. Take a few deep breaths. Cast your magical circle if that is your tradition. Call upon the blessings of Kwan Yin (no Chinese businessperson would be without the beneficent presence of Kwan Yin in the office or shop), Jupiter, Juno, and Thor if applicable. Place oil on your fingertips and hands and anoint the candles with the oil, top to bottom, while meditating on the idea of success. Now light the candles and the incense. Rub your hands together to distribute the oil.

As the smoke from the incense wafts over you, close your eyes and ask your inner voice if you really want the job you are interviewing for. If the answer is a definite yes, continue the ritual.

Now open your eyes. Position your-self so that you are able to gaze at your-self in the mirror. Really see yourself as the best person for the job. See all of your good characteristics—those that make you a valuable employee. Speak them aloud if you are comfortable do-ing so. For example, you might say, "I am a highly motivated, highly skilled in-dividual. I know I can be an outstand-ing employee." Use words to describe yourself such as well educated, caring, efficient, and capable—whatever words best describe the qualities you have to offer the employer. Now, still gazing

into the mirror, see yourself as the person the employer wants to hire. See yourself through the interviewer's eyes. Imagine that the person you are looking at is the best qualified person for the job, the person who would fit perfectly within the organization, a person of outstanding qualities and integrity.

By looking at yourself through the interviewer's eyes you will get a perspective on yourself that you did not have before. The person you see in the mirror is the person the interviewer will want to hire. Now close your eyes again, take a few more deep breaths, breathing in through the nose and letting out all the air through your mouth. As you do so, relax, and send the positive energy you have summoned out into the universe. Thank the powers you have called upon, open the circle, and you are done.

Before dressing for the interview itself, women can apply a drop of lavender or carnation oil wherever she might wear per-fume. If you buy cologne, make sure the fragrance is natural, not synthetic. Men can wear a drop of heliotrope oil, which has a very light scent that is not at all flowery. The lady at my local botanica recommends rubbing a drop of John the Conqueror oil into your hands before you go to the interview. If you do this, make sure you shake hands with your interviewer!

Now you're ready. If the job you are interviewing for is the one you are meant to have, you will get it. Good luck!

A Spell for Acing
Your Job Interview

By Edain McCoy

Nothing feels less magical than having to work for a living, but the fact is that most of us have to go out and labor for our sustenance. This means that at some point we must endure the humiliation of the infamous job interview, a sadistic compulsion on the part of employers intended to reduce us to sniveling doormats of subservience before they grudgingly allow us to work for them.

With all the stiff competition for employment, a little magic can help you project your best image. For this spell you will need one green candle, one orange one, and one yellow or gold one. You will also need some ground or whole cloves and a small tiger's eye stone. Your tiger's eye will become charged in this spell to turn its most beneficial energies to you and will become a talisman to draw wealth to you while allowing you to project your best image. It may even give you the confidence you need to outshine the competition.

On your altar or other work area set up the three candles in some semblance of a small circle, placing the green candle nearest you. Spend a moment centering yourself and concentrating your thoughts on your goal. When you are ready to begin, start lighting the candles, starting with the green one and moving clockwise around the circle.

As you light the green candle, focus on its energies of prosperity and abundance, qualities you want drawn to you through the job you hope to secure. Make a statement to affirm this such as:

Fire of green, abundance bright, drawing prosperity by your light.

As you light the orange candle focus on its qualities of attraction, particularly between forces that are already in sympathy with one another. Make a statement such as:

Simpatico permeates the meeting place, making me seem an interesting face.

As you light the yellow or gold candle, think of its qualities of projecting energy and competence, allowing you to show your best side. As you do this affirm your action with a statement such as:

From deep within my positives come through, debits hold back while credits shine true.

Place the tiger's eye in the center of the candles and spend several minutes sensing the energy of the candles filling the stone, programming it to your will. Take the cloves, an herb with energies corresponding to wealth and employment, and make a clockwise circle around the candles. Visualize this as a circle containing all the energies on your altar, helping to filter them into the tiger's eye.

Spend some more time focusing on your goal. This is a good time to practice interview scenarios or to focus your energies on a brief chant such as:

Stone of light, earth and fire, send the image that says, "please hire."

Extinguish the candles when you feel ready, or leave them sit so that you can repeat the spell on another night to give it added strength. When you are done, carry the tiger's eye in your right pocket, on the projective side of your body, during job interviews.

INTEGRATING WORK AND MAGICAL LIFE

BY CERRIDWEN IRIS SHEA

You have all these really neat tools. There are candles in every corner of the house, incense burning all the time. You're initiated or at least dedicated. You read the books, you dutifully mark your calendar to the various holidays and festivals you feel are important to you. Now what?

Now comes the time to make it real. A magical life is lived in each moment. It isn't done once a week, or on the New Moon, or on the holidays. It's a day-by-day, moment-by-moment commitment.

How to do that? It's tough enough for those practicing a mainstream religion to integrate it into their daily lives. How are we supposed to do it?

Get ready. It takes work. It also takes time. It doesn't happen quickly. You can make the decision to live a magical life, but to actually integrate will take a number of years. Fortunately, the time spent during those years will be informative, and hopefully fun, and suddenly it will be second nature.

I hope you already have an altar space set up. The best altars are in a space where they can be left out and don't have to be taken apart and packed away in between workings. If it's not, consider buying a small trunk or decorative box, or even a hatbox, and building the altar in that. When you open it, your altar is set up. If you want to hide it, you close the lid, toss a scarf or place a book on it, and no one knows what's in there.

On a monthly basis, honor the changes in the Moon cycles. The New Moon, the Full Moon, and the dark of the Moon. If you are unable to perform a ritual, then at least light a candle and some incense to honor the time. After a year or two, you will be able to feel how the cycle of the Moon changes (separate from seeing it in the sky), and can be pleasantly surprised how accurate your body calendar is in relation to it.

On a daily basis, there are all kinds of things you can do. If you try to change everything in your life all at once, it can overwhelm and discourage you. Just do one or two things reguarly until they become second nature, and then start adding more.

UPON AWAKENING: Greet the day. It can be as elaborate as a daily devotional, or as simple as lighting the candle on your altar.

SHOWERING: I bought a little spice rack shelf and fastened it to the wall in the bathroom. I have a small votive candle, some incense, and some other watery, magical, decorative items on it. I always light the candle and some incense when I shower, or even if I'm only in the bathroom to put on my makeup. If I'm running late, I combine the daily greeting with the shower, and use it as sacred time to plan the best way to live my day. I find that having the candle burning while I put on my makeup means I'm less critical of myself, and the makeup tends to go on better.

WHILE YOU'RE GETTING DRESSED: Instead of watching or listening to the news, put on some music that will set you in a mood where you feel you can achieve anything.

ON YOUR WAY TO WORK: Read the newspapers or listen to the news if you like, but try not to get pulled into all the terrible things that are happening in the world. Think about what actions you as an individual can take to make a difference: vote, go on jury duty, write a letter to the editor, donate some time to a cause important to you, make a phone call, sign a petition. Make sure that the last section you read contains the comics.

Don't be afraid to use your protective shields when you commute, but also remain aware of what is going on around you. There is just as likely to be something good happening as something bad. Be pleasant but firm with people who annoy you. The keyword is "balance," and self-confidence is one of the traits that a magical life requires and causes to blossom.

AT WORK: This one can be a bit tricky, can't it? I am lucky. Where I work now, on a Broadway show, I have a little altar on a shelf in the dressing room. The actresses I dress love it—it makes them happy and it makes me happy. Almost everyone knows who I am and what I do—there is no reason for me to be in the broom closet. If someone asks me a specific question, I answer it. I'm not out to convert anyone.

I didn't have dressing room space in the show I worked off Broadway prior to this one, so I used a corner of my shelf space to put down a cloth, a candle, a few crystals, and some pretty objects. It was called "The Quiet Space" and everyone working on the show would come to it when they needed renewal.

When I worked in an office, even as a temp, I had a portable altar that I would take with me, wherever I worked. Along with my own coffee mug (who wants to cause more pollution by using styrofoam cups?), I carried with me a small square of blue velvet. On the velvet, I placed an oversized clam shell. Inside the clam shell I set a scented tea light (air and fire), a small pine cone, and several crystals. I did not light the candle, but I liked having it there. No one ever challenged me (and I temped at over a hundred corporations over the years, all across the country). I often received comments about how lovely the setup was! It was something wonderfiul to have—a place of retreat on a busy desk. No matter how stressful things got, I could always look over at my mini-altar, take a few deep breaths, and come back to center.

If you work in a place where you don't have a desk, but you do have a locker, consider using part of a shelf for your altar, or fasten a box to the back or side of the locker and put a few meaningful objects into it.

Be as pleasant and firm with your colleagues as possible. We've all worked for psycho-bosses. They only have as much power over you as you allow them. Yes, they can control your working conditions, but they cannot control you. Be pleasant, reliable, and do your job well. Make sure you retain a life outside of your job. If your job is your life, your boss will have more control over you.

If the situation at work gets abusive, start keeping a log of every incident. Go to the person who is bothering you and gently but firmly let it be known that this is not acceptable and it must stop. If that doesn't work, go to the head of the department. File a complaint with the appropriate city or federal agency. Tell a friend outside of the work environment so that a shamed silence cannot be used against you later.

If the situation escalates, get out of it. The economy is improving. Look for another job. With luck, there will be an overlap. Remove yourself from a dangerous situation.

HOME: Take a look around your home and see what you can do to make it reflect your magical self. It doesn't have to be an oogie-boogie cliché. You don't have to paint your walls black and draw silver pentagrams and put a neon sign over your door saying "House of Witches." Use fabrics and notions and objects that make you happy to create an environment that makes you feel good whenever you walk through the door. My favorite items were thrift store finds, gifts, or sale items. My home is a jumble of eras and textures that makes me happy. The minute I walk through the door, I feel better. No matter how frustrating my day was, I'm now home.

THE PEOPLE AROUND YOU: This can be a tough one, and you may not like what I have to say about some of it. My spirituality is an integral part of who I am, and I have no intention of denying it. I also don't force people to listen to me spout off about it.

Those who do not accept my spirituality tend to drift away. I can work cordially with almost anyone—we are all professionals, and can maintain professional demeanor. The people I choose to have in my life, such as friends or lovers, don't just deal with my spirituality, they accept it.

Does this mean I only hang out with other Pagans? Not at all. I have friends involved in all types of religions. I am invited to plenty of church-related events. Mutual respect works every time.

Now for the part many of you may hate: If you are not around people who tolerate and respect you, remove them from your life. As magical people, we cannot stay in unhealthy relationships. You must change your situation. Work on a compromise and guidelines of respect and tolerance or move on. This is not merely a religious question—it has to do with basic life principles. It's not about conversion, it's about compromise. The more you integrate magic into your life, the more harmful people tend to fall or drift away anyhow. When you take responsibility for your own actions and stop allowing yourself to be manipulated, many negative people will pack up their toys and go home.

AT THE END OF THE DAY: I spend a few minutes at my altar, with candles and incense, giving thanks for the day and thinking about what I want to be. I do a "thank you" and an evening blessing, then snuff the candles and go to sleep.

Living a magical life is a constant process of discovery and growth, which is what makes it more exciting. Things that you used to have to think about become second nature after a while, and then you grow and expand and integrate. One day, you realize that you are living each day mindfully, and everything you do has more joy and meaning.

Magical Mishaps, No Worries

By Silver RavenWolf

I don't know about you, but I've done some major magical bloopers in my time. Here are some tips to prevent mishaps, or if you have made a boo-boo, ways to fix the problem. Let's run over a few standard reminders first.

Consider carefully the ramifications of any magical act, and proceed accordingly. Spontaneous ritual for acts of honor are fine, but if you have a specific magical working in mind, take some time to determine exactly what you want to accomplish, and why.

Always be specific in wording chants, charms, spells or rituals. Remember, words carry power.

Never call on a deity or archetype that you have not researched first.

If your working has several intricate steps that are new to you, write them down on a 3 x 5 card. No one will fail you for magical crib notes.

Compose two basic rituals, one for honor and one for a magical working, tailored to your personal tastes and energies. Use these rituals as templates for more advanced workings. This way, when you are ready to perform unfamiliar activities or read new passages, the ritual energies will not drag.

Compose a quickie ritual tailored to your own personal tastes and energies. We're all busy people and there are times when we cannot take a half hour or more out of our day to perform a specific working. If you have a short basic format that you know works, you will be able to do successful magic faster.

Never work magic in anger. It is okay to be angry, and each of us must learn to process anger in a positive way. One particular magical group I know waits seven days before working magic on issues that have aroused volatile emotions. Of course, you can't always wait seven days, but this is a good rule of broomstick for many of the situations we may encounter.

Fire elementals are not toys. Of the four earthly elements (earth, air, fire, and water) fire demands respect whether you are a novice or skilled practitioner. Let's face it, your bowl of salt is not going to jump up and bite you in the nose, but your fire candle can shoot a flame up your arm and into your hair in less than two seconds with disastrous results. (I kid you not, I've seen it happen.) I always encourage my students to incorporate flat stones on their altars as a way of connecting with the Earth, as well as providing a fire retardant surface for magical workings Even if your fire candle does explode (and it can happen) you will have fewer worries if you've been working on a large, flat stone. Keep a fire extinguisher nearby. Save the long-sleeved, long-tailed exotic robes for a festival and stick to safe, smart clothing when working around any type of fire. Be careful, also, of synthetic sweaters. I was conducting a ritual in St. Louis when the flames literally jumped from the cauldron and flew up a girl's sleeve, raging across her chest. The fuzz on the synthetic sweater popped and crackled with blue flame. Luckily, she was okay, but better to be safe than sorry!

Do not use cinnamon oil to anoint yourself or anyone else. Cinnamon oil burns the skin. I had the privilege to be in circle with Raymond Buckland where he and I were asked to anoint everyone in the circle. The maiden handed me the oil and I went about my business, anointing each individual. Mr. Buckland anointed me with the same oil. Several minutes later I thought my head was on fire. I realized with a sniff or two that the maiden had handed me cinnamon oil. Ouch!

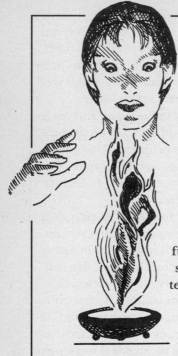

When a magical mishap does happen, don't immediately think that bad spirits or someone you don't like is trying to keep you from succeeding. Most mistakes are simply errors in judgment. That's all. When I get a letter from someone who tells me they are cursed, or they lost their power to someone else, or that another magical person is working against them and their entire brain matter is in a tizzy, I know that this person hasn't fully studied magic, and doesn't understand the underlying principles of the system they have chosen to work with. When things in your life turn to garbage, you most likely had a hand in it. Sometimes Spirit presents us with unfortunate circumstances because we are not following our life mission, or we have chosen the wrong path. Spirit most likely has been giving us warnings along the way, but we've not paid attention. Thus, the whopper hits us right between the pentacle and the broomstick. Better to design a ritual to ask the Lord and Lady to assist you in choosing the right path, and to assist you in cleaning up the problems you encounter. Asking your spirit guide or guardian angel to help is also a good idea.

If you goof in circle, keep going. The Sun will not explode because you said the wrong word, walked in the wrong direction, or used an incompatible deity. The worst that could happen is nothing at all, so don't sweat it.

Laughter in the circle is a good thing. If you trip over your own tongue, or your delicate little feet, laugh and keep going.

If you forgot an item or a tool, think twice before you cut the door to go get the missing item. Perhaps you weren't meant to use it in the first place.

Let the words "be prepared" be your Witch-Scout motto, and if you do mess up, just breeze right through it. You'll be fine.

Growth of
a Coven

By Cerridwen
Iris Shea

How does a coven grow? How are bonds built? How is power built? How does it grow beyond the small group that meets once or more a month for circles?

It can't be forced. It's sort of like love; you can't make someone love you. You have to let them love you.

Close to the Autumn Equinox of 1995 I started a study group called the Circle of Muses. I started it because enough women approached me over the months seeking knowledge that I felt we could start a working group. I was excited about the work I was doing in a coven of my peers, and I wanted to share what I had learned over the years with women who were interested.

We started as an elastic group and kept the circle open for thirteen meetings, which brought us to the following July. At one point, we were thirteen. People flowed in and out, but there was a core group that was extremely committed. We did our homework outside of circle, we read everything twe could get our hands on, we experimented on our own, and we brought in ideas to share. Several members had to take time off due to work and other commitments, but as long as they kept doing the work on their own time and submitting it, keeping up, they were still considered part of the circle. When we closed, there were nine of us. Now that everyone has been initiated, there are eight. Members were initiated over the course of a year, with no one being pushed into it before they were ready.

One of the most important policies we have, in addition to the circle being safe space (but not therapy) and working in an atmosphere of love and trust, is that everyone participate from the beginning. Each person is assigned a task at each ritual, and the tasks are rotated so that everyone can experience every task and learn it. As a group, we came up with some slightly modified ways of doing things, like calling the directions, that work better for us. The best way to learn is by doing, and the more one does, the more confidence one has in the ritual proceedings, and the more excited one is about learning new things.

Of course, it was only a matter of time before we wanted to share what we were doing with those around us. At first, it was only other circles and study groups, but in the last year, we felt the need to share more with the community, and with men as much as with women. We started holding open sabbats, not just for other Pagans, but for our friends and family who were curious and interested in what we do.

We do not forbid the members to work with other circles. Many circles I have come into contact with have a rule that one can only be a member of one circle. I understand the need not to split one's focus. I understand an online friend's explanation that there are those practitioners who collect degrees and coven memberships like scalps on a belt. I think that experiencing and learning from as many sources as possible is positive, not negative, though. Members come back excited about something newly learned, and share it. We all benefit. I have no reason to feel threatened by someone working with another circle. I'm not in any sort of competition. I encourage mutual growth and a wealth of experiences. If I disagree or feel uncomfortable with a new technique brought into circle, I talk about what I'm feeling and why. Sometimes, someone will have a different perspective, and I'm willing to try it. If it continues to remain uncomfortable, I simply won't do it.

Circle of Muses continues to work with the community. When someone we know needs help, we help. When one of us needs help, we are there 100 percent. One of the women in Muses is functioning as "Auntie Witch" to a brand new circle that's forming, and we dedicated that circle at the last Imbolc, welcoming them to the community. We include the men in our lives, both our friends and lovers, whenever possible. At our open circles, there are often people who have never attended a ritual before, and, without exception, they have felt welcomed, nurtured, and safe.

We operate on principles of love, joy, and laughter. We are honest, but not harmful. Too often, people use the label of "honesty" as a reason to say something intentionally harmful to someone else. We have found ways to be honest and loving, instead of honest and cruel. We are not afraid to say, "I'm tired," "I'm sick," "I hurt," or "I need help." We know that negative feelings will be honored and healed. We also don't get involved in inter-coven politics. We have no reason to get territorial. We know who we are, and we don't have to prove anything to anyone else. Our direct connection to divinity is clear and strong, and we are secure in it.

Does this mean that everything is hunky dory and there's never a disagreement? Of course not. We are eight strong-minded, individualistic women. There's bound to be conflict, but we have found that trusting in our own bonds and our own love for each other allows us to work things out. Sometimes it takes days, weeks, or months, but we are persistent.

Our open circles are growing. I am sure that most of the women will eventually begin circles of their own. This will not diminish the bonds of Circle of Muses. It will strengthen them. Once they are all elevated to third degree, I will probably start another circle myself, if there are enough students who request it. We welcome all those with open minds and open hearts, and promise to honor and nurture those who truly understand the freedom and responsibility involved in "Do what you will, an it harm none."

How does a coven grow? With force, ego, nurture, respect, and love. Blessed be.

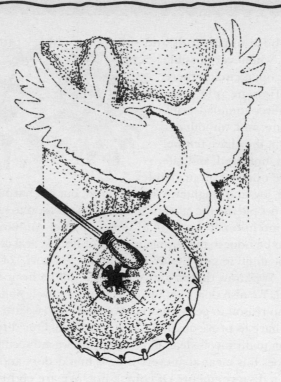

Soul Retrieval

By Ken Johnson

H as anyone offered to retrieve your soul lately? The subject of soul retrieval has recently become quite popular. There are any number of practitioners who claim to be able to perform this act. But what exactly is it?

In almost all shamanic cultures and traditions, there is a soul that lives within the body, and another, wandering soul that hovers nearby. This wandering soul is what occultists call the astral body.

According to shamanic beliefs common all over the planet, this traveling soul separates from us when we die, and walks alone down the long road to the Otherworld. Yet its journey thence begins even before our last breath; if we are deeply ill, our soul has already begun to separate from the body, and has taken its first few tentative steps along the road of no return. It is at such a moment that the shaman may intervene.

As long as there is still some particle of life within the body, the soul can be coaxed back, persuaded to return to the land of the living. The shaman beats the drum, falls into trance, and sends his or her own soul down the Otherworld road in search of the patient's soul. Perhaps it will be too late, and the patient will already be too far ahead on the road, perhaps even past the gates of no return. Or perhaps the journey will be successful—the shaman will find the patient's soul, wandering in the dark, and succeed in bringing it back home, to life, to health.

For the shaman, soul retrieval is a dangerous act. The road to the land of the dead is dark and cold and filled with perils. The shaman may easily come to harm there, attacked by evil spirits. He or she may return from the journey with some sort of illness. Hence soul retrieval is an act of courage, performed out of the shaman's love and devotion as a healer, as a service to his or her tribe, to the people.

Current practitioners of soul retrieval believe that any imbalance, whether it be physical illness or a psychological problem, may indicate that the soul and the body are no longer linked in proper harmony, and that the wandering soul is drifting. Modern soul retrieval ceremonies operate on this premise. They employ a number of neo-shamanic techniques to retrieve the soul, some of which are of fairly recent vintage.

Are these new, non-traditional methods valid? Are they safe? Should you allow your own soul to be retrieved?

While soul retrieval can be a valuable ritual remedy for those who are seriously disconnected, it requires a practitioner who operates with a great deal of skill and integrity. There are many who have such skills, but soul retrieval remains a risky business nevertheless, and one that may throw you (and the practitioner) severely out of whack. Perhaps the best rule of thumb is: If it isn't broken, don't fix it. Make sure your soul is really lost before you let someone else find it for you.

The Life of the Soul

By Susan Sheppard

It is hard to imagine the soul without hands,
and yet, it is so.

It is hard to imagine the soul without a mouth,
and yet, this is so.

There are souls that pause quietly
inside the body like little children on chairs.

There are souls that twang and stutter,
ones that shudder as nerves on air.

When the soul flies, it flies
as an owl in darkness,

A stir of white feathers
descending in pity upon the earth.

Where the soul swims, it is
limbless, within a lake of many gems.

When we count the burning stars, these
are the souls that cannot be

Extinguished. They thrive on light, not air.

The soul is most beautiful
without the body

when it cannot be counted being here.

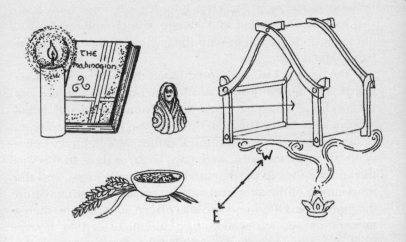

ANCESTORS AND HOUSE SPIRITS

BY RAVEN GRIMASSI

The old ways of our ancestors are intimately linked to our ancestors themselves. We bear within us this ancient connection, in part because our DNA is derived from those who came before us. As occultists, Witches, and Pagans, we understand that in a metaphysical sense everything is linked together, one thing influencing another in an endless repeating cycle.

In modern society there is a tendency to separate the dead from the living by establishing cemeteries in areas often far away from "people traffic." Individuals tend to die in hospitals and the "system" carries them away, sight unseen. In ancient times people often died in their own homes and the body was prepared for burial or cremation by the family. The dead were remembered at various times of the year, just as we celebrate the birthdays of friends and loved ones today.

Remembering and honoring your ancestors is an act of connection to your roots. In this fast-paced and ever-changing word, this one celebratory act truly belongs to you. Through it you can draw power and vigor, for it is in knowing where you came from that you can understand who you are. Understanding who you are today prepares you to reap the harvest of what you can become tomorrow.

The ancient Etruscans worshipped their ancestors as *Lasa* spirits. The ancient Romans called such spirits *Lare,* and saw them as household spirits, guardians of home and family. Small shrines were set by the hearth or on the mantel in remembrance of departed loved ones. Candles were lighted when a family member was born, wed, gave birth, or died. In this way the ancestral spirits participated in the family event, and the momentum of the ancestral current was kept flowing within the family line. Offerings were also placed at the shrine when a new venture was undertaken or a dilemma faced the household. This was performed in a belief that family spirits in the otherworld had power to influence the world of the living.

By lighting a candle at your ancestral shrine and simply reading out loud the myths or legends associated with your heritage, a personal alignment to the old ways can be established. The spoken voice creates vibrations carrying the passion of your blood up into the ether. This creates a ripple within the astral plane connecting you with times long forgotten.

To strengthen this connection, place symbols or icons typically associated with your nationality in or around the shrine. It is also useful to take on a personal name that may have been used in ancient times among your ancestors. This helps to further connect yourself with the energies of antiquity. Reading books and viewing movies that reflect cultural heroes is also an excellent aid to alignment. These tales often transmit the link to the collective conscious of the ancient peoples who created them. Therefore, by incorporating them into your own consciousness you become a part of the spiritual heritage of your ancestors.

PREPARATION OF AN ANCESTRAL SHRINE

Select a suitable shrine structure to reflect the ancestral memory. In effect this will be the home of your house spirit, so make it attractive and inviting. Place it upon a wall or on a mantle. An alignment of the shrine within your home to the west or east connects the shrine symbolically to the rising and setting of the Sun and Moon. In this way you create a connection to the cycles of life, death, and rebirth. Set an image in the shrine to represent the indwelling spirit.

Place a small offering bowl or vase in front of the shrine. Offerings of grain, milk, or flowers are good to set at your shrine. To "activate" the shrine, light some incense of either pine, sandalwood, or a similar "earthy" scent. Pass the smoke beneath the shrine so that the smoke rises up through and around the shrine. While doing this say:

Spirits of the ether, awaken, gather the ancient ones here, who were of old known to my Clan. I bless this shrine in the names of (give your deity names). *As it was in the time of the beginning, so is it now, so shall it be.*

At this point the shrine has been blessed and consecrated. Sit quietly before the shrine and visualize a small soft blue light around the figurine or statue in your shrine. In time you will actually see this light come and go within the shrine. This is assuming that you provide an offering at each Full Moon and all family occasions such as birthdays and marriages. Light a candle each time you sit before the shrine. Ask for assistance in personal matters and work toward establishing a good rapport with your household spirit. In time you will find you have nurtured protective spirits of home and family, as well as establishing a living current from the past.

THE MAGIC OF OLD PLACES

BY ED FITCH

Here are some exercises that will greatly enrich some of your outings into old places or into the wilderness.

HOUSES AND BUILDINGS

There is a power and a strength to be drawn from things that are old. Perhaps the veils between the dimensions are thin, or perhaps events long past have left an imprint and a charge on a piece of land or a building. It's the feeling we get when we walk through a semi-ruined ghost town in the West, or among the restored houses and shops of an Eastern Colonial village. In Britain and Europe the sensation comes even stronger and more often as we walk through castles, cathedrals, or houses that are several hundred of years old and have known generations upon generations within their walls.

As you pass through an old, out-of-the-way place, preferably alone, take a while to get the feeling of the place as it was in times past. Look around you and consider that the walls, the windows, and the very paving-stones that are there now and that you are gazing at have been viewed in exactly the same way by others who lived a hundred years ago, two hundred, or more. Much more. Perhaps their feelings were the same as yours are now, and their own lives as immediate and vital as your own. Simply stand there and listen with your mind and your psychic senses.

Bear in mind that your impressions don't have to be totally accurate. We all interpret psychic and past-life impressions through our own personal frames of reference. The details might vary, but the basic meaning behind it all will be the same.

Let's say you're standing in front of an old abandoned house. Look at it and estimate its age. Look at the trees around it, and imagine them being much smaller and much younger. You might want to say something like the following:

In the Name of the Gracious Lady
And the Lord of Life,
May only the good and the magical
Come to me while I am here.
And may I see and hear ever more clearly
The past of this place and those who once lived here.

Look at the dark windows, and imagine what they were like when a family gave the place a warmth and a life. Good times and bad, they will all be there, in the cracked walls and empty doorways. Go into the old house and pick up a piece of plaster, wood, or something else that has long been a part of the house. Hold it up to your forehead, and for a minute or more let yourself spontaneously sense psychically what is in the relic. Let your mind and thoughts freewheel, and grasp the impressions that you get. Sense the families, the scenes, the loves, the sorrows, and the joys. Feel and listen! Walk from room to room, touching, feeling, and sensing everything. Take your time as you put yourself more and more back into another time, another place, another century.

When you are finished and finally walk out of the house, you might want so say something like this:

I return, safe and secure
And locked firmly within
The here and the now.
I may return to the past,
Be it in this place or some other,
Though only when I so desire.
I may see much and experience much,
But only when I do desire.
And may the blessings of the Ancient Ones
Be on those who once lived here.
Blessed Be!

Take your time. Such experiences are to be savored.

DRAWING THE POWER OF THE PAST

Once you have been in and around an old, special place that has its own particular strength and vitality and that appeals to you greatly, try the following exercise to draw power and presence within yourself. Breathe in ten times slowly, saying:

I draw from all about myself
From this old and powerful
place.
May the Lord and the Lady be
with me,
So that only the good and the
beautiful
May be with me.

Inhaling deeply, imagine that you are drawing in a strength and a power that has been accumulating in this place for decades or even centuries, pulling it in through every pore in your body and holding it there.

Feel yourself immersed in the past. Feel great strength building within every part of your body, renewing and regenerating your body.

Then hold the feeling of strength, wonder, and the feeling of the past within you as you say, in these or similar words:

I now look through space and through time,
Seeing and feeling and knowing
The times of the past, the people,
Their words, and their feelings
All the more clearly.

Breathe out ten times, imagining very clearly that you are leaving the past and letting it go from within you, but that the strength you have drawn within yourself is staying, and will always be with you. Imagine that you are exhaling this power out through every pore in your body, and sending it back into the old, unique place in which you stand. When you feel that you have given back all the power, say in these words or in similar ones:

My questing is now done.
I have drawn the power of time,
And have become far stronger thereby.
I ask the blessings of the Lady and the Lord,
And give them thanks.
Blessed Be!

Leave quietly and in your own time.

SAMHAIN 10/28/96
BY CHRISTIE M. WRIGHT

All Hallow's Eve.

I hear Them calling.

The wind moans and wails like a banshee,
*   sending icy shivers down my spine.*
Shadows are everywhere.
The moon sails on the cloudy seas of night,
*   casting a magical light upon the countryside.*
Time stands still,
*   listening,*
*   waiting.*

The Veil thins,
*   and an eerie mist rises off the sea.*
Listen!
They come!
The Wild Hunt rides!

The Feast of the Dead begins!

Bouncing in the Otherworld

By Ken Johnson

There are many ways of journeying to the Otherworld. Perhaps the most popular form of journey work these days involves the use of creative visualization. Here is a completely different technique for the Otherworld journey. This one was taught to me by traditional sorcerers in Eastern Europe who still preserve a deep core of Pagan European practice.

First, drive out to the woods and take a hike. Take a friend, too, so that you won't hurt yourself doing this exercise.

Find a sapling, one that is just strong enough to support your weight, but that you can push against. Don't worry about what kind of tree it is. That's not important, and besides, the sorcerers say that all trees are good. For the sake of your own comfort, however, you may wish to choose one with very few branches, or one where the branches start farther up the tree, like a birch or certain types of pine.

Lean your back against the sapling. Close your eyes and relax, letting all thoughts leave your mind. Allow your awareness of the whole physical world to disappear.

Now, begin to bounce gently, back and forth. This is where the friend comes in. He or she should be close enough to catch you, just in case you lose your balance or the sapling breaks.

As you bounce gently back and forth, get your consciousness out of your head and put it in your heart. If this is too difficult, at least try to focus your awareness in your heart. Rest there for a moment, still bouncing.

Imagine that your arms are infinite, and that you are reaching out into the universe, embracing all the spirits, gods, and beings who live there, showering them with love from your heart.

That's basically all there is to it.

But what's supposed to happen, you ask? It varies from person to person. Some just float with a sense of joy and bliss, for this exercise will turn off your lower mind and awaken your third eye as well as your heart. Others, perceiving the world with the heart and the third eye as they reach out to embrace the Otherworld, may feel the inhabitants of the Otherworld reaching back to embrace you in return, to shower you with love.

You may feel inclined to stop bouncing for a while and just listen to and feel everything around you, which is fine. You may even hear the voices of the Otherworld inhabitants, speaking to you, or, as you stand there with your physical eyes closed and your inner eyes open, you may see some of the Otherworld beings, which is what usually happens to me.

Finally, you may wish not only to stop bouncing, but to open your physical eyes. You just may learn to see the world with your own Otherworldly vision. Everything will be shining with a special glow, the auras of the plants and trees will be visible, and you might even see the elves and plant devas themselves, hiding shyly behind the nearest bush, watching you with curiosity.

Samhain Pie

By Anne Marie Garrison

Samhain is traditionally the third and final harvest holiday of the Wiccan wheel of the year. Because the bulk of the year's fresh produce is long gone by late October, Samhain is at a turning point where traditional recipes begin to dip into the winter's store of dried fruits and nuts.

The recipe below contains both freshly harvested fruits as well as dried fruits and nuts. The essential flavor "kick" comes from rum. If possible, go to the liquor store and buy a small bottle of the real stuff (rather than getting rum extract from the grocery store). That way you should have plenty left to leave out for the ancestors on Samhain night. The ancestors get very thirsty, and in many traditions rum or whiskey is one of their favorite treats.

Basic Ingredients

- ¾ cup brown sugar or ⅛ cup honey
- 2 tablespoons white or whole wheat flour
- ¼ teaspoon salt
- ½ cup water
- 1 teaspoon cinnamon
- 1 teaspoon allspice or nutmeg
- 1 cup raisins
- 3–4 tart apples, peeled and sliced
- ¼ cup rum
- 2 (9-inch) pastry pie crusts

Recommended Extras

Use one less apple if you choose one of these options

- 1 cup fresh raspberries
- ½ cup dried and diced fruits: apricots, apples, craisins, peaches, or other
- ½ cup sliced almonds or chopped mixed nuts

Heat oven to 400°F. In a large saucepan, blend sugar or honey, flour, and salt. Stir in the water, spices, and dried fruits. Cook over medium heat, stirring constantly, until the mixture thickens (about 5 minutes). Add the apples, raspberries, nuts, and rum. Stir. Remove from heat. Place one pie crust into an ungreased 9-inch pie plate, and carefully push dough into the bowl of the plate, leaving an even amount of extra dough all around the edges. Fill with stove-top mixture, spreading evenly. Arrange the apple slices on top of the stove-top mixture so they lie as flat as possible. Carefully lay the top pie crust over the pie. With a sharp knife, trim the pie dough that hangs over the lip of the pie tin. (In other words, put your knife vertically against the pie tin, and turn the pie, cutting as you go.) Save the scraps of dough. Pinch the two crusts together. A "fluting" design can be achieved by placing your hands at an angle from the pie as you are pinching.

With a very sharp, pointy knife, pierce and then saw through the top crust, being careful not to disturb the fruit mixture underneath (see illustration). Cut two circular eyes, a triangle nose, and a crooked mouth. The two circular pieces of crust that were cut out to make eyes now become cheeks at the corners of the mouth. With the reserved dough, cut out two triangles to form eyebrows, one rectangle for a pumpkin stem, and two small bits for the pupils of the eyes. Carefully press these loose pieces of dough into place. With the pointy knife, lightly draw the pumpkin ridges into the dough (see illustration). Cover the edges of the pie with strips of aluminum foil to prevent them from burning before the pie is done. You might also want to put some foil across a rack on the lowest setting of the oven to catch any spills if the pie bubbles over. Bake in the oven for 20 minutes, then remove the aluminum foil. Bake approximately another 20 minutes. Set on a rack or wooden bread board to cool, then enjoy!

MORRIGAN

By Christie M. Wright

The skies are red as blood,
  a painter's pail o'erturned,
  spilling chaos across the calm skies.

Fingers playfully draw images in the scarlet flow,
  frightful images
    that cause men's eyes to roll back into their fevered heads,
    and foam at the mouth,
    to fall writhing on the ground,
    screaming in their madness.

The keening cry of mourning rises over the blackened and bloodied land,
  a terrible sound to cause blooded warriors to cringe
    and babes to cry in their lonely cradles.

Ravens blacken the sky,
    their dark shimmering colors a contrast to the
    blooded clouds above.

White lightning flashes,
    illuminating the plains below:
    the still corpses of those who lived before,
    their sightless eyes wide in terror,
    their bodies covered with ther kinsmans' blood.

Black thunder peals across the sky,
    and scarlet and black clouds mingle,
    blood and dirt running together as one.

Lightning flashes and thunder booms
    as the winds race over the land in fury,
    adding to the keening dirge sung by the cursed living

Lightning flashes,
    playing upon the cold features of a woman
    astride a black warhorse.
The beast's eyes roll in terrible fury,
    and his restless hooves paw the ground.

The woman's emerald eyes flash
    and ruby lips part over even white teeth.
Soft, harsh laughter trickles from Her slender white throat.
The raging winds whip Her long black hair,
    twined about with scarlet ribbons the color of blood.
A gleaming sword of white fire
    burns in Her hand,
    fed by the fury of the storm.

She is the Lady of Battle,
    horrible to behold in Her beauty.
She is the Wild Creature unleashed,
    bearing with Her the unbridled savagery of the gods.
She is beautiful in Her countenance,
    terrible in Her vengeance.

She is the Morrigan,
    Goddess of War.

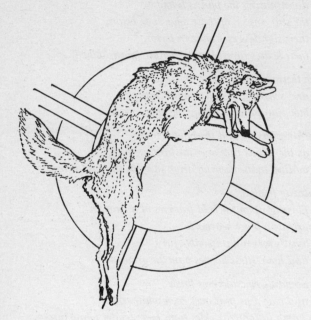

TRICKSTER

BY JIM GARRISON

I kindle the fire you stole for us. Be welcome at my fire, be welcome, Trickster.

I bring light into the darkness, even as you did. I share my light with you as you brought light to my people. Be welcome, Trickster.

I stir the pot, and from a single stone I make stew for us all. This is a secret you taught to us all long ago when we were hungry. Come, share my stew. Be welcome, Trickster.

Be welcome, Trickster.

We laugh around the fire, telling stories from the old days. We tell the stories and jokes you whispered to us before we were born.

We sing the songs of our ancestors, even as you did. We share our songs with you, even as you teach us new ones.

We dance and play in the night. We ask you to come, dance and play along with us. Be welcome among us, Trickster.

Be blessed, Trickster.

You question our words, turn our jokes back upon us, show us the other side to our actions, and reveal our motivations.

We honor you, Trickster.

You show us the way to laugh and to live, you teach us wisdom when we will not listen, and confront us with the fears we will not face.

We respect you, Trickster.

You bring mirth to our reverence, joy to our games, and ecstasy to our rites. Our souls are enriched and our lives made better by your grace.

We adore you, Trickster.

Be welcome. You always have a place at our circle; around our fire. We share your laughter and save for you a libation and a portion of the feast.

You are among friends.

Be blessed. We offer you our friendship, our camaraderie, and our joy.

You are among friends.

When our rite is done and we must return to the world of stone and steel, we bid you good hunting, good health, and much laughter! Remember us in friendship that we might enjoy each other's company on another night such as this. Our blessings go with you as we take our leave of your fair company, but rest assured that we will return. Let there always be peace and love between us.

Blessed be.

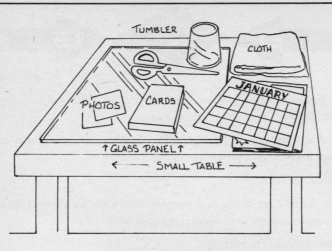

TUMBLER
CLOTH
PHOTOS
CARDS
JANUARY
↑ GLASS PANEL ↑
← — SMALL TABLE — →

HOW TO CREATE
YOUR OWN OUIJA BOARD

BY SUSAN SHEPPARD

A storm outside blows in with chilly passion. Late afternoon shadows sweep long and deep. Freshly cut wood crackles in the fire. It's just you and a few special friends sitting around. What an ideal time for intimacy and introspection! And what better way to wile away the hours than to contact both the spirit world and the higher self?

Years ago, my aunt fascinated me with stories of past days when she and her sisters made their own Ouija board. Such simple efforts yielded amazing results, even to the point of predicting the first name of the man my aunt would eventually marry.

My aunt and her sisters made their own Ouija, of course, because they were poor and didn't own a Ouija board. Anyone who is initiated into the ways of magic knows that spiritual instruments fashioned by the practitioner carry not only more mystical power, but also more spiritual nuance. Perhaps when we make something with our own hands we unlock its mystery and begin to understand it more completely.

The history behind the Ouija board is clouded in mystery, but the first commercial version was introduced by Elijah Bond in 1892. Bond later sold his invention/discovery (evidence points to the fact that planchettes and rolling tables were used to contact spirits in much the same way centuries earlier) to William Fuld, who in turn sold it to Parker Brothers in 1966.

Since then the Ouija board has become a popular parlor game—or is it? Many famous mediums, such as Jane Roberts, got their start using Ouija boards. Dare we remember how the book *The Exorcist* started out with what was meant to be a childish game?

Does the Ouija board's use as a game make it less credible as a divinatory tool? Not necessarily. Rather, it seems to point out the fact that Ouija boards can unlock doorways into alternate realms of consciousness, not to mention contacting higher guides, deceased relatives, and spirits of the dead. Perhaps this is why conventional religions ban their use.

When using the Ouija, a spiritually strong and balanced person should always be present. This helps repel any bad vibrations that enter the room or sitting area. Individuals who are highly impressionable or under stress should not use the Ouija board. Also, hard liquor should be avoided during Ouija sessions.

MATERIALS

To make your own Ouija board requires no special artistic ability. It takes only a few odds and ends and your own unique twist of imagination. To fashion your own self-styled Ouija, you will need:

1. A small but sturdy table. A kitchen table is fine.

2. Old calendars, plus a few used magazines with clear black lettering. (Cheap calendars given away by banks and drugstores at Christmas time work well because the lettering isn't too fancy.)

3. A dark cloth. Silky fabrics or velvet are gorgeous, especially in midnight blue, priestly purple, or bewitching black.

4. A piece of glass approximately eighteen by twenty-four inches, or something thereabouts. (It has to be big enough to include the numbers and letters of the alphabet.) Glass from an old picture frame should do just fine. Plexiglass also works well.

5. A clear wineglass or a tumbler that isn't too heavy.

6. Other symbols or pictures meaningful to you.

7. Astrological glyphs, tarot cards, and runes might add a further dimension for those familiar with them.

Directions

1. To begin, cut out letters of the alphabet from an old calendar. (You will need to find the letters K, Q, W, X, and Z from magazines, or make them yourself.)

2. Cut out numbers 0 through 9.

3. Create YES and NO out of the unused letters from your calendar. Place the dark cloth on the table. Put the letters in alphabetical order just like a regular Ouija board. They should take up two lines. You may also wish to shape the letters into an arc. Make sure there is spacing between the letters.

4. Below your alphabet, place a line of numbers 0 through 9. Near the bottom, put YES in the left-hand corner. Put NO in the right corner. (You may choose to include pictures, tarot cards, astrological glyphs, or runic symbols.)

5. Carefully place your piece of glass over your home-made Ouija board. (The glass should hold everything in place.) Consider polishing your rectangular glass with a bit of wax furniture polish after putting it down. Next, turn over your wine glass or tumbler and use it as your planchette.

Holding a Ouija Session

Before each Ouija session you will need to "white light" your "board." (Imagine flooding your board and table area with an aura of pristine white light.) Consider burning a white novena candle for added protection.

Having a third person available to take dictation is a good idea. When genuine contact with the spirit world ensues, the planchette tends to move quickly and you can lose entire words and sentences. Catch the phrases as best you can or you won't be able to make sense out of what the spirit is telling you later.

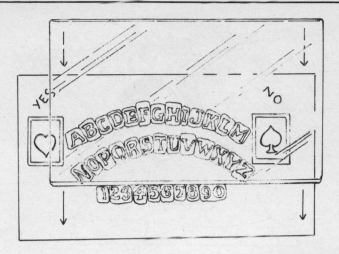

You may also wish to link hands with your partner and say a small blessing or prayer before beginning. As you and your partner proceed, ask specific questions, like "Spirit, are you here?"

Allow the board time to respond. If the planchette/glass moves to YES, you may then want to say, "By the powers of light and all that is good, please state your name!"

If the session goes smoothly and you feel you have made genuine contact with the spirit world, consider asking questions to which only you know the answer. If your board begins to curse or make negative predictions that inspire fear (such as deaths, rumors you know to be false, or threats) immediately end your session. Before leaving the table, clap your hands three times over the board and say: "Unfriendly and foul spirits of air. Be gone! You are not wanted here!"

Consider keeping a journal or a log to test the outcome and accuracy of the predictions. Be specific in your questioning. Unless you are specific, the Ouija and its guiding spirit cannot answer in a clear way. An open and light-hearted atmosphere is always a good idea since spirits are drawn to wise and whimsical people.

The Ouija is a masterful tool and is probably not meant for uninitiates fooling about with the dark side of the occult. Respect the spirits behind the board and they will respect you. When ending each Ouija session, it's a sound idea to give your blessings and also your thanks.

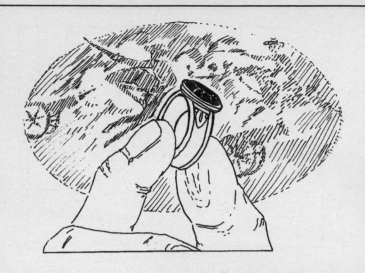

Psychometry: The Art of Seeing Through Touch

By Edain McCoy

Inanimate objects are anything but silent bystanders in the lives of their owners. Like the living beings who own them, they each have stories to tell us if we learn to let them. The way they communicate with us is through touch, or what is known as the art of psychometry.

Psychometry (pronounced si-COE-meh-tree) is the art of seeing through touch; of being able to accurately gather and interpret data about other people and events that are psychically transmitted by handling objects that were in intimate contact with those things, people, or events.

We humans are surrounded at all times by our own electro-magnetic energy fields. Objects that come into contact with these fields for extended periods of time—such as happens with jewelry, furniture, or clothing—inevitably have some of that energy imprinted upon them. When this happens, some of the life story of an object's owner can be "read" when the object is held by someone who has learned this type of psychic communication.

Experiments suggest that our electromagnetic energy fields become stronger during the times when our emotional levels are fluctuating the most. This makes for a stronger imprint on an object, and why the majority of information about someone obtained through using psychometry is often one of extremes. Most often a psychometrist gets clear images of weddings, deaths, or other moments when the emotions of the object's owner were high.

Because of this emotional imprinting, psychometry has become useful for law enforcement agencies. The idea of psychics in partnership with modern detectives, once sneered at by orthodox police forces, has proven to be the key to solving many crimes involving missing persons. In cases where an object belonging to a missing person has been discovered, but not the actual person or their body, psychics skilled at psychometry have been able to take the item and allow it to tell where to find the missing person. Using psychics skilled in psychometry is still not commonplace in most law enforcement venues, but occasionally it has proven to be the key to otherwise unsolvable crimes, and we are likely to see more acceptance of psychic assistance over time.

Psychometry is not an easy skill to master, and those who are naturally empathic seem to learn it more quickly. For example, if you find yourself crying inexplicably at an old battleground or while touring historic homes, or you become moody and temperamental while strolling through antique shops and impulse-buy unusual items claiming they seemed to be "calling out" to you, then you may already possess plenty of natural skill.

The best items to begin experimenting with are pieces of jewelry, items that are more likely than others to have spent long periods of time in direct contact with their owners. Many antique stores have a collection of inexpensive costume jewelry with which you can begin. An ideal situation is to work with a partner. Each of you can provide items owned by your ancestors. In this way you can not only experiment with psychometry together, but you can each get some immediate feedback on the accuracy of the information you receive.

You'll need a quiet time and place where you won't feel distracted by other people or obligations. Sit still, keeping good

posture while still remaining relaxed. Hold the object to be psychometrized in your non-dominant hand. This is usually defined as the hand you do not write with. This is your receptive hand, the one most easily able to receive impressions and energy transfers.

Close your eyes and take several deep breaths. Will yourself to relax and be open to the energies imprinted on the object. Don't try to force the process. Just stay focused on the object and remain relaxed and open.

Impressions may pop into your mind in a variety of ways, so reserve judgment until you're finished. Some people are sound-oriented and will hear things. Others are visually oriented and will see scenes played out in their minds, and some pick up on the emotional content and can become very agitated. Still others will get only the most basic sense of what the object is trying to tell them, but once they go to sleep their subconscious will take over and flesh out the details. It's also helpful to write down any mental impressions obtained in your psychometry experiments. What seems like nonsense to you may make perfect sense to the person whose belonging you hold and will be the key to showing you that you're learning to see through touch.

How to Hug a Tree

By Ed Fitch

Pick out a tree that looks special and is unique in some way, perhaps at the highest spot on a hill or next to the ruins of an old house, or perhaps a pine or an oak that strikes you as being old and noble-looking. Go to the tree with an offering of water and pour the water around the base, saying:

> *Tree friend, accept this offering as a token of my friendship.*
> *May the water join us, here and now.*

Put your arms around the tree, holding onto it. Put your forehead against the bark and close your eyes. Imagine feeling, vividly, your personal flow of life force merge with the life force that flows up through the trunk of the tree. Within yourself, try to feel what the tree feels, deep within the ground in its roots, and what it feels and senses from its highest branches.

Don't expect this being to be interested in you. It has a totally different type of life, and things that are important to human beings will not be of interest to it. Nonetheless, try to see the surrounding area as the tree has seen it far back when it was a seedling, and a sapling. Sense its relations with the other trees nearby. Visualize in your mind as though you can see from the high branches, and feel as though your feet were its roots. Take your time. When you are finished, step back and say the following or similar words:

> *I thank you, tree friend, and I give you blessings.*
> *Farewell and Blessed Be!*

Then go on your way, but it is good to drop by and visit the tree when you are nearby in the future.

DOWSING WITH A PENDULUM

BY JIM WEAVER

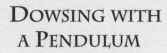

See if this sounds familiar: You can't find a favorite piece of jewelry, or you've lost your eyeglasses—again. You've turned the house upside down without any luck. What do you do? Reach for your trusty pendulum!

Few magical tools are as easy to use or as portable as a pendulum. Although pendulums are frequently used to predict future events by giving a "yes" or "no" answer, they are equally useful in locating lost objects.

When a pendulum is used in this manner you are practicing an ancient form of divination known as dowsing. Traditionally, dowsing was performed with a "divining rod" made of wood or metal to find water or minerals. As the dowser approached the area that held whatever was being searched for, the divining rod would tremble or jerk, signaling that the desired substance had been found.

The type of pendulum you use for dowsing is up to you. It could be purchased from an occult shop, or perhaps hand-made with a cord or chain and weighted with a coin, stone, or faceted crystal. A pendulum that you already possess and use for other magical purposes would be ideal, since it will already be "tuned" into you.

Whatever pendulum you decide to use, just be sure that it has been blessed and consecrated according to your spiritual path. Also, be sure that you already know what directions it will swing when it answers yes or no. Remember, each pendulum is different.

The procedure for pendulum dowsing is very simple. First, while holding the pendulum in your hand, ask the Divine Power to lead you to the lost object that you are looking for. Next, visualize the lost item.

Then move to the area where you suspect the item might be located. For example, if you think you lost a ring in your living room, stand quietly in the middle of that room. Ground and center. With your power hand, raise the pendulum to eye level, and, while holding it by the end of the chain or cord, think "stop," so the pendulum doesn't move for a moment. Now, begin to ask your questions. Aloud or silently, you might ask something like, "Did I lose my ring in the living room?" The pendulum will begin to swing, and give you a yes or no answer. If it is yes, then follow with a more detailed question, such as, "Is it under the sofa?" and so on. Let the pendulum tell you where to go next.

If you received a no, just move to another room or area and start over. I once found an important receipt in this manner. My pendulum finally led my to my bedroom, where I found the receipt tucked in a jewelry box.

It's fun to watch how your pendulum will react to your questions. Sometimes mine will give me a stronger "yes" as I move closer to the lost item. On some occasions my pendulum has trembled with a sudden quivering motion as I've approached the object that I was searching for.

There will be some instances when it won't be practical for you to physically go to the site you suspect a lost item might be located. Perhaps the area is too large, or maybe you lost something outside. No problem.

In such cases, simply sketch a map or outline of the area. It doesn't have to be fancy. Then hold the pendulum over your map on the spot you think the object might have been lost. Once again, ask your questions. You might ask something like, "Is it by the road?" or "Is it farther north?" When you dowse in this way you can cover large areas quickly.

No matter what method you choose, when you find the lost item, pause for a moment and give thanks to the Divine Power for bringing the misplaced object back to you. Thank your pendulum, too.

TAROT MEDITATIONS

By Estelle Daniels

Tarot cards are wonderful for telling fortunes, but they are also an important esoteric tool. Many occultists use meditation as a way of discovering information about themselves and the world. One meditation technique is to use a tarot card as the focus for the meditation.

A traditional tarot deck has seventy-eight cards and is divided into two parts: the major arcana or trumps, composed of twenty-two cards with names and pictures; and the minor arcana, composed of fifty-six cards in four suits from ace to king, with a fourteenth card, the page, in between the ten and knight (modern jack). The minor arcana correspond to the cards in a regular deck. Of the major arcana, only the fool survives in a modern deck of playing cards.

The major arcana of a tarot deck are also known as the keys. They are more important than the minor arcana. Each has a specific name and meaning. They also have esoteric meanings and can indicate spiritual matters. Of the minor arcana, the court cards represent people, but also events or conditions. Each suit corresponds to an element. Wands are fire, cups are water, swords are air, and pentacles are earth. However, apart from any divinatory meaning, each card of the tarot depicts a story in itself. These symbols and pictures have evolved over time and have acquired a life of their own.

When you choose a tarot deck for meditation, it is best to choose a deck where each of the cards has a separate picture. Some decks have merely a number of symbols (like three cups for the Three of Cups) for the minor arcana, but others have a distinct picture for each card. All have pictures for the major arcana. Using non-traditional tarot decks can bring good results, but for the beginner, a standard tarot deck (seventy-eight cards; twenty-two major arcana and fifty-six minor arcana in four suits) is best.

The most popular tarot deck up through the 1970s was the Rider-Waite deck, illustrated by Pamela Coleman Smith. This was drawn shortly after 1900 under the auspices of the Golden Dawn. For many years this was the only tarot deck readily available. The Robin Wood tarot is a more recent deck, drawn in the 1980s, and it is beautiful. It is a deck that borrows some symbology from the Rider Waite, but is more Celtic in flavor. The drawings are more realistic and less "cartooney" than the Rider-Waite. There are many other decks available, many of which use the word "tarot," yet are not traditional tarot decks. Some add extra cards to the major arcana. Some add extra cards to each suit. Some add extra suits. Try to see the cards in a deck before buying it. At least see a few cards so you get an idea of the flavor of the deck. There are hundreds of decks to choose from, and many people have several decks, for different purposes.

There are many ways to use tarot cards as meditation tools. The major arcana have pictures. They all form a progression, from 1, the magician, to twenty-one, the world, and then zero (unnumbered or twenty-two) the fool and back to one again. Meditate on the progression, what a soul has to work through before attaining mastery, and then descended back into another cycle of learning and mastery. Meditate on each individual card, what it means, what the symbols and colors in the card mean, and how each symbol or color adds to the totality of meaning for the card.

Tying the tarot to the Qabala, each of the major arcana corresponds to a pathway between the sephiroth. Keep in mind the

Tree of Life as a whole and the meaning of each of the sephiroth. Look at each card and try to understand how it can be a bridge between those two sephiroth. See how the nature of the card corresponds with and is a blend of their natures.

Using the minor arcana, meditate on each suit as a whole. How does each card fit into the progression of the suit, from ace to king? Work backward from king to ace. Are there similarities in symbols, colors, themes used in the cards? The Rider-Waite deck has a story for each suit of the minor arcana. Lay out each suit and work it out for yourself.

Look at each card individually. Look at the symbols and colors used in the card. What do they mean to you? How do they fit with the message of the card? Place yourself within the scene depicted in the card. Look around, and see if you can discover things that are "hidden" from view. Talk to the people in the card. What do they have to tell you?

Look at all four aces, twos, and so on together. How do they differ, how are they similar? What themes are duplicated? How does each family of court cards fit together? Are they compatible? Is there symbology repeated in each?

Groups can use the tarot as a basis for long-term study. Take a different card each week, look at it, discuss its meaning, symbols, where it occurs in the deck, how it fits into the progression. Use the picture on the card as a basis for a guided meditation, with one member of the group guiding everyone into the card to explore further. Let each member report back what they discovered while on their journey.

Comparing and contrasting different tarot decks can also be enlightening. Check out the similarities and differences. Which decks appeal to you, and why? Get together with several people and look at different decks. It's fun and a good way to get to know each other. It's a good way to see what different decks are available without having to buy each deck.

Tarot is more than just for fortune telling. The cards are universal symbols and can bring new insight and spiritual knowledge.

SMOKING THE BILLET

BY EDAIN MCCOY

One of the easiest of all divination techniques remains suprisingly little-known. It involves only a single lighted candle, a small square of white paper, and the person who has a burning question to be answered. The unusual name of the divination comes from the nineteenth-century spiritualist practice of using small squares of paper, known as billets, to trigger a medium's psychic connection with the spirit world.

When you are in a quiet, dark place, light the single candle, and take the square of paper and press it between your palms. You may rub the paper, or move it about in any way that feels right to you. While you are doing this, allow yourself to relax and focus on your question or issue at hand. Slow your mind, and allow your subconscious to come forward and do the work. When you feel ready, hold the paper tautly in both hands a few inches above the flame. Be careful not to let the paper become scorched, but do allow the smoke from the flame to mark the paper. Again, you may move the paper about in any manner that feels right to you. When you sense that your question has been answered, extinguish the candle and take a critical look at the smoke patterns under good light. The patterns and symbols you see can be interpreted to determine the response to your question. A good book on symbolism, such as might be found in a dream interpretation guide, can help you read your answers if you have trouble understanding them.

Stang Blessing:
A Spell of Consecration

By Jim Garrison

This rite is intended as a solo one, though a working group, grove, or coven might modify it to suit themselves. Gather the following items:

Purification incense. Whatever herbs or resins you prefer will be fine.

Matches. Wooden farmer matches are the best bet.

String or garland of oak leaves (summer to winter) or holly (winter to summer).

Your newly made stang. (A stang is a forked tree branch or stick that acts as a vertical altar. Stangs are usually made of ash or rowan, but you can also use an old garden fork.)

Wine or some other libation beverage. This need not be alcoholic. Cider works fine, though I'd recommend Jagermeister or strong wine or beer/wine/ale, especially if it is home brewed.

Whatever ritual regalia or tools you feel inclined to use in creating sacred space outdoors and don't mind carrying along on the trip. (It might be best to just dress all in black and skip the robes. An athame is nice, but could be problematic if you must cross public land, so it may be easier to just rely on your own fingers.)

Go to an empty, wild, deserted place—be it a vacant lot, a state park, a gravel pit, or the back forty of a neighboring farm (if you have permission—don't trespass). Make your trip during the night if possible. It's preferable to do this rite during the waxing or Full Moon. This rite is supposed to take place outdoors. The stang is, by its very nature, an outdoor tool. You don't want to consecrate a tool dedicated to the Horned God, Lord of the Wild Hunt, inside, do you? You might consider doing this ritual during a campout.

When you have found the place you plan on using for this rite, prepare a campfire at the center of the space. Use whatever dead wood you have available in the area, though it is nice to have ash, oak, or birch in the mix. Once you have the fire going and you're ready to proceed, pick up your stang and salute the north (the stang is often associated with the north). You can salute the other directions if you wish.

Take a deep breath and do whatever technique you use for grounding and centering—perform the Lesser Banishing Ritual of the Pentagram, or whatever helps. Go to the north and present the stang to the Moon high above you, reciting the following, or something similar:

> *Lady, I ask that you look down upon me here, observe and witness this rite and the spirit in which it is performed. I ask for your blessing and guidance in this undertaking. Know that my heart is right, that I am a true member of your people, and I come before you now to renew the ancient bond, to reclaim what aspects of the old ways still remain open to me in this place and in this time. Blessed Be.*

Walk, or dance, around the perimeter of your space three times widdershins (counter-clockwise), carrying the stang. Visualize each trip around the fire leaving a trail of black, then red, then white light. Recite, chant, or mentally echo the following, or something similar:

> *I come before the Mighty Ones—ancestors and guides, you who stand watching. I am (say your magical name), and it is my intention to dedicate this stang to the service and honor of the Horned God. May this stang serve as my standard, my sign of respect and fellowship with the god of my ancestors. The old ways are faint—nearly lost to us. I ask that this stang renew the connection between our worlds. Horned One, Great God of my people, I (your magical name) call to you. If it please you, bestow your blessing upon me, and upon my craft, the path that has brought me here before you.*

Go to your fire and toss in as much of the herbs/resinous incense as you prefer to use. You could use a sand-filled bowl and charcoal, if you want, but the fire can be so much more dramatic. For a bit of fun mix the herbs with handfuls of baking powder or talcum. When you toss the mixture into the fire it will flash. Some folks like that sort of theatricality, and if it serves to establish the mood and atmosphere, go for it. Setting is an essential component to ritual. Always use your available resources for greatest effect.

Pass the stang through the smoke, visualizing the fire destroying any and all impurities, burning away anything no longer appropriate for a tool dedicated to the God. Visualize the stang taking on the capacity for, and quality of, destruction. This is a weapon of the God, and there must be an ending before there can be a beginning.

It makes things much more interesting and satisfying—if you are so inclined—to dance around the fire as you pass the stang through the smoke—just don't try this with too

Stang Sigil

many other people around who are likewise swinging forks around the place—it could hurt. This is the reason this rite is designed as a solo working, though if you use some common sense, it could be made to work for a group.

Once you've cleansed the stang in fire and incense smoke, take it to the north and stick it into the ground. Libate the fork with liquor or cider. Take a good, deep drink of the libation brew yourself—don't offer something to the gods that you wouldn't drink yourself. Visualize the stang taking on the qualities of balance and harmony—however you relate to these forces yourself. You might find it useful and instructive to contemplate the nature of sacrifice, the exchange of energy that makes life a dance, the interaction of forces that makes up existence, or you may just want to take another drink—as you will. After a silent moment, recite something like the following:

> *As I offer this libation unto the north, unto the Ancestors, Mighty Ones, and Watchers, I offer this stang as my standard, my sign of faith and fellowship with the God of my ancestors. Horned One, Lord of the Gates of Death, Lord of the Gates of Life— Father and Master of the Earth—I ask for your blessing upon this humble tool I bring before you. Let this stang be a key, a mark of my covenant with you, and a symbol of the bond that I seek to establish between us. Let this stang be my guard, my guide, my steed, and the symbol of your love and protection for those of us who would rebuild your following. You are ever at the heart of my tribe, my clan, my people. By my*

Stang Sigil

blood, my sweat, my tears, and my work, I claim allegiance to the old Horned God as a priest/ess of the old ways, the new ways, the eternally changing, ever living ways of the Witches.

Pour out a libation to the Horned God. Don't be stingy—you can't ask for the blessing of a deity you're too cheap to show a good time. Offer the libation as a gift of the heart, with a smile, and without expecting to establish some sort of cosmic tab with the God. You're building a relationship, so treat the Horned One with respect, not demands and expectations. You'll be the better for it. Now is a good time to drape the stang with a string of oak leaves, or garland. Sit there facing the stang looking out toward the north, and meditate upon the Horned God, or go dance around the fire and work yourself into an ecstatic frenzy—whatever is appropriate for you. Visualize the stang taking on the qualities and energies of creation and fertility—however you personally relate to these universal forces.

Stang Sigil

Once you've had enough, go to the north and thank the Mighty Ones, the Horned God, and the Goddess. Take the stang from out of the ground and hold it up to the Moon. Visualize the stang soaking up moonlight and storing it like a battery. Clean up your campsite and head on back to home with your newly consecrated stang.

Once you have performed this rite, you may want to do something similar once a year to re-consecrate and dedicate the stang to the Horned God. This is purely voluntary and not at all necessary. You may wish to store your stang in a closet or other dark place—some folks like to use a shroud or old cotton sheet to wrap the stang when it is not in use. Others hang the stang over the fireplace, or leave it leaning against the back porch. You'll have to decide for yourself what is appropriate for you and act accordingly.

The stang embodies the forces of creation, destruction, and balance as a weapon/tool of the God. Meditation and reflection, contemplation and sudden inspiration will show you what you need to know, and teach you how to use the stang. May the ecstasy of the sabbat be yours—Blessed Be!

Stang Sigil

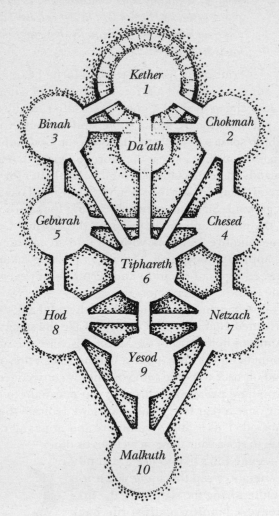

BASIC QABALA

BY ESTELLE DANIELS

This diagram shows the Tree of Life, which is central to the esoteric magical system known as Qabala.

The Qabala is a system developed sometime during the Middle Ages by Jews as an explanation of the structure of the mystical universe. The teachings were originally oral, but by the 1300s they were written down and solidified into a somewhat uniform set of doctrines. The symbol of the Tree of Life was standardized around that time. During the Renaissance, Christian mystics and magicians took the system and added more doctrine and teachings and adopted Qabala into their magical workings. During the 1700s Eliphas Levi made a connection between the pathways of the Tree of Life and the tarot trumps. The secret societies of the 1800s and 1900s, especially the Golden Dawn, made Qabala the foundation for their magical systems. The system of high magic is based on the Qabala in various forms.

For those not familiar with Qabala it seems almost too simplistic. How can life, the universe, and everything be contained in and explained by ten circles and twenty-two lines between them? Like any symbolic language, Qabala seeks to categorize things into similarities, thereby allowing fuller understanding by experiencing the commonalities each group of things exhibits.

Even the name Qabala isn't standard. There are about twenty-seven ways to spell this word, which is a transliteration from Hebrew, and therefore only approximate anyhow. Cabalah, Kabbala and QBL are three of the more common ways to "spell" this word.

The heart of the Qabala is the ten spheres, or sephiroth. Each governs an area of life and experience. By traveling up and down the tree one can gain wisdom and knowledge and experience what each sphere has to offer. One studies and works with each sphere and its correspondences and thereby refines one's character and soul with the endpoint of returning to God—one aspect of the Great Work.

THE SEPHIROTH

STARTING AT THE BOTTOM, SPHERE 10 IS MALKUTH (mal-kooth), The Kingdom, which is earth, solid matter, where we are. The colors associated with Malkuth are black, citrine, russet, and olive (a blending of the other colors). It is the tangible world, the here-and-now, and the material plane. Everybody starts here. Malkuth represents the contact between the body and external world experienced through the senses. Its virtues are discrimination and skepticism, and its vices are inertia and avarice.

MOVING UP TO SPHERE NINE IS YESOD (yay-sod), the foundation, which corresponds to the Moon, emotion, and instinct. Its color is purple. Yesod can also be likened to the unconscious mind, the energy of the sexes, and the past. Its virtue is independence, and its vices are idleness and stagnation.

SPHERE EIGHT IS HOD, glory, which corresponds to Mercury, mind, thought, and intellect. Its color is orange. Here is our stream of consciousness, awareness of self, and learning. Its virtue is truthfulness, and its vices are falsehood and dishonesty.

SPHERE SEVEN IS NETZACH (net-tsakh; with a soft "ch"), victory, which corresponds to Venus, feelings, the senses, beauty, artistic expression, and appreciation. Its color is green (or pink). Netzach can be linked to that which is beautiful and pleasant. Its virtues are selfnessness and altruism, and its vice is lust. Hod and Netzach form a polarity of thinking and feeling. The ideal is to balance between the two.

SPHERE SIX IS TIPHARETH (tiff-err-eth), beauty or harmony, which corresponds to the Sun, personal identity, self-awareness, center, and soul. Its color is golden yellow. Its virtue is devotion to the Great Work, and its vices are pride and selfishness. Tiphareth is the center of the Tree, and symbolizes the center of the self. It has paths directly linking it to all the other spheres except Malkuth.

SPHERE FIVE IS GEBURAH (gay-boo-rah), strength or severity, which corresponds to Mars, personal will or power, and doing. Its color is red. Its virtues are energy and courage, and its vices are cruelty and restriction.

SPHERE FOUR IS CHESED (khes-edd, soft "ch"), mercy or love, which corresponds to Jupiter, personal love, awareness, and being. Its color is blue. Its virtue is obedience to love, and its vices are bigotry and hypocrisy. Geburah and Chesed form a polarity of severity and mercy, sternness and love, and again a dynamic balance is desirable, for too much or too little of either can lead to various undesirable traits.

NEXT ON THE TREE IS A BLANK SPACE, THE UN-NUMBERED SPHERE CALLED DA'ATH (day-ath), the abyss, knowledge without understanding. Da'ath is the abyss that separates man from Deity, that which corresponds to a person's link with the collective unconscious. Above the Abyss, all opposites are reconciled, below the Abyss everything is duality. Da'ath connects the upper and lower spheres, and there are many correspondences that have to do with this link. Some attribute Pluto to Da'ath, while others attribute Chiron.

SPHERE THREE IS BINAH (bee-nah), understanding, which corresponds to Saturn, spiritual awareness, and love. Its color is black, which absorbs all other colors, representing the lower spheres on the tree. Its virtue is silence, and its vices are avarice and greed. Binah represents the eternal receptive feminine principle.

SPHERE TWO IS CHOCKMAH (Hokh-mah, soft ch), wisdom, which corresponds to Uranus or Neptune and to the fixed stars—the zodiac itself. It is spiritual will or purpose. Its color is gray, the color of emerging light, or the mixture of the black of Binah and the white of Kether. Its virtue is devotion to the Great Work. It has no vice, for the illusion of duality has been transcended. Chockmah represents the eternal active male principle, also the principle of fully knowing oneself.

SPHERE ONE IS KETHER (key-thur), The crown, which corresponds to Neptune or Uranus and what is beyond the sphere of the zodiac (deity). It is union with deity, and is attributed to the pure spirit of the transpersonal self. Its color is white brilliance, which obscures what Kether really is (deity). Its virtue is attainment and completion of the Great Work, and it has no vice.

The spheres can be divided into groups, by triangles, the three pillars, pairs, and then studied and better understood within the context of the groupings. All these combinations, and some which are not obvious (like the hidden pathways between sephiroth that are not on the tree, and the Qliphoth [cliff-off], a mirror-image Qabala or the "dark side," that still ends up at Kether) add to the complexity and depth of understanding that can be obtained by studying Qabala.

There are whole books written about the Qabala, and this short article can only be a very brief introduction, but this mystical construct of the universe has been studied and analyzed for centuries, and still fascinates seekers. There is much we could all learn from the Qabala, and if you are a magical seeker, it is worth a look. Blessed Be.

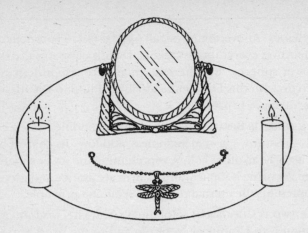

THE ENCHANTMENT OF GLAMOURY

BY EDAIN MCCOY

The 1996 occult movie *The Craft* featured a spell that allowed one of the lead characters to radically alter her appearance in order to show herself in the guise of someone else. They referred to the spell as a "glamour," and made it look delightfully easy. As with most depictions from Hollywood, this was overly simplified and overly fanciful, yet it was still based on an ancient Celtic concept.

When the Celts came to Ireland, legends tell us they found the Emerald Isle inhabited by a divine race of beings known as the Tuatha De Danaan. Unable to withstand the Celtic invasion, the Tuatha went underground and became the mythic faery race of Ireland. Stories abound about faery beings who come up from their underground burghs, appearing in deceptive guises to lead hapless humans into dangerous situations.

This was known as *glamoury,* the veil of illusion the Danaan wore as needed to befuddle their human foes. The word eventually came into modern English as glamour, a term often used for a woman who adopted stylish tastes in make-up and hairstyle. In other words, she was wearing a veil of illusion.

Glamoury spells are still part of Celtic magic, though its original purpose has been largely forgotten. This was a Celtic version of shapeshifting. While under the enchanted veil of a glamoury spell we can enhance our rituals by becoming the deities. We can use it to melt into the background and appear nearly invsible, or we can shape it so that it enhances our personal appearance and charisma.

To perform this last type of glamoury spell you will need a mirror (preferably one used only for magic), a red candle, a green candle, and something to use as a talisman to trigger the spell's action when you need it. A necklace is ideal since it can lie close to the center of your body and still be seen by others. Silver pieces work well for this, and so does jewelry with opal, diamond, or jade gemstones. A bottle of favorite scent also works well in this capacity.

Do this spell at night, and in as much darkness as you can manage. Cast a small circle and sit in its center facing west, the traditional Celtic direction of the otherworld land of the Tuatha. Place the mirror in front of you and the two candles behind you, one to each side, so that the candles and the mirror form a triangle around you. The green candle is associated with the planet Venus, which rules personal beauty. The red candle is the color of passion, and will help you project charisma. Keep these color associations in mind, but keep the candles themselves out of sight. The idea is to have just enough light to almost see into the mirror, but not enough to clearly illuminate your reflection.

Grasping your chosen talisman firmly between your hands, take several deep breaths to become fully relaxed, then gaze into the mirror while visualizing your image changing to the image you wish to project. As you do this, also pour your energy into charging the talisman as a trigger to activate your spell. As you continue to work at molding your image you may notice it start to change to reflect your desired appearance. Don't be alarmed if your reflection seems to take on a life of its own.

When you are satisfied that you have molded your image as much as you can for one session, place the talisman over your heart area and pour into it the energy of the image you created. Visualize it becoming a trigger that will release the energy of your spell when it is worn. Seal the spell by putting the talisman on and repeating this charge:

From burrow dark and lake-world deep,
Faries slumbering rise from sleep,
Sometimes here, now sometimes there,
What I will is the face I wear.

Extinguish and cover the candles to protect their energy until it is time to do the spell again. Repeat the spell as often as you need to reinforce the mental image you want to project. Follow this up with as many physical world efforts as you wish to use to change your image.

COMMON SCENTS
BATH SALTS

BY RON RHODES

It is very easy to prepare your own magical bath salts. I've made it even easier by formulating recipes with commonly available ingredients. All the fragrances used can be found in your local pharmacy, craft shop, or department store. I'll suggest amounts for the fragrances, but you can vary these according to personal taste. Just don't use too much, or your bath salts will be soggy. I am also suggesting a color for each bath salt. Just use regular food coloring for this. If you need to blend colors such as red and blue to get purple, do so in a teaspoon before you add it to the bath salts.

To use these bath salts, simply add ¼ to ½ cup to your regular bath water. Bathe as usual, while visualizing your goals and desires as already fulfilled. Because the magical intentions are released with the vapors of the fragrance, the hotter the water, the shorter the duration the bath needs to be. Because steam draws out the actual fragrance from the water, there is no need to stay in the water any longer than fifteen minutes.

Follow these easy steps for all of the recipes. Just vary the fragrance according to each bath salt made.

1. Try to keep your mind on the purpose of the bath salt as you prepare it.

2. For a base salt, you can use plain epsom salts or a blend of epsom salts and table, sea, or mineral salts.

3. Place approximately 2 cups of base salt into a clean, dry quart jar.

4. Add fragrances and coloring.

5. Place lid onto jar, tighten, and shake jar vigorously until well blended.

6. Store bath salts in an airtight, well-labeled glass container to prevent the salts from going stale as well as avoiding future identification problems.

SACRED RITES

Use before any spell or ritual work

10   drops lemon oil

10   drops lavender oil

 5   drops cinnamon oil

 5   drops jasmine oil

 5   drops anise oil

    Color: dark blue or green

BRIGHT AURA

To clean the "bad vibes" from one's personal energy

15   drops peppermint oil

10   drops lavender oil

10   drops vanilla extract

 5   drops almond extract

    Color: None

SPELL BREAKER

Use when you think someone has zapped you

10   drops clove oil

10   drops peppermint oil

10   drops lemon oil

10   drops eucalyptus oil

    Color: dark green

PASSAGES

To help cope with major life changes

10   drops lime oil

10   drops lemon oil

10   drops peppermint oil

10   drops almond extract

    Color: your choice

DREAM TIME
To enhance your dream recall

10 drops jasmine oil
5 drops lavender oil
5 drops orange oil
Color: light blue

HELP
Use when you need help

15 drops peppermint oil
10 drops cinnamon oil
10 drops lemon oil
10 drops vanilla extract
10 drops almond extract
Color: orange

ASTRAL FLIGHT
When attempting astral projection

10 drops orange oil
10 drops anise oil
5 drops jasmine oil
5 drops eucalyptus oil
5 drops wintergreen oil
Color: light blue or yellow

BLESSING

To help you connect to your divine source

20 drops almond extract
10 drops rose oil
5 drops lavender oil
5 drops lemon oil
5 drops cinnamon oil
Color: blue

ANGEL

Use when contacting the angelic realms

15 drops lavender oil
10 drops almond extract
10 drops vanilla extract
Color: pink or light green

PERSONAL POWER

Use to increase personal energy levels

10 drops of your favorite fragrance/scent
10 drops lemon oil
5 drops peppermint oil
5 drops orange oil
Color: your choice

NOTE: You may want to clean your bathtub with a baking soda paste after your magical bath.

Hawaiian Sacred Sites

By Bernyce Barlow

It can be argued the whole of Hawaii is sacred simply by nature, but there are some places on the islands that carry an imprint that cannot be denied. Riding on a seismic conveyor belt, these islands emit energies found nowhere else on the globe. There are many sacred sites scattered among the islands, sites that display powerful energies that tease and mingle with the human psyche.

CITY OF REFUGE: The City of Refuge is an ancient site that islanders still consider an active sanctuary. It was the place where the royal bones of the kings and chiefs were kept in a *heiau* or temple. Hawaiians believed *mana* or power, stayed in the bones even after death, and called upon this power from time to time. The City of Refuge was also a place one could go to be absolved of a crime through prayer and penitence.

HILL OF THE WHALE: Located at Spencer Beach, this prophecy temple was built to honor Ku, the war god of the Kameameha lineage. It was said if Kameameha could build this temple according to prescription he would reign over all of the islands. Upon the completion of this temple Kameameha did indeed unite all of the Hawaiian islands under his rule.

MO'OKINI HEIAU: Although this heiau is one of the largest on the island, it took less than twenty-four hours to construct. A human chain of thousands passed rocks hand by hand from over fourteen miles away to build this temple. Mo'okini became a place of sacrifice and the imprint there is very, very strong.

IAO VALLEY, MAUI: This valley has been considered sacred by the Hawaiians for as long as can be remembered. The valley was used as an internment site for royal bones as well as a

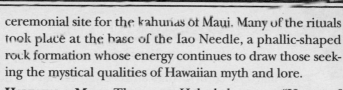

ceremonial site for the kahunas of Maui. Many of the rituals took place at the base of the Iao Needle, a phallic-shaped rock formation whose energy continues to draw those seeking the mystical qualities of Hawaiian myth and lore.

HALEAKALA, MAUI: The name Haleakala means "House of the Sun." It is in this dormant volcano that Maui, the trickster and god of the fisherman, resides. Before Maui, Pele was the resident spirit of place. The energies there are magnetic and pull you inward. Black Hill and White Hill, both on the rim of Haleakala, are two sacred sites used by the Hawaiians to invoke ancestral spirits.

THE ROAD TO HANA, MAUI: It's the pilgrimage to Hana that is sacred. Hana is simply the end of the journey. Along the way, mystic waterfalls spill from jungle formations, tropical forests whisper their secrets, and green-blue pools of water invite you to dive in and renew yourself. Each curve brings into view a new vista, cove, or jungle flower to appreciate. The road is more than a gateway to the other side of Maui, it is a portal to what Maui was like before settlement.

HALAWA VALLEY, MOLOKAI: There is a trail that leads through the center of this valley that leads to the sacred ruins of Iliiliopae. The ruins are a testament to the warriors of Molokai. The kahunas of this island had found favor with the poison-war goddess Kawela and sought her favor at the heiau Illiliopae. Her spirit is said to reside in the forests of the Halawa valley.

TOMB OF PUUPEHE, LANAI: The tomb of Puupehe faces the Auau Channel on the east side of Lanai. In a sea cave, the Maui princess waited for her betrothed, Makakehau, a chief of Lanai. Before their union, Puupehe was swept into the Pacific by a storm and drowned. Upon finding his princess, Makakehau lept from the lava rock formation to join his lover in death.

ORANGES AT YULE

BY LYNNE STURTEVANT

E arlier this century, children received oranges in their Christmas stockings. How exotic it must have been to have fresh citrus fruit in the dead of winter. Oranges in December are no longer a rare and special treat. However, as we mark the winter solstice and celebrate Yule, we can use oranges in a variety of ways to decorate our homes. Because of their shape and color, oranges are a natural symbol of the returning Sun.

POMANDERS

Fragrant orange pomanders will fill your rooms with pleasant scents throughout the Yule season. In order to make a pomander, you need oranges, whole cloves, and a small finishing nail or push pin. Whole cloves are available in the grocery store or can be purchased in bulk at specialty stores. You need about half ounce of whole cloves for each medium-size orange pomander.

To make a pomander, punch holes in the orange skin with the nail, and then insert the cloves into the holes. The blending of the spice and citrus scents is heavenly. You can cover the orange completely or create designs with the cloves. Possible patterns include stripes, spirals, runes, snowflakes, crescent Moons, stars, and, of course, Suns.

Within a few weeks, the orange will completely dehydrate. The cloves help draw the juice from the fruit. As the orange dries, it will turn dark, shrink and become very light in weight. Keep this in mind as you insert the cloves. Leave some space between them to allow for shrinkage.

While the orange pomander is drying, it will continue to release its beautiful, spicy fragrance. Turn it every few days so that it will dry evenly. When the pomander is completely dry, it can be saved for next year's celebration. Refresh your pomander with a little clove oil and store it

340

in a sealed sandwich bag. It should last for years and will be a nice reminder of Yules passed.

Dehydrated Orange Slices

Dehydrated orange slices are very pretty and easy to make. Dehydration results in a bright peel and translucent flesh. It preserves and sets the color. Select small oranges with thin, smooth skin. Large, fleshy oranges with thick skins are difficult to dehydrate properly and may spoil. Cut the oranges into slices no more than one quarter of an inch thick. The end slices are not suitable for dehydrating.

The orange slices can be dehydrated in either a conventional oven or a microwave. For the conventional oven, arrange the slices in a single layer on a cookie sheet. Place them in a 200° oven and leave the oven door ajar. Air must circulate in the oven in order for the oranges to dehydrate. Turn the orange slices every ten to fifteen minutes. The entire process will take from two to five hours depending on humidity and the thickness of the slices. Three hours is average.

If you use the microwave, place the slices in a single layer on a double thickness of paper towels. Set the microwave on defrost or its lowest power setting. Turn and rearrange the slices every three minutes. The entire process will take from fifteen to thirty minutes depending on the microwave, humidity, and the thickness of the slices. You must monitor this process very closely! When the slices have dehydrated, if you continue to microwave them, they will blacken and burn in a matter of seconds.

Regardless of the type of oven you use, the slices are done when the peel is leathery. Don't wait until the peel becomes brittle. The fleshy part of the orange will still be a little moist. Remove the slices from the oven or microwave and lay them on paper towels to cool and continue drying overnight.

You can create a garland by passing a heavy thread, twine or fishing line through the center of the slices. Add cinnamon sticks, pine cones, bay leaves or cedar greens for a lovely solstice decoration. Individual orange slices can be hung on the Yule tree or used to decorate wreaths. When we use them as solar symbols, oranges in December are still special!

THE WITCHES' LADDER

BY JIM GARRISON

K nots, cords, beads, feathers, bones, sticks and stones— the Witches' ladder is made up of any combination of these things. Simple and effective, the Witches' ladder incorporates basic knot magic with elemental correspondences to create a distinctive and powerful talisman that you can hang in your home for protection or give as a gift to your friends for one of the sabbats.

A Witches' ladder is a length of cord that is knotted to hold feathers or other objects. It is used in multiple-part spell or consecration practice that takes place over the span of a lunar month, though you could constructon based on planetary hours, or tie it at the same time each day, or link it to a certain sabbat or Full Moon, etc. The important thing is to remain consistent and to repeat the same procedure each time so that you keep charging the ladder the same way each time. This is part of the power of this particular charm, as it is a highly charged and potent resevoir for certain very specific energies reinforced by selected correspondences. Thus you can make a Witches' ladder for home protection, fertility, prosperity, and so on.

To make a Witches' ladder, first cut a length of stout cord. Colored silk cords are attractive, but leather strips or macrame can also be used. Be sure to pick a color that corresponds to your goal, such as green for prosperity, blue for healing, and white for protection. I prefer to keep things manageable, so I recommend that you cut the cord at about eighteen inches or thereabouts. Cut as many lengths as you plan to make ladders with. If you are planning on braiding your ladder, you'll need as many lengths as you care to braid together. Whether you want three, five, seven or more is up to you, though I'd stick with three or five. You might want to seal the ends of your cords with candle wax.

Loosely roll up each length of your cord and use a small piece of scrap cord to tie it into a bundle. Fumigate the little bundles with incense smoke and ritually cleanse them with the elements. Then place each set of cords into a black fabric sack, or wrap them in a square of cloth or handkerchief. If you like, you can add a few pieces of gemstone, some herbs, or whatever other purification or blessing materials you care to include at this time. Store the unfinished ladder components in this bag, a cloth, or somewhere dark and safe until it's time to work on the ladder.

When the time is right, take your packet of cords into sacred space and begin tying them onto rings or tie a loop into the top part. Select the objects you intend to incorporate into your ladder—feathers, shells, beads, crystals, etc. Be sure to pick objects that relate best to your goals, like tiny brass bells for a ladder of protection or small scraps of hand-made paper on which you've sketched a sigil or set of runes, rolled up and tied into the ladder. You might like to try using feathers that you braid into the the ladder, much like is done for a a prayer stick. Use your imagination and creativity.

Tie one object—such as a feather or piece of rock crystal—into the cord, or braid the cord a bit, and then insert the object. As you do this, you may wish to use a chant or visualize your intentions as vividly as possible and thus embed this energy into the cords as you then tie them or braid them to seal in the power. If working with a group, you could have the group raise power to charge the ladder and then complete the whole piece in one session. If you're on your own, you'll probably want to do a section at a time. There's something to be said for slowly accumulating power and letting something like this develop and grow over a period of time.

If you are doing the ladder in stages, be sure to clamp or twist-tie the braid and return it to the bag or cloth. Repeat this every night for a month, or whenever the timing is right, whether that's once a month, once a year, or every odd-numbered day—select the scheme that works best for you and stick with it.

PAINTED SPIRIT STONES

BY SILVER RAVENWOLF

Among the dancing fire drakes a wise old woman speaks tales of myth and reality, of power and strength in days of old.

"There are stones," she says, "of ordinary make, like those you tread upon each day. No one knows that these stones, when clapped together, can call forth the powers of the Universe. These are the wise stones of the elements." She nods her head slowly. "They are gifts from the ancestors." The light of the fire plays across her withered face, undulating power and mystery.

"Find two smooth, flat stones that are slightly larger than the palm of your hand," she says. "Better it be when the Moon is Full."

"You will paint upon the back of the stones those magical symbols that are dear to you. One stone should represent your power animal, whether it be a creature of the land, air, or sky. Forget not to add your own special sigil and then seal the power inside with the sign of our holy pentacle. When the Moon is Full, empower these stones to call the magical skill and wisdom you need. It may come as a dragon, a wolf, a maid, or a man. Do this within the magic circle, round thrice about to keep bad spirits out. Henceforth, when the need is upon you, call forth their magic by clapping the stones together and saying:

Once to call my Lady, and once to call my Lord
And once to call the magic in which I'll be restored!"

DIRECTORY
OF PRODUCTS
AND SERVICES

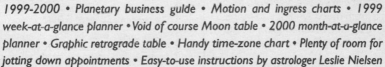

Experience the Enchantment

Invocation to Isis (cassette)
An Egyptian Journey, harp & flute
Heart (cassette)
Solo pedal harp to touch the heart
happenstance dance (CD & cassette)
Harp with many other instruments
Erin's Harp (CD)
Traditional Celtic music to stir the soul

Melissa Morgan Music

To order send $10 per cassette, $15 per CD to:
Melissa Morgan
4822 Santa Monica Ave. #108
San Diego, CA 92107
(619)699-0305 (M-F 8AM-6PM)

New Poetry Contest
$48,000.00 in Prizes

The National Library of Poetry to award 250 total prizes to amateur poets in coming months

Owings Mills, Maryland – The National Library of Poetry has just announced that $48,000.00 in prizes will be awarded over the next 12 months in the brand new North American Open Amateur Poetry Contest. The contest is open to everyone and entry is free.

"We're especially looking for poems from new or unpublished poets," indicated Howard Ely, spokesperson for The National Library of Poetry. "We have a ten year history of awarding large prizes to talented poets who have never before won any type of writing competition."

How To Enter

Anyone may enter the competition simply by sending in *ONLY ONE* original poem, any subject, any style, to:

The National Library of Poetry
Suite A1241
1 Poetry Plaza
Owings Mills, MD 21117-6282

Or enter online at www.poetry.com

The poem should be no more than 20 lines, and the poet's name and address must appear on the top of the page. "All poets who enter will receive a response concerning their artistry, usually within seven weeks," indicated Mr. Ely.

Possible Publication

Many submitted poems will also be considered for inclusion in one of The

Gordon Steele of Virginia, pictured above, is the latest Grand Prize Winner in The National Library of Poetry's North American Open Amateur Poetry Contest. As the big winner, he was awarded $1,000.00 in cash.

National Library of Poetry's forthcoming hardbound anthologies. Previous anthologies published by the organization have included *On the Threshold of a Dream*, *Days of Future's Past*, *Of Diamonds and Rust*, and *Moments More to Go*, among others.

"Our anthologies routinely sell out because they are truly enjoyable reading, and they are also a sought-after source-book for poetic talent," added Mr. Ely.

World's Largest Poetry Organization

Having awarded over $150,000.00 in prizes to poets worldwide in recent years, The National Library of Poetry, founded in 1982 to promote the artistic accomplishments of contemporary poets, is the largest organization of its kind in the world. Anthologies published by the organization have featured poems by more than 100,000 poets.

Work at Home
Be a Medical Billing Specialist
Earn up to $40,000 a year!

**No previous experience needed...learn at home.
Prepare medical claims for doctors, hospitals, clinics.**

This exciting money-making opportunity is wide open. So if you want to make a good living at home—without commuting, without selling...and working the hours you choose—call the toll-free number below or mail the coupon for free facts about what could be the greatest job opportunity of your life! There are plenty of high-pay office jobs, too!

COMPARE THESE ADVANTAGES WITH ANY OTHER PROFESSION!

- You can work as much as you want
- You can earn $10 to $20 an hour
- Choose your hours...any time of day
- No time wasted traveling to work
- Be your own boss
- Continuing graduate support throughout your career
- Work wherever you want to live
- Prestige of working in the medical profession
- Plenty of high-pay office jobs, too

**GET FREE FACTS!
NO COST! NO OBLIGATION!
MAIL COUPON TODAY
OR CALL TOLL-FREE**

Experts train you step by step...you can be ready to work in just four months!

The medical profession is in need of skilled medical claims and billing specialists...and you can make almost as much money as you want because there is so much work. You learn medical terminology, procedures and how to prepare medical claims for Medicare, Medicaid and private patients. Experts show you how to do your work to meet the exacting standards of the medical profession.

Compare the money you can make at home as a Medical Claims and Billing Specialist with any other job.

What other job can you start with just four months of training at home and start earning up to $40,000 a year? Plus, you get these extra benefits—no transportation cost or time wasted going to and from your job, no expensive clothes because you can do all your work at home, no child day care costs, work whatever hours you choose...early mornings, late at night, any time, and take "breaks" whenever you want them. And it's not only the money you make that's important—you'll be working in a prestigious job making a valuable contribution to the medical profession.

THAT REALLY WORK
BIBLICAL KING SOLOMON

Solomon's Luck & Good Fortune Talisman

This ancient and very powerful talisman has the power to help its owner prosper and become very lucky in life. As the owner of this marvellous ancient talisman you will be blessed with endless good fortune and receive celestial guidance whenever you compete in games of chance e.g. Competitions, Lotteries, or Bingo. This is an ancient talisman of considerable power that will attract **(like a magnet)** untold Luck and Good Fortune to its owner, and if need be, it can also create job opportunities and Career advancements. We are so convinced of the beneficial power of this talisman that we **guarantee** it to be **truly** the luckiest talisman on the face of the earth.

Solomon's Money & Wealth Talisman

This ancient talisman is now considered by many to be one of the most **powerful** and **successful** Money/Wealth **magnets** ever created. It has proved itself so successful in creating **real** and **visible** financial independence for all its owners, that we can say, that on receipt of this powerful money magnet you will soon start to experience real financial independence and security, these financial and monetary blessings will continue to grow and multiply throughout the years ahead. As the owner of this powerful talisman you will be assured of a future free of all **real** money/financial worries.

Solomon's Mind & Body Rejuvenation Talisman

Solomon created this talisman to help promote and restore the overall good health and well-being of its owner. As well as being one of the **oldest** and **most effective** Health and Well-being talismans known to man, it is also said to have the power to create an outward youthful appearance, by magically rejuvenating the mind and body. Clients who have already benefitted from its **powerful healing and rejuvenating** qualities, have reported that within six months, they actually started to look and feel **visibly healthier, younger** and **physically stronger** than their years. It is now a historical fact that King Solomon had an **unusually long and healthy life span,** today scholars of cosmic law put this down to his possession of this wondrous talisman. On a magical level this rejuvenation talisman is simply a very powerful and effective cosmic re-charger of the human battery/Soul.

The Enlightened Path (ML), P.O. Box 6205, Basingstoke, Hants, RG24 7YP, England

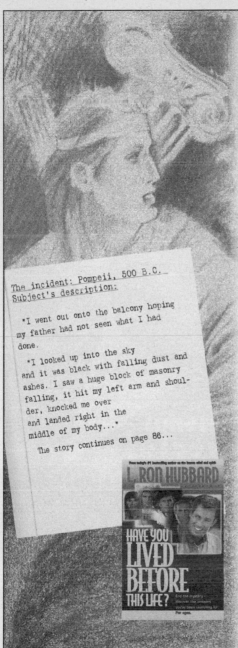

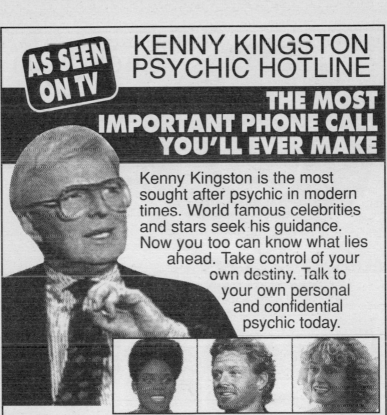